"Compared to even the simplest verse, the rhythmic structure of prose seems haphazard, unconsidered. The poet, unless he is writing the freest of free verse, organizes his rhythmic structures; these structures include rhyme, stanzaic form, tone color, and most importantly, meter. The study of those principles that guide the poet's use of rhythmic structures is called prosody. The largest part of prosodical study concerns itself with meter. This anthology does not, however, neglect prosody in its larger meaning, perhaps best defined by Ezra Pound as the "articulation of the total sound of a poem."

—from the author's Introduction

Harvey Gross teaches at the University of California, Irvine. He attended the University of Vienna for a year and received his Ph.D. from the University of Michigan. A contributor to the PMLA, Centennial Review, and the Virginia Quarterly Review, he is the author of SOUND AND FORM IN MODERN POETRY, *published in 1964.*

LITERATURE AND IDEAS SERIES

Irving Howe, General Editor

THE STRUCTURE OF VERSE

Modern Essays on Prosody

EDITED WITH AN INTRODUCTION
AND COMMENTARY BY

Harvey Gross

A Fawcett Premier Book

Fawcett Publications, Inc., Greenwich, Conn.
Member of American Book Publishers Council

Acknowledgments

I wish to thank Bea Gottlieb for finding out-of-print items in the New York Public Library. Mr. Louis B. Wright, of The Folger Shakespeare Library, has graciously permitted quotation from the Library's 1570 edition of Ascham's The Scholemaster. Mrs. Betty Becker helped type the introductory sections.

H.G.

CONTENTS

Introduction: Prosody and Literary Study   7

PART ONE

PROSODY: PURVIEW, HISTORY, AND DEFINITION

Rene Wellek and Austin Warren **Euphony, Rhythm, and Metre**   21

I. A. Richards **Rhythm and Metre**   42

Robert Graves **Harp, Anvil, Oar**   52

George Saintsbury **"The Mothers"**   72

Robert Bridges **A Letter to a Musician on English Prosody**   86

Ezra Pound **Treatise on Metre**   102

PART TWO

THEORIES OF METER

Otto Jespersen **Notes on Metre**   111

Yvor Winters **The Audible Reading of Poetry**   131

W. K. Wimsatt, Jr. and Monroe C. Beardsley
     The Concept of Meter: An Exercise in Abstraction   150

Northrop Frye **The Rhythm of Recurrence: Epos**   168

Ronald Sutherland **Structural Linguistics and English Prosody**   181

PART THREE

THREE ESSAYS IN CRITICISM

Arnold Stein **Meter and Meaning** 193

Harvey Gross **T. S. Eliot and the Music of Poetry** 202

Theodore Roethke **What Do I Like?** 218

APPENDIXES

R. M. Alden **The Foot and the Verse** 235

Glossary of Terms 265

INTRODUCTION

Prosody and Literary Study

Prosody, unlike "literary history" or the New Critical methods of close reading and *explication de texte*, has been slow in establishing its respectability as a proper literary study. I use *respectability* and *proper* with some emphasis. Many cranks and faddists have taken up prosody; they resemble those passionate and humorless bands of anti-Stratfordians who devote their energies to the disestablishment of Shakespeare as the author of his own plays. The politics of prosodical study might well dismay the student anxious to discover necessary facts and basic principles. Bitter feuding between rival schools of prosodists—the linguists versus the aestheticians, the "timers" versus the "stressers," the quantifiers versus the strict foot-and-syllable scanners—has done little to clarify the issues or even to furnish a simple map of the terrain.

The bafflement and contention besetting prosody as a study may be traced to bad heredity. From its beginnings in the Elizabethan age, prosody mistook its subject, misjudged what it saw (and did not *hear*), and developed a bad temper. The bad temper is rooted in an easily deduced psychological fact: no man wants the sensitivity of *his* ears impugned. Roger Ascham, well brought up on the classics and knowing what he liked, fulminated against "the Gothic . . . barbarous and rude Ryming" of the early Tudor poets. He conceded that the Earl of Surrey did passably well as a poet, but complained that Surrey did not understand "perfite and trewe versifying"; that is, Surrey did not compose his English lines according to the principles of Latin and Greek quantitative verse. Ascham tells us:

> . . . here is the fault, that their feete be feete without ioyntes, that is to say, not distinct by trew quantitie of sillabes: And so soche feete be but numme feete, and be euen as vnfitte for a verse to turne and runne roundly withall as feete of brasse or wood be vnweeldie to go well withall. And as a foote of wood is a plaine shew of a manifest maime, euen so feete in our English versifing without quantitie and ioyntes be sure signes that the verse is either

7

borne deformed, vnnaturall, and lame, and so verie vnseemlie to
looke vpon, except to men that be gogle eyed them selues.[1]

Ascham instigated a lengthy argument, continued by suc-
ceeding theorists and poets, on the nature of English prosody.
This discussion was clouded over by two overwhelming impulses: to explain accomplished English poetry by the rules
of short and long, and to draft laws of quantity by which
English verse might move in Virgilian hexameters or in
Horatian Sapphics. Sir Philip Sidney, Gabriel Harvey, Edmund Spenser, and Thomas Campion all (to use Saintsbury's
phrase) committed whoredom with the enchantress of quantitative metric. While this hanky-panky had no adverse effects
on poetry itself (Campion's superb musicality owes much to
his impeccable sense of quantity), it produced misbegotten
twins of confusion and discord, whose heirs, however named,
are still apparent today. Thus those who still talk about "long"
and "short," those who perpetuate a punitive legalism, and
those who regard prosody as an account of what poets should
have done and didn't, trace their ancestry back to Elizabethan
dalliance and illicit classicizing.

The prosodist's job is empirical. What "laws" he thinks he
discovers must be deduced from the verse itself, and must not
be a set of a priori formulations. The student should carefully
study Jespersen's approach to the structure of the iambic line;
his method is a model of sensitive listening and objective
description. As a matter of policy, I have rejected for this
collection any essay animated by a theoretical monism: that
English verse is entirely a matter of quantity, of "isochronous
intervals," or bar lengths of music in duple or triple time.
English verse has been written in many ways, some metrical,
some nonmetrical. Metrical verse appears in two basic forms:
the strong-stress (or Old English meter) and the syllable-stress
(or accentual-syllabic) form; these distinctions are carefully
made by Bridges, Winters, and Wimsatt and Beardsley. No
one "law" explains all English verse; no single principle of
stressing, isochronism, syllabic length or syllabic number, accounts for the rhythmic impetus in English verse—from
Beowulf to Robert Lowell.

This collection has been designed to emphasize fundamental
clarifying distinctions. These distinctions may be noted in the
three-part arrangement of the table of contents. Part One
begins with general statements on the function of sound in

[1] Roger Ascham, *The Scholemaster*, Book II, 1570. From the copy in
the Folger Shakespeare Library. Used with permission.

literary structure and the psychological effects of rhythmic organization. History, charmingly fanciful and equally charmingly sensible, is represented in the selections from Robert Graves and George Saintsbury. Bridges narrows in on the subject matter of prosody with great learning and theoretical vigor.

Part Two is devoted to metrical theory. I have tried to select leading hierophants of the three major faiths: the traditional scanners of syllable and stress, the musical or temporal scanners, and the linguists. Finally, Part Three includes essays in literary criticism, mainly nontechnical in nature, but proceeding on the assumption that fruitful discussion of poetry must take cognizance of rhythmic form.

Rhythm itself is a mysterious fact of aesthetic experience. To talk about it at all recalls a story frequently told of Louie Armstrong. Some earnest seeker-after-truth challenged Louie to define jazz: to tell what it really was. Louie raised a fierce eyebrow and bellowed, "Why man, if you don't know what it is, I can't tell you!" Other versions of this story exist; it may even be mythical. To define the nature of rhythm raises a similar problem. Most human beings know what rhythm is; most can produce rhythmic noises and make rhythmic gestures. Many can even push their bodies around to music in those patterns called dancing. But the precise definition of rhythm has so far eluded aesthetics and psychology.

This is no cause for despair. We all know rhythm without being able to understand its essential nature. The "knowledge" of rhythm and jazz rests on experience prior to rational, verbal explanations; the earnest seeker-after-truth could "know" nothing of jazz unless he had made previous response to it. Louie's outraged answer was not only a crushing response to a foolish question; it was exactly and theoretically the only possible answer. Unless the seeker-after-truth had physical and emotional experience of jazz, he did not know it; the knowledge of music lives in the response to it.

We know rhythm only through response to it. Know is put into qualifying italics because it is obvious that rhythmic knowledge is a very special form of knowledge, finally not translatable into words. Rhythm is the way our bodies and our emotions respond to the passage of time. Seasons recur; autumn follows summer, and "If winter comes, can spring be far behind?" We speak, then, of "the rhythm of the seasons."

Biological process is rhythmic. Birth, growth, decay, and death
are patterns in time—patterns experienced as rhythms. Human
psychological process is also rhythmic. The buildup of inner
tension, produced by powerful feelings of expectation, and the
release of these tensions through fulfillment of expectation is
characteristically rhythmic.

Rhythm in the arts imitates and expresses physiologic and
psychologic response to the passage of time. The experience
of the flow of life makes patterns in time; the temporal arts,
music and poetry, thus move in time, and their rhythmical
shapes of sound ultimately symbolize biological nature and
the tensions of inner, psychological life. In infancy the
response to the rhythms of poetry and music is entirely physical. It seems human beings are born with what Aristotle calls
"the instinct for harmony and rhythm;" parents discover one-
year-olds wagging their diapered bottoms to the beat of Count
Basie or Beethoven. As we grow older, we take more sophisticated pleasures in rhythmic effects, but at any age the rhythms
of poetry may appeal directly to our physical beings. Whether
we are chanting a nursery rhyme,

> Ding, dong, bell, pussy's in the well.
> Who put her in? Little Johnny Green. . .

or bringing the good news from Ghent to Aix,

> I sprang to the stirrup, and Joris, and he;
> I galloped, Dirck galloped, we galloped all three.
> "Good speed!" cried the watch, as the gate-bolts undrew;
> "Speed!" echoed the wall to us galloping through. . .

our bodies will involuntarily make inward gestures appropriate
to drawing water or galloping down the highway.

Rhythm not only imitates physical action, it can also express
the most delicate feelings and moods. No words can adequately
paraphrase the effect of hopeless, absolute despair conveyed
by the final line of the stanzas of Keats' *La Belle Dame Sans
Merci*:

> O what can ail thee, Knight at arms
>   Alone and palely loitering?
> The sedge has withered from the Lake,
>   And no birds sing!

The final line is half the length of the preceding three. We
have been prepared to find the final line rhythmically sym-
metrical with the others. Compelled by the rhythmic vacancy,

our defeated expectation produces a desolation of spirit no other poetic device could produce. The economy of Keats' line contributes to the total poetic response; a rhythm can create effects with maximum efficiency and minimum means. We can think of poetic rhythm as analogous to those stylized gestures in athletics—the "follow-through" in golf and tennis—which increase the efficiency of driving or serving.

No example of poetic economy surpasses that one line in *King Lear*, uttered when the shattered old man realizes that Cordelia will

> . . . come no more,
> Never, never, never, never, never!

Never, five times repeated, sets up a falling rhythm more emotionally effective than any passage of the most flaming rhetoric. It is a stroke of utmost simplicity and utmost genius. Shakespeare expresses the inexpressible, the grief of a father for a beloved child, through rhythmic structure.

Rhythms in poetry imitate and express; they are the muscles and nerves of the poetic organism. Good prose, of course, also displays rhythmical structure; those magnificent descriptive passages of Dickens surge and sway in great rolling cadences:

> Fog everywhere. Fog up the river, where it flows among green aits and meadows; fog down the river, where it rolls defiled among tiers of shipping, and the waterside pollutions of a great (and dirty) city. Fog on the Essex marshes, fog on the Kentish heights. Fog creeping into the cabooses of collier-brigs; fog lying out on the yards, and hovering in the rigging of great ships; fog dropping on the gunwales of barges and small boats. *(Bleak House)*

Equally rhythmic, but in a different way, is the classic prose of Dr. Johnson. In the passage below, the rhythm depends on Johnson's ingenious handling of syntax, the delaying prepositional phrases which come between the beginning and the end of a long but graceful clause:

> In the character of his *Elegy* I rejoice to concur with the common reader; for by the common sense of readers uncorrupted with literary prejudices, after all the refinements of subtilty and the dogmatism of learning, must be finally decided all claim to poetical honours. *(The Life of Gray)*

Compared to even the simplest verse, the rhythmic structure of prose seems haphazard, unconsidered. The poet, unless he is writing the freest of free verse, organizes his rhythmic structures; these structures include rhyme, stanzaic form, tone color, and most importantly, meter. The study of those principles that guide the poet's use of rhythmic structures is called prosody. The largest part of prosodical study concerns itself with meter. This anthology does not, however, neglect prosody in its larger meaning, perhaps best defined by Ezra Pound as the "articulation of the total sound of a poem."

An analysis of a very short poem reveals a complex rhythmic organism, a life sustained by meter, rhyme, and stanzaic shape:

TO ELECTRA

> I dare not ask a kiss;
>> I dare not beg a smile;
> Lest having that, or this,
>> I might grow proud the while.
>
> No, no, the utmost share
>> Of my desire, shall be
> Only to kiss that air,
>> That lately kissèd thee.
>>> (Robert Herrick, 1648)

We note first the meter, the regular recurrence of phonetically stressed syllables. Here the meter is *iambic trimeter*, a pattern of six syllables to each line, arranged *unstressed, stressed, unstressed, stressed, unstressed, stressed*. Each group of unstressed and stressed syllables is called a foot; three such feet make a trimeter line. Scansion, the use of visual symbols to describe the phonetic facts of meter, is more convenient and more accurate than clumsy verbal analysis:

> Ĭ dáre | nŏt ásk | ă kíss;
>> Ĭ dáre | nŏt bég | ă smíle;
> Lĕst háv | ĭng thát, | ŏr thís,
>> Ĭ míght | grŏw próud | thĕ whíle.
>
> Nó, nó, | thĕ út | mŏst sháre
>> Ŏf mý | dĕ síre, | shăll bé
> Ón lў | tŏ kíss | thăt áir,
>> Thăt láte | lў kís | sĕd thée.

Since the scansion of traditional English meter has become a controversial matter, the student should carefully study Part Two of this collection. It may be observed now that the pattern of unstressed, stressed, ($\smallsmile/$) is not invariable; the first foot of the fifth line contains two stresses; the first foot of the seventh line reverses the iambic movement. These departures from the prevailing meter are expressive; they modify and control feeling.

Another prosodic element is movement or pace. The pace of a poem is controlled by the length of the syllables. In English length of syllable alone cannot form meter; unlike Latin and Greek, our language has no fixed rules for determining which syllables are long, which short. In English a stressed syllable is generally long, and stress tends to lengthen short syllables. But we often find unstressed long syllables, as in the second foot of this line:

$$\text{Í might} \mid \text{gro͝w próud} \mid \text{th͝e whíle} \ldots$$

The ow of grow and the ou of proud are approximately equal in length or quantity; the quantities of vowel and diphthong in the second foot make us linger briefly, slowing the movement of the line.

The printed line itself controls the poem's movement. It is conventional to pause slightly at the end of lines; this pause has rhythmic effect. Rhyme appears at the end of lines, although in English verse rhyme may occur within, and at the head of lines. Rhyme is also rhythmic; its regular recurrence makes us pause and throws our attention back to the rhyming word. Length of line and pattern of rhyme together form the stanza. The four-line stanza of Herrick's little poem is a quatrain; its alternately rhyming lines define the scheme abab.

Meter, pace, the appearance of the lines on the page, rhyme, and stanzaic shape all serve "the articulation of the total sound of a poem." But analysis itself brings us far from "knowing" the poem's rhythm. The dissection of a human brain can tell us very little about the intelligence of its owner; prosodic analysis points out only general rhythmic anatomy. A poet's rhythmic style is a matter of voice, of subtle phrasing, and elements too tenuous and variable for exact analysis. Two lines of blank verse, scanning exactly alike, may be miles apart rhythmically:

> But look, the morn in russet mantle clad,
> Walks o'er the dew of yon high eastward hill.
> *(Hamlet)*

> To reign is worth ambition, though in Hell:
> Better to reign in Hell than serve in Heaven.
>   *(Paradise Lost)*

An experienced reader comes to know the rhythms of Shakespeare and Milton. We learn a poet's rhythmic style subconsciously; it works on us subtly, evoking feelings we can scarcely frame in words. The prosody of a great poet, the style he achieves in the rhythmic handling of language, is like his handwriting: immediately recognizable and ultimately inimitable.

How can students learn to recognize the poet's prosodical handwriting? First by developing, preferably at an early age, their "instinct for harmony and rhythm." Unfortunately, too many students arrive at college with this basic part of their education sadly neglected. Northrop Frye remarks:

> Ideally, our literary education should begin . . . with such things as "this little pig went to market"—with verse rhythm reinforced by physical assault. The infant who gets bounced on somebody's knee to the rhythm of "Ride a cock horse" does not need a footnote telling him that Banbury Cross is twenty miles northeast of Oxford. . . . All he needs is to get bounced. If he is, he is beginning to develop a response to poetry in the place it ought to start.[2]

It would scarcely do for college instructors to bounce students on their knees. The damage of culture and the omissions of education must be repaired with more dignified if less pleasurable expedients. An effective audible reading—not an "oral interpretation"—can do much to clarify metrical structure. Of course, the teacher himself must read with an awareness of rhythmic organization. Too often the student has been taught to read verse by programatically suppressing the meter: to make it sound as much like prose as possible. This is doubtless the reaction to pre-educationist education, when students were expected to bang out the meter as they read:

> O YOUNG Loch-in-VAR is come OUT of the WEST
> Through ALL the wide BOR-der his STEED was
>   the BEST . . .

Despite the crudity of this as a performance, it showed the student the structure of anapestic tetrameter.

There exists a widespread notion that if a poem is read metrically, that is, with an underlying sense of the metrical

[2] *The Well-Tempered Critic* (Bloomington, 1963), p. 25.

paradigm, there can be no projection of rhythmic nuances: those variations from the metrical norm that are the expressive elements of prosodic structure. A young lady once asked the great pianist and teacher, Artur Schnabel, whether she should play in time or in accordance with her feelings. Schnabel answered, with characteristic wit, "Why not feel in time?" The best readers of verse *feel in time*; they read with a careful regard to the metrical accent and, at the same time, allow the curve of feeling, the rhythm itself, to rise and fall above the subtly emphasized metrical checkpoints.

A superb example of this kind of reading may be heard in Ezra Pound's recording of *Canto I*.[8] Pound uses Old English strong-stress meter, scanning four strong beats to the line with a heavy caesura after the second beat:

> ... We sét up mast and sáil || on that swárt shíp,
>
> Bóre sheep a boárd her, || and our bó dies álso
>
> Héa vy with weép ing, || and the wínds from stérn wárd ...

Pound's reading carefully marks the strong beats. His delivery is highly stylized: a heavy Irish intonation and a narrow range of dynamic intensity. The effect is midway between chant and outright song—completely metrical yet with a full realization of every expressive opportunity the verse offers. *Feeling in time*.

Readings such as Pound's do much to explain the nature of metrical structure and exemplify the proper reading of verse. The phonograph can contribute immensely to the ear-training of students. It must, of course, be used with discretion. A sophomore suffering from overexposure to Dylan Thomas may be ruined, prosodically speaking, for life. Thomas' magnificently sonorous voice imposed similar rhythms on all the poetry he read; it was the besetting weakness of his delivery. The phonograph, valuable though it is, must be supplemented by theoretical study (the essays contained in this volume) and excursions into practical craftsmanship.

The student who aspires to prosodical sophistication might first study R. M. Alden's "The Foot and the Verse" and then spend some hours fashioning twenty lines of unrhymed iambic pentameter. Music students begin their theoretical studies with the writing of simple melodies and basic harmonic pro-

[8] On Caedmon Record TC 1122.

gressions. Students of literature, alas, have little technical training in the art they study. Many students enter graduate school overinformed on such matters as The Reform Bill of 1832 or The Objective Correlative; only a handful can write a passably correct sonnet. The student who has struggled with octet and sestet, with iamb and trochee, with caesura and rhyme, gains an insight into the art of poetry no amount of historical background or theoretical savvy can supply.

All this seems elementary enough—including the observation that scansion comes considerably easier after the student has learned to write even a line of bad verse. Scansion is also made easier when the student recognizes the metrical paradigm the poet uses. Is the poet writing traditional syllable-stress meter, of which the characteristic form is iambic pentameter; or is he writing strong-stress meter, of which the characteristic form is the four-beat line of Old English verse? Or is he writing one of the rarer metrical forms: purely syllabic verse such as Marianne Moore writes; or quantitative verse, such as many generations of English poets tried to write and failed? These four forms represent the kinds of verse that can be named as metrical. The rest, I suppose, is "free verse." I myself, however, prefer the term *nonmetrical* prosody to describe the long lines of Whitman and D. H. Lawrence, or the short lines of William Carlos Williams.

This collection, I have previously noted, emphasizes distinctions and clarity. It makes no attempt at democratic representation of all possible opinions; and while an occasional polemical chord is struck, this anthology generally avoids the harsher harmonies that grind and grate in so much prosodical discussion. After I completed the selection of essays, I discovered that one-third of the authors writing on prosody were themselves skillful poets; two of them, Ezra Pound and Theodore Roethke, transcendent figures in the history of modern literature. Long ago Dryden observed, "Poets themselves are the most proper, though I conclude not the only critics. . . . I . . . think it reasonable that the judgment of an artificer in his own art should be preferable to the opinion of another man; at least where he is not bribed by interest or prejudiced by malice." [4]

Little in these essays has been motivated by malice, though

[4] Quoted in Ralph Cohen's *The Art of Discrimination* (Berkeley and Los Angeles, 1964), p. 29.

Graves, Bridges, and Winters take positions, reasonably enough, defending the kind of poetry they themselves write. Roethke, with charm and relish, explains procedures in his poetry by appealing, not to interest or malice, but to the history of his subject: to the origins of persistent and catchy rhythms in nursery rhymes and early Tudor song. My own "'position" reveals itself in the selection of the essays and the continuity suggested by their arrangement. The student should pay some attention to the linking material between the essays; these remarks are synthetic rather than merely explanatory, attempting to position the essays in a theoretical direction. The theory that emerges is eclectic, empirical, and descriptive rather than proscriptive. But given the nature of the subject, I cannot imagine it otherwise.

Part One

PROSODY: PURVIEW, HISTORY, AND DEFINITION

RENÉ WELLEK AND AUSTIN WARREN

Euphony, Rhythm, and Metre

[*Few books have had as pervasive and as salutary an effect on literary study as René Wellek and Austin Warren's Theory of Literature. A work of comprehensive scholarship, it also sustains a method of precise critical discrimination.*

[*This essay outlines prosody in its largest dimensions: the function of sound structure in the "work of literary art." It then proceeds to clarification and systematic analysis. A salient contribution is the distinction "between performance and pattern of sound." Metrics, as such, becomes a study of paradigms: the abstract, given series of phonetically identical items; and the variations and departures from the paradigm.*

[*Wellek and Warren divide metrical study into "graphic prosody," musical scansion, and "acoustic metrics." The student should note that these three approaches are represented by the essays in Part Two of this collection.*]

EVERY work of literary art is, first of all, a series of sounds out of which arises the meaning. In some literary works, this stratum of sounds is minimised in its importance; and it becomes, so to speak, diaphanous, as in most novels. But even there the phonetic stratum is a necessary precondition of the meaning. The distinction between a novel by Dreiser and a poem like Poe's "The Bells" is in this respect only quantitative and fails to justify the setting up of two contrasting kinds of

From Theory of Literature. Copyright 1942, 1947, 1949, © 1956 by Harcourt, Brace & World, Inc. Reprinted by permission of the publisher.

literature, fiction and poetry. In many works of art, including of course prose, the sound-stratum attracts attention and thus constitutes an integral part of the aesthetic effect. This is true of much ornate prose and of all verse, which by definition is an organization of a language's sound-system.

In analysing these sound-effects, we have to bear in mind two principles, important but frequently ignored. We must, initially, distinguish between performance and pattern of sound. The reading aloud of a literary work of art is a performance, a realisation of a pattern which adds something individual and personal and, on the other hand, may distort or even entirely ignore the pattern. Hence a real science of rhythmics and metrics cannot be based only on the study of individual recitals. A second common assumption, that sound should be analysed in complete divorce from meaning, is also false. It follows from our general conception of the integrity of any work of art that such a divorce is false; but it follows also from the demonstration that mere sound in itself can have no or little aesthetic effect. There is no "musical" verse without some general conception of its meaning or at least its emotional tone. Even listening to a foreign language which we do not understand at all, we do not hear pure sound but impose our phonetic habits on it as well as hear, of course, the meaningful intonation given to it by the speaker or reader. In poetry, pure sound is either a fiction or an extremely simple and elementary series of relationships such as those studied in Birkhoff's *Aesthetic Measure*,[1] which cannot possibly account for the variety and importance possessed by the sound-stratum when seen as integral to the total character of a poem.

We must first distinguish between two very different aspects of the problem: the inherent and the relational elements of sound. By the former, we mean the peculiar individuality of the second a or o, or l or p, independent of quantity, since there cannot be more or less a or p. Inherent distinctions in quality are the basis for the effects which are usually called "musicality" or "euphony." Relational distinctions, on the other hand, are those which may become the basis of rhythm and metre: the pitch, the duration of the sounds, the stress, the frequency of recurrence, all elements permitting quantitative distinctions. Pitch is higher or lower, duration shorter or longer, stress stronger or weaker, frequency of recurrence greater or smaller. This fairly elementary distinction is important, for it isolates a whole group of linguistic phenomena:

[1] Birkhoff, *Aesthetic Measure*, Cambridge, Mass., 1933.

those which the Russians have called "orchestration" (*instrumentovka*) in order to stress the fact that the sound-quality is here the element which is being manipulated and exploited by the writer.[2] The term "musicality" (or "melody") of verse should be dropped as misleading. The phenomena we are identifying are not parallel to musical "melody" at all: melody in music is, of course, determined by pitch and hence is vaguely parallel to intonation in language. There are actually considerable differences between the intonation line of a spoken sentence, with its wavering, quickly changing pitches, and a musical melody with its fixed pitches and definite intervals.[3] Nor is the term "euphony" quite sufficient since, under "orchestration," "cacophony" needs to be considered in poets like Browning or Hopkins who aim at deliberately harsh, expressive sound-effects.

Among the devices of "orchestration" we have to distinguish between sound-patterns, repetition of identical or associated sound-qualities, and the use of expressive sounds, of sound-imitation. Sound-patterns have been studied by the Russian formalists with particular ingenuity; in English, W. J. Bate has analysed the elaborate sound-figures in the verse of Keats, who himself rather curiously theorized about his practice.[4] Osip Brik [5] has classified the possible sound-figures according to the number of repeated sounds, the number of repetitions, the order in which the sounds follow each other in the repeated groups, and the position of the sounds in the rhythmical units. This last and most useful classification needs further division. One can distinguish repetitions of sounds closely placed within a single verse, of sounds which occur in the beginning of one group and at the end of another, or at the end of one line and the beginning of the next, or at the beginning of lines, or simply in final position. The next to last group is parallel to the stylistic figure of anaphora. The last will include such a common phenomenon as rhyme. Accord-

[2] The Russian *instrumentovka* is a translation of *instrumentation* used by René Ghil, in his *Traité du verbe* (Paris 1886). There he claims priority to its application to poetry (see p. 18). Ghil later corresponded with Valery Bryusov, the Russian symbolist poet. (See *Lettres de René Ghil*, Paris 1935, pp. 13-16, 18-20.)

[3] See the experimental work of Carl Stumpf, *Die Sprachlaute*, Berlin 1926, esp. p. 38 ff.

[4] W. J. Bate, *The Stylistic Development of John Keats*, New York 1945.

[5] Osip Brik, "Zvukovie povtory" (Sound-figures), in *Poetika*, St Petersburg 1919.

ing to this classification, rhyme appears as only one example of sound-repetition and should not be studied to the exclusion of such analogous phenomena as alliteration and assonance.

We should not forget that these sound-figures will vary in their effect from language to language, that each language has its own system of phonemes and hence of oppositions and parallels of vowels or affinities of consonants, and finally, that even such sound-effects are scarcely divorceable from the general meaning-tone of a poem or line. The Romantic and Symbolistic attempt to identify poetry with song and music is little more than a metaphor, since poetry cannot compete with music in the variety, clarity, and patterning of pure sounds. Meanings, context, and "tone" are needed to turn linguistic sounds into artistic facts.

This can be demonstrated clearly through a study of rhyme. Rhyme is an extremely complex phenomenon. It has its mere euphonious function as a repetition (or near-repetition) of sounds. The rhyming of vowels is, as Henry Lanz has shown in his *Physical Basis of Rime*,[6] determined by a recurrence of their overtones. But, though this sound-side may be basic, it is obviously only one aspect of rhyme. Aesthetically far more important is its metrical function signalling the conclusion of a line of verse, or as the organizer, sometimes the sole organizer, of stanzaic patterns. But, most importantly, rhyme has meaning and is thus deeply involved in the whole character of a work of poetry. Words are brought together by rhyme, linked up or contrasted. Several aspects of this semantic function of rhyme can be distinguished. We may ask what is the semantic function of the syllables which rhyme, whether rhyme is in the suffix (character, register), in the roots (drink, think), or in both (passion, fashion). We may ask from what semantic sphere rhyme-words are selected: whether, for example, they belong to one or several linguistic categories (parts of speech, different cases) or groups of objects. We might want to know what is the semantic relation between the words linked by rhyme, whether they belong to the same semantic context as do many of the common doubles (heart, part; tears, fears) or whether they surprise precisely by the association and juxtaposition of completely divergent semantic spheres. In a brilliant paper [7]

[6] Henry Lanz, *The Physical Basis of Rime*, Palo Alto 1931.
[7] W. K. Wimsatt, "One Relation of Rhyme to Reason," *Modern Language Quarterly*, v (1944), pp. 323-38 (reprinted in *The Verbal Icon*, Lexington, Ky., 1954, pp. 153-66).

W. K. Wimsatt has studied these effects in Pope and Byron, who aim at the shock of confronting "Queens" and "screens," "elope" and "Pope," or "mahogany" and "philogyny." Finally one can distinguish the degree to which rhyme is implicated in the total context of a poem, how far rhyme-words seem mere fillers or, at the opposite extreme, whether we could conjecture the meaning of a poem or stanza only from its rhyme-words. Rhymes may constitute the skeleton of a stanza or they may be minimised so much that one scarcely notices their presence (as in Browning's "Last Duchess").

Rhyme can be studied, as H. C. Wyld has done,[8] as linguistic evidence for the history of pronunciation (Pope rhymed "join" and "shrine"); but for literary purposes we must bear in mind that standards of "exactness" have varied considerably with different poetic schools and, of course, in different nations. In English, where masculine rhyme prevails, feminine and trisyllabic rhymes have usually burlesque or comic effects, while in Medieval Latin, in Italian or Polish, feminine rhymes will be obligatory in the most serious contexts. In English, we have the special problem of the eye-rhyme, the rhyming of homonyms which is a form of punning, the wide diversity of standard pronunciations in different ages and places, the idiosyncrasies of individual poets, all problems which have hitherto been scarcely raised. There is nothing in English to compare with Viktor Zhirmunsky's book on rhyme,[9] which classifies the effects of rhyme in even greater detail than this sketch and gives its history in Russia and in the main European countries.

From these sound-patterns where the repetition of a vowel or consonant-quality (as in alliteration) is decisive, we must distinguish the different problem of sound-imitation. Sound-imitation has attracted a great deal of attention, both because some of the most well-known virtuoso passages in poetry aim at such imitation and because the problem is closely connected with the older mystical conception which assumes that sound must in some way correspond with things signified. It is suffi-

[8] H. C. Wyld, *Studies in English Rhymes from Surrey to Pope*, London 1923. See also Frederick Ness, *The Use of Rhyme in Shakespeare's Plays*, New Haven 1941.

[9] V. Zhirmunsky, *Rifme, ee istoria i teoriya* (Rhyme, Its History and Theory), Petrograd 1923; Valery Bryusov, "O rifme" (On Rhyme), *Pechat i revolutsiya* 1924 (I, pp. 114-23) reviews Zhirmunsky's book and suggests many further problems for the investigation of rhyme. Charles F. Richardson, *A Study of English Rhyme*, Hanover, N. H., 1909, is a modest beginning in the right direction.

cient to think of some passages in Pope or Southey or to
remember how the seventeenth century thought of actually
intoning the music of the universe (e.g. Harsdörffer in Germany[10]). The view that a word "correctly" represents the
thing or action has been generally abandoned: modern linguistics is inclined to grant, at the most, a special class of
words, called "onomatopoeic," which are, in some respects,
outside the usual sound-system of a language and which
definitely attempt to imitate heard sounds (cuckoo, buzz,
bang, miaow). It can be easily shown that identical sound-
combinations may have completely different meanings in different languages (e.g. Rock in German means "jacket," in
English, "a large stone"; rok in Russian means "fate," in
Czech, "year"); or that certain sounds in nature are very differently represented in different languages (e.g. "ring," sonner,
läuten, zvonit). It can be shown, as John Crowe Ransom has
amusingly done, that the sound-effect of a line like the "murmuring of innumerable bees" is really dependent on the meaning. If we make only a slight phonetic change to "murdering
of innumerable beeves" we destroy the imitative effect completely.[11]

    Still, it seems that the problem has been unduly minimised
by modern linguists and is too easily dismissed by modern
critics like Richards and Ransom. One must distinguish between three different degrees. First there is the actual imitation
of physical sounds, which is undeniably successful in cases like
"cuckoo," though it may, of course, vary according to the
linguistic system of a speaker. Such sound-imitation must be
differentiated from elaborate sound-painting, the reproduction
of natural sounds through speech-sounds in a context where
words, in themselves quite devoid of onomatopoeic effects, will
be drawn into a sound-pattern like "innumerable" in the quotation from Tennyson or many words in passages in Homer
and Virgil. Finally, there is the important level of sound-symbolism or sound-metaphor, which in each language has its
established conventions and patterns. Maurice Grammont has

---

[10] Wolfgang Kayser, Die Klangmalerei bei Harsdörffer, Leipzig 1932
(Palaestra, vol. 179); I. A. Richards, Practical Criticism, London
1929, pp. 232-3.
[11] J. C. Ransom, The World's Body, New York 1938, pp. 95-7. One
could, however, argue that the change made by Mr Ransom is only
apparently slight. Replacing m by d in "murmuring" destroys the
sound pattern "m-m" and thereby makes the word "innumerable"
drop out of the sound-pattern into which it had been drawn. In isolation, "innumerable" is, of course, quite onomatopoetically ineffective.

made the most elaborate and ingenious study of French verse[12] in regard to expressiveness. He has classified all French consonants and vowels and studied their expressive effects in different poets. Clear vowels, for example, can express smallness, rapidity, élan, grace, and the like.

While the study of Grammont is open to the charge of mere subjectivity, there is still, within a given linguistic system, something like a "physiognomy" of words, a sound-symbolism far more pervasive than mere onomatopoeia. There is no doubt that synaesthetic combinations and associations permeate all languages and that these correspondences have been, quite rightly, exploited and elaborated by the poets. A poem such as Rimbaud's well-known "Les Voyelles," which gives a one-to-one relationship between individual vowels and colours, though based on a widespread tradition,[13] may be purely wilful; but the fundamental associations between front vowels (e and i) and thin, quick, clear, and bright objects and, again, between back vowels (o and u) and clumsy, slow, dull, and dark objects can be proved by acoustic experiments.[14] The work of Carl Stumpf and Wolfgang Köhler shows also that consonants can be divided into dark (labials and velars) and bright (dentals and palatals). These are by no means mere metaphors but associations based on indubitable similarities between sound and colour observable especially in the structure of the respective systems.[15] There is the general linguistic problem of "sound and meaning"[16] and the separate problem of its ex-

[12] M. Grammont, Le Vers français, ses moyens d'expression, son harmonie, Paris 1913.

[13] René Etiemble, "Le Sonnet des Voyelles," Revue de littérature comparée, xix (1939), pp. 235-61, discusses the many anticipations in A. W. Schlegel and others.

[14] Albert Wellek, "Der Sprachgeist als Doppelempfinder," Zeitschrift für Ästhetik, xxv (1931), pp. 226-62.

[15] See Stumpf, quoted in note 2, and Wolfgang Köhler, "Akustische Untersuchungen," Zeitschrift für Psychologie, LIV (1910), pp. 241-89, LVIII (1911), pp. 59-140, LXIV (1913), pp. 92-105, LXXII (1915), pp. 1-192. Roman Jakobson, Kindersprache, Aphasie und allgemeine Lautgesetze, Upsala 1941, supports these results by evidence drawn from children's language and aphasia.

[16] See e.g. E. M. Hornbostel, "Laut und Sinn," in Festschrift Meinhof, Hamburg 1927, pp. 329-48; Heinz Werner, Grundfragen der Sprachphysiognomik, Leipzig 1932. Katherine M. Wilson, Sound and Meaning in English Poetry, London 1930, is rather a general book on metrics and sound-patterns.

ploitation and organization in a work of literature. The last, especially, has been studied only very inadequately.

Rhythm and metre present problems distinct from these of "orchestration." They have been studied very widely, and a huge literature has grown up around them. The problem of rhythm is, of course, by no means specific to literature or even to language. There are the rhythms of nature and work, the rhythms of light-signals, the rhythms of music, and, in a rather metaphorical sense, the rhythms of the plastic arts. Rhythm is also a general linguistic phenomenon. We need not discuss the hundred and one theories about its actual nature.[17] For our purposes, it is sufficient to distinguish between theories requiring "periodicity" as the *sine qua non* of rhythm and theories which, conceiving of rhythm more widely, include in it even non-recurrent configurations of movements. The first view definitely identifies rhythm with metre, and thus may require the rejection of the concept of "prose rhythm" as a contradiction or a mere metaphor.[18] The other and wider view is strongly supported by the researches of Sievers into individual speech rhythms and a wide variety of musical phenomena including plain-song and much exotic music which, without periodicity, are still rhythmical. So conceived, rhythm allows us to study individual speech and the rhythm of all prose. It can easily be shown that all prose has some kind of rhythm, that even the most prosaic sentence can be scanned, that is, subdivided into groups of longs and shorts, stressed and unstressed syllables. Much was made of this fact even in the eighteenth century by a writer, Joshua Steele;[19] and there is a large literature today analysing pages of prose. Rhythm is closely associated with "melody," the line of intonation determined by the sequence of pitches; and the term is frequently used so broadly as to include both rhythm and melody. The famous German philologist Eduard Sievers professed to distinguish personal rhythmical and intonational patterns, and Ottmar Rutz has associated these with specific physiological

[17] Convenient recent surveys are A. W. de Groot, "Der Rhythmus," *Neophilologus*, XVII (1932), pp. 81-100, 177-97, 241-65; and Dietrich Sekel, *Hölderlins Sprachrhythmus*, Leipzig 1937 (Palaestra 207), a book which contains a general discussion of rhythm and a full bibliography.

[18] e.g. in W. K. Wimsatt's *The Prose Style of Samuel Johnson*, New Haven 1941, pp. 5-8.

[19] Joshua Steele, *Prosodia Rationalis, or an Essay towards Establishing the Melody and Measure of Speech*, London 1775.

types of bodily posture and breathing.[20] Though attempts have
been made to apply these researches to strictly literary purposes, to establish a correlation between literary styles and
the types of Rutz,[21] these questions seem to us mostly outside
the realm of literary scholarship.

We enter the realm of literary scholarship when we have
to explain the nature of prose rhythm, the peculiarity and use
of rhythmical prose, the prose of certain passages in the English Bible, in Sir Thomas Browne, and Ruskin or De Quincey,
where rhythm and sometimes melody force themselves even
on the unattentive reader. The exact nature of the artistic
prose rhythm has caused very considerable difficulty. One
well-known book, W. M. Patterson's *Rhythm of Prose*,[22] tried
to account for it by a system of elaborate syncopation. George
Saintsbury's very full *History of English Prose Rhythm*[23] constantly insists that prose rhythm is based on "variety," but
leaves its actual nature completely undefined. If Saintsbury's
"explanation" were correct there would be, of course, no rhythm at all. But Saintsbury doubtless was only stressing the
danger of prose rhythm's falling into exact metrical patterns.
Today, at least, we feel the frequent blank verse in Dickens as
awkward and sentimental deviation.

Other investigators of prose rhythm study only one rather
distinct aspect, "cadence," the concluding rhythm of sentences
in the tradition of Latin oratorical prose for which Latin had
exact patterns with specific names. "Cadence," especially in
interrogatory and exclamatory sentences, is partly also a question of melody. The modern reader has difficulty in hearing the
elaborate patterns of the Latin cursus when imitated in English, since English stresses are not fixed with the same conventional rigidity as longs and shorts in the Latin system; but it
has been shown that effects analogous to the Latin were widely

---

[20] Eduard Sievers, *Rhythmisch-melodische Studien*, Heidelberg 1912;
Ottmar Rutz, *Musik, Wort und Körper als Gemütsausdruck*, Leipzig
1911, *Sprache, Gesang und Körperhaltung*, Munich 1911, *Mensch-
heitstypen und Kunst*, Jena 1921; Gunther Ipsen and Fritz Karg,
Schallanalytische Versuche, Heidelberg 1938, lists the literature on
this question.

[21] O. Walzel, *Gehalt und Gestalt in dichterischen Kunstwerk*, Pots-
dam 1923, pp. 96-105, 391-94. Gustav Becking, *Der musikalische
Rhythmus als Erkenntnisquelle*, Augsburg 1923, is an admired, but
fantastic attempt to use Sievers's theories.

[22] W. M. Patterson, *The Rhythm of Prose*, New York 1916.

[23] G. Saintsbury, *A History of English Prose Rhythm*, London 1913.

attempted and occasionally achieved, especially in the seventeenth century.[24]

In general, the artistic rhythm of prose is best approached by keeping clearly in mind that it has to be distinguished both from the general rhythm of prose and from verse. The artistic rhythm of prose can be described as an organization of ordinary speech rhythms. It differs from ordinary prose by a greater regularity of stress distribution, which, however, must not reach an apparent isochronism (that is, a regularity of time intervals between rhythmical accents). In an ordinary sentence there are usually considerable differences of intensity and pitch, while in rhythmical prose there is a marked tendency towards a levelling of stress and pitch differences. Analysing passages from Pushkin's The Queen of Spades, Boris Tomashevsky, one of the foremost Russian students of these questions, has shown by statistical methods[25] that the beginnings and ends of sentences tend towards greater rhythmical regularity than do the centres. The general impression of regularity and periodicity is usually strengthened by phonetic and syntactical devices: by sound-figures, by parallel clauses, antithetic balancings where the whole structure of meaning strongly supports the rhythmical pattern. There are all kinds of gradations from almost non-rhythmical prose: from chopped sentences full of accumulated stresses to rhythmical prose approaching the regularity of verse. The main transitional form towards verse is called ver set by the French and occurs in the English Psalms and in such writers who aim at Biblical effects as Ossian or Claudel. Every other accented syllable in the ver set is stressed more strongly, and thus groups of two stresses are created similar to the groups in dipodic verse.

We need not enter into a detailed analysis of these devices. They clearly have a long history which has been most profoundly influenced by Latin oratorical prose.[26] In English literature, rhythmical prose climaxes in the seventeenth century with writers like Sir Thomas Browne or Jeremy Taylor.

[24] Oliver Elton, "English Prose Numbers," A Sheaf of Papers, London 1922; Morris W. Croll, "The Cadence of English Oratorical Prose," Studies in Philology, xvi (1919), pp. 1-55.

[25] B. Tomashevsky, "Ritm prozy (po Pikovey Dame)" (Prose Rhythm, according to The Queen of Spades), O Stikhe. Statyi. (Essays on Verse), Leningrad 1929.

[26] Eduard Norden, Die antike Kunstprosa, Leipzig 1898, two vols., is standard. See also Albert de Groot, A Handbook of Antique Prose Rhythm, Groningen 1919.

It gives way to a more simple colloquial diction in the eight-
eenth century, even if a new "grand style"—the style of
Johnson, Gibbon, and Burke—arose towards the end of the
century.[27] It was variously revived in the nineteenth century by
De Quincey and Ruskin, Emerson and Melville, and again,
though on different principles, by Gertrude Stein and James
Joyce. In France, there is the splendour of Bossuet's and
Chateaubriand's prose; in Germany, there is the rhythmical
prose of Nietzsche; in Russia, there are famous passages in
Gogol and Turgenev and, more recently, the "ornamental"
prose of Andrey Byely.

The artistic value of rhythmical prose is still debated and
debatable. In accordance with the modern preference for
purity in the arts and genres, most modern readers prefer their
poetry poetic and their prose prosaic. Rhythmical prose seems
to be felt as a mixed form, as neither prose nor verse. But this
is probably a critical prejudice of our time. A defence of
rhythmical prose would presumably be the same as a defence
of verse. Used well it forces us into a fuller awareness of the
text; it underscores; it ties together; it builds up gradations,
suggests parallelisms; it organizes speech; and organization is
art.

Prosody, or metrics, is a subject which has attracted an
enormous amount of labour through the centuries. Today it
might be supposed we need do little more than survey new
metrical specimens and extend such studies to the new techniques of recent poetry. Actually, the very foundations and
main criteria of metrics are still uncertain; and there is an
astonishing amount of loose thinking and confused or shifting
terminology even in standard treatises. Saintsbury's *History of
English Prosody*, which in its scale has never been surpassed or
equalled, rests on completely undefined and vague theoretical
foundations. In his strange empiricism, Saintsbury is even
proud of his refusal to define or even to describe his terms.
He speaks for instance of longs and shorts, but cannot make up
his mind whether his term refers to distinctions in duration
or stress.[28] In his *Study of Poetry*, Bliss Perry speaks confusedly
and confusingly of the "weight" of words, "the relative loudness or pitch, by which their meaning or importance is indi-

[27] See William K. Wimsatt's *The Prose Style of Samuel Johnson*,
New Haven 1941.
[28] G. Saintsbury, *History of English Prosody*, three vols., London
1906-10.

cated."[29] Similar misconceptions and equivocations could be easily quoted from many other standard books. Even when correct distinctions are made, they may be disguised under a completely contradictory terminology. Thus T. S. Omond's elaborate history of English metrical theories and Pallister Barkas's useful survey of recent theories[30] must be welcomed as attempts to straighten out these confusions though their conclusions support an unwarranted scepticism. One must multiply these distinctions many times when we consider the enormous variety of metrical theories on the Continent, especially in France, Germany, and Russia.

For our purposes it will be best to distinguish only the main types of metrical theories without getting involved in the finer differences or in mixed types. The oldest type can be called "graphic" prosody and is derived from Renaissance handbooks. It works with graphic signs of longs and shorts, which in English usually are meant to represent the stressed and unstressed syllables. Graphic prosodists usually attempt to draw up metrical schemes or patterns which the poet is assumed to observe exactly. We all have learned their terminology in school, have heard of iambi, trochees, anapaests, and spondees. These terms are still the most widely understood and the most useful for ordinary descriptions and discussions of metrical patterns. Yet the insufficiency of the whole system is today widely recognized. It is obvious that the theory pays no attention to actual sound and that its usual dogmatism is completely mistaken. Everybody today understands that verse would be the dullest of monotones if it really fulfilled the graphic patterns exactly. The theory lingers mostly in classrooms and elementary textbooks. It has, however, its merits. It concentrates frankly on metrical patterns and ignores the minutiae and personal idiosyncrasies of the performer, a difficulty which many modern systems have been unable to avoid. Graphic metrics knows that metre is not merely a matter of sound, that there is a metrical pattern which is thought of as implied or underlying the actual poem.

The second type is the "musical" theory, based on the assumption, correct as far as it goes, that metre in poetry is analogous to rhythm in music and thus best represented by musical notation. An early standard exposition in English is

---

[29] Bliss Perry, A Study of Poetry, London 1920, p. 145.
[30] T. S. Omond, English Metrists, Oxford 1921; Pallister Barkas, A Critique of Modern English Prosody, Halle 1934 (Studien zur englischen Philologie, ed. Morsbach and Hecht, LXXXII).

Sidney Lanier's *Science of English Verse* (1880); but the
theory has been refined upon and modified by recent investigators.[31] In America, at least among teachers of English, it
seems the accepted theory. According to this system, each
syllable is assigned a musical note, of undesignated height.
The length of the note is determined rather arbitrarily by
assigning a half-note to a long syllable, a quarter-note to a
semi-short syllable, an eighth-note to a short syllable, and so
on. Measures are counted from one accented syllable to another; and the speed of reading is indicated rather vaguely
by choosing either ¾ or ⅜, or in rare cases 3/2 measures. With
such a system it is possible to arrive at the notation of any
English text, e.g. an ordinary English pentameter line like
Pope's

> Lo, the poor Indian whose untutored mind

can be written out as three-eight thus

According to this theory, the distinction of iambus and trochee
will be completely reinterpreted, the iambus being merely
characterized by an anacrusis, which is considered extrametrical or counted with the preceding line. Even the most complex metres can be written out in such a notation by a judicious
introduction of rests and the handling of longs and shorts.[33]

The theory has the merit of strongly stressing the tendency
of verse towards subjectively felt isochronism, the ways in
which we slow down or speed up, lengthen or shorten the
reading of words, introduce pauses to equalize measures. The

[31] See esp. M. W. Croll, "Music and Metrics," *Studies in Philology*,
xx (1923), pp. 388-94; G. R. Stewart, Jun., *The Technique of English
Verse*, New York 1930.
[32] This notation comes from Morris W. Croll, *The Rhythm of English Verse* (mimeographed pamphlet, Princeton 1929), p. 8. It seems
a highly artificial reading to substitute a rest for a primary accent.
[33] The most elaborate theoretical book, with hundreds of examples, is
William Thomson's *The Rhythm of Speech*, Glasgow 1923. A recent
subtle exponent is John C. Pope, *The Rhythm of Beowulf*, New
Haven 1942.

notation will be most successful with "singable" verse, but it seems highly inadequate in dealing with colloquial or oratorical types of verse and is usually helpless when it has to deal with free verse or any verse which is not isochronic. Some propounders of the theory simply deny that free verse is verse.[34] Musical theorists can handle ballad metre as "dipodic," or even double compound measures successfully,[35] and can account for some metrical phenomena by the introduction of the term "syncopation." In Browning's verses

> The gray sea and the long black land
> And the yellow half-moon large and low

"sea" and "black" in the first line and "half" in the second can be noted as syncopated. The merits of the musical theory are obvious: it did much to defeat the usual schoolroom dogmatism; and it allowed the handling and notation of metres unprovided for in textbooks, e.g. some of the complex metres of Swinburne, Meredith, or Browning. But the theory has serious deficiencies: it gives free reign to arbitrary individual readings; it levels out distinctions between poets and schools of poetry by reducing all verse to a few types of monotonous beats. It seems to invite or imply chant-like oral performance of all poetry. And the isochronism it establishes is little more than subjective, a system of sound and rest sections perceived as equalized when compared with each other.

A third metrical theory, acoustic metrics, is today widely respected. It is based on objective investigations, frequently employing scientific instruments such as the oscillograph, which allows the recording and even photographing of the actual events in the reading of poetry. The techniques of scientific sound-investigation were applied to metrics by Sievers and Saran in Germany, by Verrier, who used mostly English materials, in France, and, in America, by E. W. Scripture.[36] A brief statement of some basic results can be found in Wilbur L. Schramm's *Approaches to a Science of English Verse*.[37] Acoustical metrics has clearly established the distinct elements

---

[34] e.g. Donald Stauffer, *The Nature of Poetry*, New York 1946, pp. 203-4.

[35] George R. Stewart, Jun., *Modern Metrical Technique as Illustrated by Ballad Meter* (1700-1920), New York 1922.

[36] See bibliography, section III, 2.

[37] W. L. Schramm, University of Iowa Studies, Series on Aims and Progress of Research, No. 46, Iowa City, Ia. 1935.

constituent of metre. Today, therefore, there is no excuse for
confusing pitch, loudness, timbre, and time, since these can
be shown to correspond to the physical, measurable factors of
frequency, amplitude, form, and duration of the sound-waves
emitted by the speaker. We can photograph or draw the findings of the physical instruments so clearly that we can study
every minute detail of the actual events of any recitation. The
oscillograph will show us with what loudness, and what time,
with what changes of pitch, a given reader recited this or that
line of poetry. The first line of *Paradise Lost* will appear as a
figure similar to the violent oscillations on a seismograph during an earthquake.[38] This is indubitably an achievement; and
many scientifically inclined people (among whom, of course,
are many Americans) conclude that we cannot go beyond
these findings. Yet laboratory metrics obviously ignores, and
has to ignore, meaning: thus it is concluded that there is no
such thing as a syllable, since there is a continuum of voice;
that there is no such thing as a word, since its limits cannot
appear on the oscillograph; and that there is even no melody
in the strict sense, since pitch, carried only by the vowels and
a few consonants, is constantly interrupted by noises. Acoustic
metrics also shows that there is no strict isochronism, since the
actual duration of measures varies considerably. There are no
fixed "longs and shorts," at least in English, for a "short"
syllable may be physically longer than a "long"; and there are
even no objective distinctions of stress, for a "stressed" syllable may be actually pronounced with less intensity than an
unstressed one.

But while one may acknowledge the usefulness of these
results, the very foundations of this "science" are open to
grave objections which greatly minimize its values for literary
students. The whole assumption that the findings of the
oscillograph are directly relevant to the study of metrics is
mistaken. The time of verse-language is a time of expectation.[39]
We expect after a certain time a rhythmical signal, but this
periodicity need not be exact nor need the signal be actually
strong so long as we feel it to be strong. Musical metrics is
indubitably correct in saying that all these distinctions of time
and stress as well as pitch are only relative and subjective. But

[38] See the title-page of Henry Lanz, *The Physical Basis of Rime*, Stanford Press 1931.
[39] Vittorio Benussi, *Psychologie de Zeitauffassung*, Heidelberg 1913,
pp. 215 ff.

acoustic and musical metrics share one common defect or, rather, limitation: they rely exclusively on sound, on a single or many performances of reciters. The results of acoustic and musical metrics are conclusive only for this or that particular recitation. They ignore the fact that a reciter may or may not recite correctly, that he may add elements or may distort or completely disregard the pattern.

A line like

Silent upon a peak in Darien

can be read by imposing the metrical pattern: 'Silént upón a péak in Dárién"; or it may be read as prose: "Sílent upón a péak in Dárien"; or it may be read in various ways reconciling the metrical pattern and the prose rhythm. In hearing "silént" we shall, as English speakers, feel the violence done to "natural" speech; in hearing "sílent" we still shall feel the "carry-over" of the metrical pattern from the preceding lines. The compromise of a "hovering accent" may be anywhere between the two extremes; but in all cases, whatever the reading, the specific performance of a reciter will be irrelevant to an analysis of the prosodic situation, which consists precisely in the tension, the "counterpoint," between the metrical pattern and the prose rhythm.

The pattern of verse is inaccessible and incomprehensible to merely acoustic or musical methods. The meaning of verse simply cannot be ignored in a theory of metrics. One of the best musical metrists, George R. Stewart, formulates, for example, that "verse can exist without meaning," that since

> metre is essentially independent of meaning, we may with propriety attempt to reproduce the metrical structure of any particular line entirely apart from its meaning.[40]

Verrier and Saran have formulated the dogma that we must take the viewpoint of a foreigner who listens to the verse without understanding the language.[41] But this conception, which in practice is quite untenable and is actually deserted by Stewart,[42] must result in disastrous consequences for any

---

[40] G. R. Stewart, *The Technique of English Verse*, New York 1930, p. 3.

[41] Saran, *Deutsche Verslehre*, loc. cit., p. 1; Verrier, *Essai* . . . , Vol. 1, p. ix.

[42] Stewart has to introduce the term "phrase," which implies an understanding of meaning.

literary study of metrics. If we ignore meaning, we give up the concept of word and phrase and thus give up the possibility of analysing the differences between the verse of different authors. English verse is largely determined by the counterpoint between the imposed phrasing, the rhythmical impulse, and the actual speech rhythm conditioned by phrasal divisions. But the phrasal division can be ascertained only upon familiarity with the meaning of the verse.

The Russian formalists[43] have therefore tried to put metrics on an entirely new basis. The term "foot" seems to them inadequate, since there is much verse without "feet." Isochronism, though subjectively applicable to much verse, is also limited to particular types and, furthermore, is not accessible to objective investigation. All these theories, they argue, wrongly define the fundamental unit of poetic rhythm. If we see verse merely as segments grouped around some stressed syllable (or long syllable, in quantitative systems), we shall be unable to deny that the same groupings, and even the same order of groupings, can be found in types of linguistic pronouncements not describable as poetry. The fundamental unity of rhythm is, then, not the foot but the whole line, a conclusion which follows from the general Gestalt theory which the Russians embrace. Feet have no independent existence; they exist only in relation to the whole verse. Each stress has its own peculiarities according to its position in the verse, that is, whether it is the first, the second, or the third, etc., foot. The organizing unity in verse varies in different languages and metrical systems. It may be "melody," that is, the sequence of pitches which, in certain free verse, may be the only mark distinguishing it from prose.[44] If we do not know from the context, or the arrangement of print which serves as a signal, that a passage of free verse is verse, we could read it as prose and indeed not distinguish it from prose. Yet it can be read as verse and, as such, will be read differently, i.e. with a different intonation. This intonation, they show in great detail, is always two-part, or dipodic; and if we eliminate it, verse ceases to be verse, becoming merely rhythmical prose.

In the study of ordinary metrical verse, the Russians apply

[43] See bibliography and Victor Erlich, Russian Formalism, The Hague 1955.
[44] Jan Mukařovsky, "Intonation comme facteur de rythme poétique," Archives néerlandaises de phonétique expérimentale, VIII-IX (1933), pp. 153-65.

statistical methods to the relation between the pattern and the speech rhythm. Verse is conceived as an elaborate contrapuntal pattern between the superimposed metre and the ordinary rhythm of speech, for, as they strikingly say, verse is "organized violence" committed on everyday language. They distinguish "rhythmical impulse" from pattern. Pattern is static, graphic. "Rhythmical impulse" is dynamic, progressive. We anticipate the signals which are to follow. We organize not only the time but all the other elements of the work of art. Rhythmical impulse, so conceived, influences the choice of words, the syntactical structure, and hence the general meaning of a verse.

The statistical method used is very simple. In each poem or section of a poem to be analysed, one counts the percentage of cases in which each syllable carries a stress. If, in a pentameter line, the verse should be absolutely regular, the statistics would show zero percentage on the first syllable, one hundred per cent on the second, zero on the third, one hundred on the fourth, etc. This could be shown graphically by drawing one line for the number of syllables and another, vertically opposed to it, for the percentages. Verse of such regularity, is of course, infrequent, for the simple reason that it is extremely monotonous. Most verse shows a counterpoint between pattern and actual fulfilment, e.g. in blank verse the number of cases of accents on the first syllable may be rather high, a well-known phenomenon described either as the "trochaic foot," or "hovering" accent, or "substitution." In a diagram, the graph may appear flattened out very considerably; but if it is still pentameter and intended as such, the graph will preserve some general tendency towards culmination points on syllables 2, 4, 6, and 8. This statistical method is, of course, no end in itself. But it has the advantage of taking account of the whole poem and thus revealing tendencies which may not be clearly marked in a few lines. It has the further advantage of exhibiting at a glance the differences between schools of poetry and authors. In Russian, the method works especially well, since each word has only a single accent (subsidiary accents are not stresses but matters of breathing), while in English good statistics would be fairly complex, taking into account the secondary accent and the many enclitic and proclitic words.

Great stress is laid by Russian metrists on the fact that different schools and different authors fulfil ideal patterns differently, that each school or sometimes author has its own metrical norm, and that it is unfair and false to judge schools and authors in the light of any one particular dogma. The history of versification appears as a constant conflict between different norms, and one extreme is very likely to be replaced by another. The Russians also stress, most usefully, the vast differences between linguistic systems of versification. The usual classification of verse systems into syllabic, accentual, and quantitative is not only insufficient but even misleading. For instance, in Serbo-Croat and Finnish epic verse, all three principles—syllabism, quantity, and accent—play their part. Modern research has shown that the supposedly purely quantitative Latin prosody was, in practice, considerably modified by attention to accent and to the limits of words.[45]

Languages vary according to the element which is the basis of its rhythm. English is obviously determined by stress, while quantity, in English, is subordinated to accent, and the word limits also play an important rhythmical function. The rhythmical difference between a line made out of monosyllables and one entirely made out of polysyllabic words is striking. In Czech, the word limit is the basis of rhythm, which is always accompanied by obligatory stress, while quantity appears as merely an optional diversifying element. In Chinese, pitch is the main basis of rhythm, while in ancient Greek, quantity was the organizing principle, with pitch and the limits of words as optional diversifying elements.

Within the history of a specific language, though systems of versification may have been replaced by other systems, we should not speak of "progress" or condemn the older systems as mere clumsy doggerel, mere approximations to the later established systems. In Russian, a long period was dominated by syllabism, in Czech, by quantitative prosody. The study of the history of English versification from Chaucer to Surrey could be revolutionized were it realized that poets such as Lydgate, Hawes, and Skelton did not write imperfect verse but followed conventions of their own.[46] Even a reasoned defence of the much-ridiculed attempt to introduce quantitative metre into English by men of such distinction as Sidney, Spenser, and Gabriel Harvey could be attempted. Their abortive movement was at least historically important for the break-

[45] Eduard Fraenkel, *Iktus und Akzent im lateinischen Sprechvers*, Berlin 1928.
[46] Some beginnings are to be found in Albert H. Licklider, *Chapters on the Metric of the Chaucerian Tradition*, Baltimore 1910.

ing down of the syllabic rigidity of much earlier English verse.

It is also possible to attempt a comparative history of metrics. The famous French linguist, Antoine Meillet, in his *Les Origines indo-européenes des mètres grecs*, compared ancient Greek and Vedic metres for the purpose of reconstructing the Indo-European metrical system;[47] and Roman Jakobson has shown that the Yugoslav epic verse is very close to this ancient pattern which combines a syllabic line with a curiously rigid quantitative class.[48] It is possible to distinguish and to trace the history of different types of folklore verse. The epic recitative and the "melodic" verse used in the lyric must be sharply differentiated. In every language, epic verse seems to be far more conservative, while song verse, which is most closely associated with a language's phonetic features, is liable to far greater national diversity. Even for modern verse, it is important to keep in mind the distinctions between oratorical, conversational, and "melodic" verse, distinctions ignored by most English metrists, who, under influence of the musical theory, are preoccupied with song verse.[49]

In a valuable study of nineteenth-century Russian lyrical verse,[50] Boris Eikhenbaum has attempted to analyse the role of intonation in "melodic," "singable," verse. He shows strikingly how the Russian romantic lyric has exploited tripodic measures, intonation schemes such as exclamatory and interrogatory sentences, and syntactical patterns such as parallelism; but, in our opinion, he has not established his central thesis of the forming power of intonation in "singable" verse.[15]

We may be doubtful about a good many features of the Russian theories, but one cannot deny that they have found a way out of the impasse of the laboratory on the one hand, and the mere subjectivism of the musical metrists on the other. Much is still obscure and controversial; but metrics has today

---

[47] A. Meillet, *Les Origines indo-européenes des mètres grecs*, Paris 1923.

[48] Roman Jakobson, "Über den Versbau der serbokroatischen Volksepen," *Archives néerlandaises de phonétique expérimentale*, VIII-IX (1933), pp. 135-53.

[49] Thomas MacDonagh (*Thomas Campion and the Art of English Poetry*, Dublin 1913) distinguishes between song, speech, and chant verse.

[50] Boris E. Eikhenbaum, *Melodika lyricheskovo stikha* (*The Melody of Lyrical Verse*), St Petersburg 1922.

[51] See the criticism of Eikhenbaum in Viktor Zhirmunsky's *Voprosy teorii literatury* (*Questions of the Theory of Literature*), Leningrad 1928.

restored the necessary contact with linguistics and with literary semantics. Sound and metre, we see, must be studied as elements of the totality of a work of art, not in isolation from meaning.

I. A. RICHARDS

Rhythm and Metre

[Coleridge defined aesthetic form as "the fulfillment of expectation." Taking his cue from Coleridge, I. A. Richards develops a closely argued account of the mind's response to
rhythm and meter. Richards observes that sound alone can
have little effect on psychological process; it is pattern of sound
in conjunction with "its contemporaneous other effects"—
chiefly meaning or propositional sense—that produces a
unique impact on our nervous structure.

[Richards is the thorough "contextualist"; he points out
that everything that happens in a poem depends on the poem's
organic environment. He acknowledges the complexity of the
sound-sense relationship; the meter may qualify, embellish, or
comment on the meaning of the words. Perhaps meter's most
important function is to provide aesthetic distance; through
the precise control of feeling, meter makes possible "the most
difficult and delicate utterances."]

> ... when it approaches with a divine hopping.
> The Joyful Wisdom.

RHYTHM and its specialised form, metre, depend upon repetition, and expectancy. Equally where what is expected recurs
and where it fails, all rhythmical and metrical effects spring
from anticipation. As a rule this anticipation is unconscious.
Sequences of syllables both as sounds and as images of speech-
movements leave the mind ready for certain further sequences
rather than for others. Our momentary organisation is adapted
to one range of possible stimuli rather than to another. Just
as the eye reading print unconsciously expects the spelling to
be as usual, and the fount of type to remain the same, so the

Chapter XVII from Principles of Literary Criticism. Used by permission of Harcourt, Brace, and World, Inc.

mind after reading a line or two of verse, or half a sentence of prose, prepares itself ahead for any one of a number of possible sequences, at the same time negatively incapacitating itself for others. The effect produced by what actually follows depends very closely upon this unconscious preparation and consists largely of the further twist which it gives to expectancy. It is in terms of the variation in these twists that rhythm is to be described. Both prose and verse vary immensely in the extent to which they excite this "getting ready" process, and in the narrowness of the anticipation which is formed. Prose on the whole, with the rare exceptions of a Landor, a De Quincey, or a Ruskin, is accompanied by a very much vaguer and more indeterminate expectancy than verse. In such prose as this page, for example, little more than a preparedness for further words not all exactly alike in sound and with abstract polysyllables preponderating is all that arises. In short, the sensory or formal effect of words has very little play in the literature of analysis and exposition. But as soon as prose becomes more emotive than scientific, the formal side becomes prominent.

Let us take Landor's description[1] of a lioness suckling her young—

> On perceiving the countryman, she drew up her feet gently, and squared her mouth, and rounded her eyes, slumberous with content; and they looked, he said, like sea-grottoes, obscurely green, interminably deep, at once awakening fear and stilling and suppressing it.

After "obscurely green" would it be possible (quite apart from sense) to have "deeply dark" or "impenetrably gloomy"? Why, apart from sense, can so few of the syllables be changed in vowel sound, in emphasis, in duration or otherwise, without disaster to the total effect? As with all such questions about sensory form and its effects, only an incomplete answer can be given. The expectancy caused by what has gone before, a thing which must be thought of as a very complex tide of neural settings, lowering the threshold for some kinds of stimuli and raising it for others, and the character of the stimulus which does actually come, both play their part.

Even the most highly organised lyrical or "polyphonic" prose raises as it advances only a very ambiguous expectation. Until the final words of the passage, there are always a great number of different sequences which would equally well fit in, which would satisfy the expectancy so far as that is merely

[1] Works, II, 171.

due to *habit*, to the *routine of sensory stimulation*. What is expected in fact is not this sound or that sound, not even this kind of sound or that kind of sound, but some one of a certain thousand kinds of sounds. It is much more a negative thing than a positive. As in the case of many social conventions it is easier to say what disqualifies than to say what is required.

In this very indeterminate expectancy the new element comes with its own range of possible effects. There is, of course, no such thing as *the* effect of a word or a sound. There is no one effect which belongs to it. Words have no intrinsic literary characters. None are either ugly or beautiful, intrinsically displeasing or delightful. Every word has instead a range of possible effects, varying with the conditions into which it is received. All that we can say as to the sorting out of words, whether into the "combed" and "slippery," the "shaggy" and "rumpled" as with Dante, or in any other manner, is that some, through long use, have narrower ranges than others and require more extraordinary conditions if they are to change their "character." What effect the word has is a compromise between some one of its possible effects and the special conditions into which it comes. Thus in Shakespeare hardly any word ever looks odd until we consider it; whereas even in Keats the "cold mushrooms" in the *Satyr's Song* give the mind a shock of astonishment, an astonishment which is full of delight, but none the less is a shock.

But with this example we have broken down the limitation to the mere sound, to the strictly formal or sensory aspect of word sequences, and in fact the limitation is useless. For the effect of a word as sound cannot be separated from its contemporaneous other effects. They become inextricably mingled at once.

The sound gets its character by compromise with what is going on already. The preceding agitation of the mind selects from a range of possible characters which the word might present, that one which best suits with what is happening. There are no gloomy and no gay vowels or syllables, and the army of critics who have attempted to analyse the effects of passages into vowel and consonantal collocations have, in fact, been merely amusing themselves. The way in which the sound of a word is taken varies with the emotion already in being. But, further, it varies with the sense. For the anticipation of the sound due to habit, to the routine of sensation, is merely a part of the general expectancy. Grammatical regularities, the necessity for completing the thought, the reader's state of conjecture as to what is being said, his apprehension in dramatic literature of the action, of the intention, situation, state of mind generally, of the speaker, all these and many other things intervene. The way the sound is taken is much less determined by the sound itself than by the conditions into which it enters. All these anticipations form a very closely woven network and the word which can satisfy them all simultaneously may well seem triumphant. But we should not attribute to the sound alone virtues which involve so many other factors. To say this is not in the least to belittle the importance of the sound; in most cases it is the key to the effects of poetry.

This texture of expectations, satisfactions, disappointments, surprisals, which the sequence of syllables brings about, is rhythm. And the sound of words comes to its full power only through rhythm. Evidently there can be no surprise and no disappointment unless there is expectation and most rhythms perhaps are made up as much of disappointments and postponements and surprises and betrayals as of simple, straightforward satisfactions. Hence the rapidity with which too simple rhythms, those which are too easily "seen through," grow cloying or insipid unless hypnotical states intervene, as with much primitive music and dancing and often with metre.

The same definition of rhythm may be extended to the plastic arts and to architecture. Temporal sequence is not strictly necessary for rhythm, though in the vast majority of cases it is involved. The attention usually passes successively from one complex to another, the expectations, the readiness to perceive this rather than that, aroused by the one being either satisfied or surprised by the other. Surprise plays an equally important part here; and the difference in detail between a surprising and delightful variation and one which merely irritates and breaks down the rhythm, as we say, is here, as elsewhere, a matter of the combination and resolution of impulses too subtle for our present means of investigation. All depends upon whether what comes can be an ingredient in the further response, or whether the mind must, as it were, start anew; in more ordinary language, upon whether there is any "connection" between the parts of the whole.

But the rhythmic elements in a picture or a building may be not successive but simultaneous. A quick reader who sees a word as a whole commonly overlooks misprints because the general form of the word is such that he is only able at that instant to perceive one particular letter in a particular place and so overlooks what is discrepant. The parts of a visual field

exert what amounts to a simultaneous influence over one another. More strictly what is discrepant does not get through
to more central regions. Similarly, with those far more intricate wholes, made up of all kinds of imagery and incipient action of which works of art consist. The parts of a growing
response mutually modify one another and this is all that is
required for rhythm to be possible.

We may turn now to that more complex and more specialised form of temporal rhythmic sequence which is known
as metre. This is the means by which words may be made to
influence one another to the greatest possible extent. In metrical reading the narrowness and definiteness of expectancy,
as much unconscious as ever in most cases, is very greatly increased, reaching in some cases, if rime also is used, almost
exact precision. Furthermore, what is anticipated becomes
through the regularity of the time intervals in metre virtually
dated. This is no mere matter of more or less perfect correspondence with the beating of some internal metronome. The whole conception of metre as "*uniformity in
variety*," a kind of mental drill in which words, those erratic
and varied things, do their best to behave as though they
were all the same, with certain concessions, licenses and equiv-
alences allowed, should nowadays be obsolete. It is a survivor
which is still able to do a great deal of harm to the uniniti-
ated, however, and although it has been knocked on the head
vigorously enough by Professor Saintsbury and others, it is as
difficult to kill as Punch. Most treatises on the subject, with
their talk of feet and of stresses, unfortunately tend to en-
courage it, however little this may be the aim of the authors.

As with rhythm so with metre, we must not think of it as
in the words themselves or in the thumping of the drum.
It is not *in* the stimulation, it is in our response. Metre adds
to all the variously fated expectancies which make up rhythm
a definite temporal pattern and its effect is not due to our perceiving a pattern in something outside us, but to our becoming patterned ourselves. With every beat of the metre a tide
of anticipation in us turns and swings, setting up as it does so
extraordinarily extensive sympathetic reverberations. We shall
never understand metre so long as we ask, "Why does temporal pattern so excite us?" and fail to realise that the pattern
itself is a vast cyclic agitation spreading all over the body, a
tide of excitement pouring through the channels of the mind.

The notion that there is any virtue in regularity or in variety, or in any other formal feature, apart from its effects upon us, must be discarded before any metrical problem can be understood. The regularity to which metre tends acts through the definiteness of the anticipations which are thereby aroused. It is through these that it gets such a hold upon the mind. Once again, here too, the failure of our expectations is often more important than success. Verse in which we constantly get exactly what we are ready for and no more, instead of something which we can and must take up and incorporate as another stage in a total developing response is merely toilsome and tedious. In prose, the influence of past words extends only a little way ahead. In verse, especially when stanza-form and rime co-operate to give a larger unit than the line, it may extend far ahead. It is this knitting together of the parts of the poem which explains the mnemonic power of verse, the first of the suggestions as to the origin of metre to be found in the Fourteenth Chapter of *Biographia Literaria*, that lumber-room of neglected wisdom which contains more hints towards a theory of poetry than all the rest ever written upon the subject.

We do great violence to the facts if we suppose the expectations excited as we read verse to be concerned only with the stress, emphasis, length, foot structure and so forth of the syllables which follow. Even in this respect the custom of marking syllables in two degrees only, long and short, light and full, etc., is inadequate, although doubtless forced upon metrists by practical considerations. The mind in the poetic experience responds to subtler niceties than these. When not in that experience but coldly considering their several qualities as sounds by the ear alone, it may well find two degrees all that are necessary. The obvious comparison with the difference between what even musical notation can record in music and the player's interpretation can usefully be made here.

A more serious omission is the neglect by the majority of metrists of the pitch relations of syllables. The reading of poetry is of course not a monotonous and subdued form of singing. There is no question of definite pitches at which the syllables must be taken, nor perhaps of definite harmonic relations between different sounds. But that a rise and fall of pitch is involved in metre and is as much part of the poet's technique as any other features of verse, as much under his control also, is indisputable. Anyone who is not clear upon this point may compare as a striking instance Milton's *Hymn on the Morning of Christ's Nativity* with Collins' *Ode to Simplicity* and both with the second Chorus of *Hellas*. Due allowances made for the natural peculiarities of different readers, the scheme of pitch relations, in their contexts, of

> That on the bitter cross
> Must redeem our loss;

and of

> But com'st a decent maid,
> In Attic robe array'd,

are clearly different. There is nothing arbitrary or out of the poet's control in this, as there is nothing arbitrary or out of his control in the way in which an adequate reader will stress particular syllables. He brings both about by the same means, the modification of the reader's impulses at what has gone before. It is true that some words resist emphasis far more than perhaps any resist change of pitch, yet this difference is merely one of degree. It is as natural to lower the pitch in reading the word "loss" as it is to emphasise it as compared with "our" in the same context.

Here again we see how impossible it is to consider rhythm or metre as though it were purely an affair of the sensory aspect of syllables and could be dissociated from their sense and from the emotional effects which come about through their sense. One principle may, however, be hazarded. As in the case of painting the more direct means are preferable to the less direct, so in poetry. What can be done by sound should not be done otherwise or in violation of the natural effects of sound. Violations of the natural emphases and tones of speech brought about for the sake of the further effects due to thought and feeling are perilous, though, on occasion, they may be valuable devices. The use of italics in *Cain* to straighten out the blank verse is as glaring an instance as any. But more liberties are justified in dramatic writing than elsewhere, and poetry is full of exceptions to such principles.[2] We must not forget that Milton did not disdain to use spelling, "mee," for example, in place of "me," in order to suggest additional emphasis when he feared that the reader might be careless.

So far we have been concerned with metre only as a specialised form of rhythm, giving an increased interconnection between words through an increased control of anticipation.

---

[2] It is worth remarking that any application of critical principles must be indirect. They are not any the less useful because this is so. Misunderstanding on this point has often led artists to accuse critics of wishing to make art a matter of rules, and their objection to any such attempt is entirely justified.

But it has other, in some cases even more important powers. Its use as an hypnotic agent is probably very ancient. Coleridge once again drops his incidental remark, just beside yet extremely close to the point. "It tends to increase the vivacity and susceptibility both of the general feelings and of the attention. This effect it produces by the continued excitement of surprise, and by the quick reciprocations of curiosity still gratified and still re-excited, which are too slight indeed to be at any moment objects of distinct consciousness, yet become considerable in their aggregate influence. As a medicated atmosphere, or as wine during animated conversation, they act powerfully, though themselves unnoticed." (*Biographia Literaria*, Chap. XVIII.) Mr. Yeats, when he speaks of the function of metre being to "lull the mind into a waking trance" is describing the same effect, however strange his conception of this trance may be.

That certain metres, or rather that a certain handling of metre should produce in a slight degree a hypnoidal state is not surprising. But it does so not as Coleridge suggests, through the surprise element in metrical effects, but through the absence of surprise, through the lulling effects more than through the awakening. Many of the most characteristic symptoms of incipient hypnosis are present in a slight degree. Among these susceptibility and vivacity of emotion, suggestibility, limitations of the field of attention, marked differences in the incidence of belief-feelings closely analogous to those which alcohol and nitrous oxide can induce, and some degree of hyperæsthesia (increased power of discriminating sensations) may be noted. We need not boggle at the word "hypnosis." It is sufficient to say, borrowing a phrase from M. Jules Romains, that there is a change in the regime of consciousness, which is directly due to the metre, and that to this regime the above-mentioned characteristics attach. As regards the hyperæsthesia, there may be several ways of interpreting what can be observed. All that matters here is that syllables, which in prose or in *vers libres* sound thin, tinny and flat, often gain an astonishing sonority and fullness even in verse which seems to possess no very subtle metrical structure.

Metre has another mode of action not hitherto mentioned. There can be little doubt that historically it has been closely associated with dancing, and that the connections of the two still hold. This is true at least of some "measures." Either motor images, images of the sensations of dancing, or, more probably, imaginal and incipient movements follow the syllables and make up their "movement." Once the metre has begun to "catch on" they are almost as closely bound up with the sequence of the words as the tied "verbal" images themselves.

The extension of this "movement" of the verse from dance forms to more general movements is natural and inevitable. That there is a very close connection between the sense and the metrical movement of

> And now the numerous tramplings quiver lightly
> Along a huge cloud's ridge; and now with sprightly
> Wheel downward come they into fresher skies,

cannot be doubted whatever we may think of the rime.
It is not less clear in

> Where beyond the extreme sea wall, and between
>   the remote sea gates,
> Waste water washes, and tall ships founder, and deep
>   death waits,

or in

> Ran on embattell'd Armies clad in Iron,

than it is in

> We sweetly curtsied each to each
> And deftly danced a saraband.

Nor is it always the case that the movement takes its cue from the sense. It is often a commentary on the sense and sometimes may qualify it, as when the resistless strength of Coriolanus in battle is given an appearance of dreadful ease by the leisureliness of the description,

> Death, that dark spirit, in's nervy arm doth lie
> Which being advanc'd declines, and then men die.

Movement in poetry deserves at least as much study as onomatopœia.

This account, of course, by no means covers all the ways by which metre takes effect in poetry. The fact that we appropriately use such words as "lulling," "stirring," "solemn," "pensive," "gay" in describing metres is an indication of their power more directly to control emotion. But the more general effects are more important. Through its very appearance of artificiality metre produces in the highest degree the "frame" effect, isolating the poetic experience from the accidents and

irrelevancies of everyday existence. We have seen how necessary this isolation is and how easily it may be mistaken for
a difference in kind. Much which in prose would be too personal or too insistent, which might awaken irrelevant con-
jectures or might "overstep itself" is managed without disaster
in verse. There are, it is true, equivalent resources in prose—
irony, for example, very frequently has this effect—but their
scope is far more limited. Metre for the most difficult and
most delicate utterances is the all but inevitable means.

ROBERT GRAVES

Harp, Anvil, Oar

[*It is hard to resist Robert Graves. He commands a vast, if idiosyncratic, scholarship; he brings a poet's imagination to both history and aesthetics. The anthropology Graves invokes to trace metrical origins need not be taken as science; however, Graves' recognition of the strong-stress and syllable-stress systems is of great value.*

[*More valuable than Graves' mythology of literary history is his wisdom as a craftsman. He has closely observed English metrical practice; his comments on Donne, Shakespeare, and T. S. Eliot deserve the student's attention. His stringent insistence on purity of genre is an echo from the Augustan Age: prose is prose and verse is verse and let us not dilute good wine with water. The principle of metrical decorum has not been better stated or more vigorously advocated.*]

LAST week I spoke about Marvan, the seventh-century poet of Connaught who revealed to the professors of the Great Bardic Academy how the poet's harp originated: namely when the wind played on the dried tendons of a stranded whale's skeleton in the time of Macuel son of Miduel. And how metre originated: namely in the alternate beat of two hammers on the anvil, while Lamiach was still alive. The three hundred professors could not follow Marvan here, having long ceased to think poetically. As historic or scientific statements his revelations are, of course, challengeable: not a grain of evidence can be cited for the existence of the whale, or even for that

of Macuel son of Miduel. Nevertheless, as poetic statements
they are exact. What is the whale? An emblem of the White
Love-goddess Rahab, Ruler of the Sea, who used yearly to
destroy her sacred kings in numerous cities from Connaught
to the Persian Gulf; until at last the god Enlil, or Marduk (or
Jehovah, according to the prophet Isaiah) killed her with the
new-fangled weapon called a sword—the Babylonians claimed
in a hymn that he sliced her like a flatfish. But the King of
Babylon still had to do ritual battle with her every year, be
swallowed, and spewed up again on the third day, as Jonah was.
And though Jehovah's prophets chanted: "O ye whales, bless
ye Adonai, praise Him and magnify Him for ever!" they knew
that Leviathan was unregenerate, uncontrollable and not to be
fished up with any hook let down. Hence the author of the
Apocalypse prophesied that one day "there shall be no more
sea"; by this he meant "no more Raham, and no more whales."

The emblems of the Muse Trinity are a white dove in the
sky, a white hind in the forest, a whale taking his pastime in
the depth of the sea. Where, then, could one find a better
figure of death than the white skeleton of a stranded whale?
And wind, North Wind, the wind that (proverbially) pigs
alone can see, the wind that, as I told you, Marvan carried in
his mantle, the wind that fertilized the windswift sacred mares
of Trojan Erichthonius and the prophetic vultures of Roman
augury—wind (*spiritus, pneuma*) is the emblem of inspiration. The bones of Rahab the Whale may lie stranded on the
shore; but, for a poet, there is more truth in her dead sinews
than in Marduk's living mouth. When Macuel son of Miduel
heard the wind howling tunefully in the Æolian harp of the
whale's skeleton, he bethought himself and built a smaller,
more manageable one from the same materials. And when he
stuck his harp and cried: "Sing to me, Muse!" this was no
formal invitation—Rahab herself sang at his plea.

A close parallel, by the bye, may be found in English popular
poetry. The ballad of the *Twa Sisters of Binnorie* tells of a
drowned woman whose hair was used for harp-strings:

> And by there came a harper fine
>   Edinbro', Edinbro'
> Such as harp to nobles when they dine.
>   Stirling for aye
> He's ta'en twa strands of her yellow hair
> And with it strung a harp sae rare
>   Bonnie St Johnstone stands on Tay.

He's done him into her father's hall,
      Edinbro', Edinbro'
And played the harp before them all,
      Stirling for aye
And syne the harp spake loud and clear
"Farewell my father and mither dear."
      Bonnie St Johnstone stands on Tay.

And syne the harp began to sing
      Edinbro', Edinbro'
And it's "Farewell, sweetheart," sang the string
      Stirling for aye
And then, as plain as plain could be,
"There sits my sister who drowned me."
      Bonnie St Johnstone stands on Tay.

The harp is the prophetic voice of the yellow-haired goddess
—the Muse-goddess was always yellow-haired—and she sings
of love, and grief, and doom. Marvan, moreover, was careful
to distinguish the fitful inspirational music of the Æolian harp
from the purposeful rhythmic clatter of the smith's anvil.

I am aware that I should here be discussing the English, not
the Irish, literary scene. But Irish poetry is to English poetry,
as—may I say?—the Pharisaic synagogue is to the Christian
Church: an antecedent which historians are tempted to forget
or belittle. The English have long despised the Irish; and
though generously ready to acknowledge their debt to Anglo-
Saxon, French, Italian, Latin and Greek literatures, are loth
to admit that the strongest element in English poetic technique (though certainly acquired at second or third hand) is
the Irish tradition of craftsmanship.

When two hammers answer each other five times on the
anvil—*ti-tum, ti-tum, ti-tum, ti-tum, ti-tum*—five in honour
of the five stations of the Celtic year, there you have Chaucer's
familiar hendecasyllabic line:

      A knight ther was, and that a worthy man
      That fro the tymë that he first began
      To ryden out, he lovéd chivalrye. . . .

But Anglo-Saxon poetry had been based on the slow pull and
push of the oar:

      Then I of myself / will máke this known
      That awhíle I was held / the Héodenings' scop,
      To my duke most dear / and Déor was my name.

The function of the Nordic *scop* seems to have been two-fold. Not only was he originally a "shaper" of charms, to protect the person of the king and so maintain prosperity in the realm; but he had a subsidiary task, of persuading a ship's crew to pull rhythmically and uncomplainingly on their oars against the rough waves of the North Sea, by singing them ballads in time to the beat. When they returned from a successful foray, and dumped their spoil of gold collars, shields, casques, and monastic chalices on the rush-strewn floor of the beer-hall, then the *scop* resumed his song. The drunken earls and churls straddled the benches, and rocked to the tune: "Over the whale's way, fared we unfearful. . . ."

Anglo-Saxon poetry is unrhymed, because the noise of row-locks does not suggest rhyme. Rhyme reached England from France. It had been brought there by Irish missionaries who recivilized Western Europe after the Frankish invasions. These missionaries wrote and talked Latin, and *The Rhythm of St Bernard of Cluny*, the first rhymed poem of high literary pretensions written by an Englishman (during the reign of Henry I or II) follows the pure Irish tradition. Its complicated series of internal and end-rhymes, and its faultless finish, leave no doubt about this. Here are four of the three thousand rhymed lines:

> *Urbs Syon aurea, Patria lactea, cive decora,*
> *Omne cor obruis, omnibus obstruis et cor et ora.*
> *Nescio, nescio, quae jubilatio, lux tibi qualis,*
> *Quam socialia gaudia, gloria quam specialis.*

Prosodists have a Latin name for the metre: *Leonini cristati trilices dactylici*. St Bernard's *Rhythm* has been translated into English, pretty well (though with a loss of all the rhyme pairs except the end ones, which have become monosyllables), by the Victorian hymn-writer, J. M. Neale:

> *Jerusalem the Golden,*
> *   With Milk and Honey Blest,*
> *Beneath Thy Contemplation*
> *   Sink heart and voice oppressed:*
> *I know not, O I know not,*
> *   What social joys are there;*
> *What radiancy of Glory,*
> *   What Light beyond Compare!*

Nordic verse-craft, as I was saying, is linked to the pull of the oar. Greek verse-craft is linked to the ecstatic beat of feet around a rough stone altar, sacred to Dionysus (or Hermes, or Eros, or Zeus Cronides), probably to the sound of the dactylic drum played by a priestess or a priest:

$$\text{--}\cup\cup/\text{--}\cup\cup/.\text{--}//\cup\cup/\text{--}\cup\cup/\text{--}\cup\cup/\text{--}\text{--}$$

The Greeks also admitted the iambic, traditionally named in honour of lasciviously hobbling Iambe, who (you may remember) tried to coax a smile from the bereaved Demeter at Eleusis. Iambic metre may have begun with Helladic totem dances which imitated the hobbling of partridge or quail:

$$\cup\text{--}/\cup\text{--}/\cup//\text{--}/\cup\text{--}/\cup\text{--}/\cup\text{--}$$

There was also the spondaic measure derived from the gloomy double-stamp of buskined mourners, arousing some dead hero to drink the libations (spondae) that they poured for him:

$$\text{--}\text{--}/\text{--}\text{--}/\text{--}/\text{--}//\text{--}/\text{--}\text{--}/\text{--}\text{--}/\text{--}\text{--}$$

A metrical line in Greek poetry represents the turn taken by a dancer around an altar or tomb, with a cæsura marking the halfway point: the metre never varies until the dancers have dropped with fatigue. Similarly in *Beowulf* and other Anglo-Saxon poems, the oars' pull and push continues mercilessly until harbour is reached, or until the drunken diners fall off their bench to the floor, unable to rise again.

The Irish concept of metre is wholly different. All poets owed allegiance to the Muse-goddess Brigid—who may be decently equated with the Helladic Moon-goddess Brizo of Delos. Brigid had three aspects: the Brigid of Poets, the Brigid of Smiths, and the Brigid of Physicians. A Brigid of Smiths may seem anomalous, because English smiths have long ranked lower in the social scale than poets and physicians. In England smithcraft ceased, with the triumph of Christianity, to be an inspired profession; it was wrested by monks from the hands of the lame Smith Wayland (who served the Goddess Freya) and registered merely as a useful trade. Even as a trade, it is dying now: wedding ring, or scythe, or steel helmet is supplied by factories where not even a superstitious vestige of the Wayland cult has gone into the making. But the pagan smith, whether goldsmith, whitesmith, or blacksmith, approached his work with enormous care and magical precaution.

The religious connexion between poetry, smithcraft, and medicine is a close one. Medicine presupposes a knowledge of times, seasons, and the sovereign properties of plants, trees, beasts, birds, fish, earths, minerals. Poetry presupposes an inspired knowledge of man's sensuous and spiritual nature. Smithcraft—for the smith was also carpenter, mason, shipwright and toolmaker—presupposes an inspired knowledge of how to transform lifeless material into active forms. No ancient smith would have dared to proceed without the aids of medicine and poetry. The charcoal used on his forge had been made, with spells, at a certain time of the year from timber of certain sacred trees; and the leather of the forge bellows, from the skin of a sacred animal ritually sacrificed. Before starting a task, he and his assistant were obliged to purify themselves with medicines and lustrations, and to placate the Spites which habitually crowd around forge and anvil. If he happened to be forging a sword, the water in which it was to be tempered must have magical properties—May dew, or spring water in which a virgin princess had washed her hair. The whole work was done to the accompaniment of poetic spells.

Such spells matched the rhythm of the smiths' hammers; and these were of unequal weight. A sledge hammer was swung by the assistant; the smith himself managed the lighter hammer. To beat out hot metal successfully, one must work fast and follow a prearranged scheme. The smith with his tongs lays the glowing lump of iron on the anvil, then touches with his hammer the place where the sledge blow is to fall; next he raps on the anvil the number of blows required. Down comes the sledge; the smith raps again for another blow, or series of blows. Experience teaches him how many can be got in while the iron is still hot. So each stage of every process had its peculiar metre, to which descriptive words became attached; and presently the words found their own tunes. This process explains Marvan's mysterious reference to Lamiach, who appears in the English translation of Genesis as "Lamech." Lamech was the father of Tubal the first smith, and Jubal the first musician. Nor did the smith (as many archæologists assume) let caprice rule the number and shape of ornaments that he introduced into his work. Whether he was forging a weapon, or a piece of armour, or a tool, or a cauldron, or a jewelled collar, every element in the design had a magical significance.

An Irish poet versified to the ring of hammers; and the fact that rhyme and regular metre had become characteristic of English poetry by Chaucer's time implies that the smithy tradition of careful thought and accurate workmanship, which these call for, had also been to some extent adopted. The metaphor of beating out one's verses on the anvil is now, indeed, a poetical commonplace. But let me put it this way: though every English poet is a smith for the greater part of the year, he takes to the sea during the brief sailing season. Chaucer may seem to be a hammer-and-anvil poet when he writes:

> A knight ther was, and that a worthy man
> That fro the tyme that he first began
> To ryden out, he lovéd chivalrye. . . .

Ti-tum, ti-tum, ti-tum, ti-tum. Then he lays down the hammer and reaches for the oar. Instead of:

> Honoùr and freédom, trùth and coúrtesy . . .

he writes:

> Trùth and honoùr / freédom and coúrtesy . . .

and this has been the English verse-tradition ever since.

Skelton also reconciled the anvil with the oar in a metre which he used in his early Lament for Edward IV, and again at the close of his life in Speke Parrot. Note the Anglo-Saxon alliteration:

> Miseremini mei / ye that be my frendis!
>   This world hath forméd me / downë to fall.
> How many I endure / when that everi thing endis?
>   What creäture is bornë / to be eternáll?

and:

> The myrrour that I tote in / quasi diaphanum,
>   Vel quasi speculum / in aenigmate,
> Elencticum, or ells / enthymematicum,
>   For logicians to loke on / somewhat sophistice:
> Retoricyons and oratours / in freshe humanyte,
> Support Parrot, I pray you / with your suffrage ornate,
> Of confuse tantum / auoydynge the chekmate.

The history of Shakespeare's blank verse is a progression from the careful anvil work of, say, The Comedy of Errors, to

The Tempest, where the oar is pulling in a very rough sea.
The Comedy of Errors begins:

EGEON:
> Proceed, Solinus, to procure my fall,
> And by the doom of death end woes and all.

DUKE OF Merchant of Syracusa, plead no more.
EPHESUS: I am not partial to infringe our laws;
> The enmity and discord which of late
> Sprung from the rancorous outrage of your Duke
> To merchants, our well-dealing countrymen,
> Who wanting guilders to redeem their lives,
> Have sealed his rigorous statutes with their bloods,
> Excludes all pity from our threatening looks. . . .

But in *The Tempest* the opening exchanges between shipmas-
ter and boatswain are recognized as blank verse only because
every now and then a regular line occurs to reassert the norm.
(Heming and Condell in their edition of the *First Folio* print
them as prose, and all cautious editors follow suit.)

(The BOATSWAIN appears when the MASTER summons him)
THE MASTER: Good. Speak to the mariners; fall to't yarely.
> Or we run ourselves aground. Bestir, bestir!
BOATSWAIN: Heigh my hearts, cheerily, cheerily, my hearts,
> yare, yare!
> Take in the topsail! Tend to the master's
> whistle!
(to the MASTER)
> Blow till thou burst thy wind, if room enough!

The rules of prosody apply only to anvil verse, or to sacred-
dance verse, in which every syllable is evaluated and counted.
Pope, for instance, says that he lisped in numbers for the numbers came; "numbers" translates the Latin *numeri*, which
imply a careful count of syllables. Pope never escaped from the
"numbers" theory: which posits an orderly sequence of metrical feet each with the same determined time value, every long
syllable being given the value of a crotchet, and every short
syllable the value of a quaver; though the Elizabethan critics,
headed by George Puttenham, had emphatically rejected this
theory. The only fundamental difference between Pope's notion of verse and Virgil's, or Horace's, was that the Latin convention of what made a syllable long or short had lapsed. Now,
in Bernard of Cluny's *Rhythm*, for instance, the Latin rules
of quantity are maintained: every syllable is regarded as long
or short by nature, though a short syllable may become long

by position; and a terminal vowel, or vowel plus *m*, will be elided and disappear. This, it must be realized, was a highly artificial convention: ordinary Latin speech, as heard in the home and Forum, seems from the scraps of camp songs penned by Suetonius to have been accentual, and the accent did not necessarily fall on the long vowel.

It amused educated English poets—such as Chaucer, Skelton, Ben Jonson, Milton, Marvell, Dr. Johnson, and Coleridge —to compose Latin verses in Classical style; but the freedom to observe natural speech stresses (as opposed to the laws of quantity) not only in vernacular verse but in Latin too, if they pleased, had already been won for them by the hymnologists and carol-makers and Goliardic song-writers of the Middle Ages. The first two lines of the famous medieval students' drinking song:

> Mihi est propositum in taberna mori;
> Vinum sit appositum potatoris ori. . . .

contain thirteen false quantities, and the first two lines of the equally famous hymn:

> Dies irae, dies illa
> Solvens saecla in favilla. . . .

contain eight. (Don't bother to count them.) This is not due to ignorance. Who would dare accuse St Thomas Aquinas of ignorance because he rhymes *natus* with *datus*? Aquinas knew well enough that rhyme was a barbarism in Classical Latin poetry—and that Cicero had made a fool of himself with the internal rhyme of:

> O fortunatam natam, me Consule, Romam!

But he also knew that these quantities had been justified by Irish metrical example; the Irish did not acknowledge quantity, they relied on accent.

Skelton, in his *Devout Trentale for Old John Clerk, Sometime the Holy Patriarche of Diss*, actually alternated correct hexameters with Goliardic verse:

> Sequitur trigintale,
> Tale quale rationale,
> Licet parum curiale,
> Tamen satis est formale,
> Joannis Clerc, hominis
> Cujusdam multinominis,
> Joannes Jayberd qui vocatur,

Clerc cleribus nuncupatur.
Obiit sanctus iste pater
Anno Domini MD, sexto.
In parochia de Dis.
Non erat sibi similis;
In malitia vir insignis,
Duplex corde et bilinguis;
Senio confectus,
Omnibus suspectus,
Nemini dilectus,
Sepultus est amonge the wedes:
God forgeue hym his mysdedes!

Dulce melos[1]
Penetrans coelos.

Carmina cum cannis cantemus festa Joannis:
Clerk obiit vere, Jayberd nomenque dedere;
Dis populo natus, Clerk cleribusque vocatus.

The Elizabethan critics, humanists to a man, were a little
uneasy about this divergence from Classical metric theory, but
there was clearly no help for it. Samuel Daniel, in his *Defence
of Rhyme* (1603), found it necessary to lay down: "As Greeke
and Latine verse consists of the number and quantity of silla-
bles, so doth the English verse of measure and accent." They
admitted, in fact, that the natural accent of current English
speech decides whether a syllable should be long or short—
even though the same word may change its value in the same
line. Thus, for instance, the pentameter:

õffĕr hĕr / ĭcĕs, õr / ā / / lõvĕlў cŏm/fõrtăblĕ / chāir

is quantitatively correct according to Ovidian rule, but does
not scan. Moreover, the Virgilian hexameter, as Thomas
Nashe forcefully explained in his answer to Gabriel Harvey's
recommendation of it, is not natural to English:

The Hexamiter verse I graunt to be a Gentleman of an auncient
house (so is many an english beggar); yet this Clyme of ours hee
cannot thriue in. Our speech is too craggy for him to set his plough
in; hee goes twitching and hopping in our language like a man running vpon quagmiers, vp the hill in one Syllable, and downe the
dale in another, retaining no part of that stately smooth gate which
he vaunts himselfe with amongst the Greeks and Latins.

[1] Melos rhyming with coelos.

And so a strong sense has grown up among practical English poets that the natural rhythm of speech decides where accents fall; and that, therefore, the less artificial the words, the truer the poem.

Tell a schoolchild that Keats's *Faery Song* is an iambic poem with three four-foot lines followed by one of five feet, another of four feet, one of two feet, and finally a five-footer, rhyming AB, AB, C, C, B—and he will read it like this:

> Ah woe / is me / poor silv/er wing
> That I / must chant / thy lad/y's dirge
> And death / to this / fair haunt / of spring
> And mel/ody / and streams / of flower/y verge.
> Poor Silv/er wing / ah woe / is me
> That I / must see
> These Bloss/oms snow / upon /thy lad/y's pall.

But if the words are spoken in the manner most natural to their sense and feeling, this is how Keats will have meant it to be said; and you realize that the laws of prosody are, to verse, very much as copperplate models are to handwriting. Keats had a poet's ear for verse; and Shakespeare had; as Donne had; as Coleridge had; as Skelton had. But Keats was easily seduced. When he put on his singing robes and played at being a Classical poet, he became gorbliminess incarnate. In his *Ode to Apollo*, for example:

> Then, through thy Temple wide, melodious swells
>   The sweet majestic tone of Maro's lyre:
> The soul delighted on each accent dwells,—
>   Enraptur'd dwells,—not daring to respire,
> The while he tells of grief around a funeral pyre.

> 'Tis awful silence then again;
>   Expectant stand the spheres;
>   Breathless the laurell'd peers,
> Nor move, till ends the lofty strain,
> Nor move till Milton's tuneful thunders cease
> And leave once more the ravish'd heaven in peace.

> Thou biddest Shakespeare wave his hand,
>   And quickly forward spring
> The Passions—a terrific band—
>   And each vibrates the string

> That with its tyrant temper best accords,
> While from their Master's lips pour forth the inspiring words.

Keats should have known that to impose an artificial word-order, or an artificial vocabulary, on poems is a lapse in poetic dignity.

There is so much to say about professional standards in verse-technique, that I shall confine myself to generalities. For instance, that though the muscular *str* and *scr* words: *strain, strength, string, strangle, stretch, struggle, strident, extravagant, screw, scrape, scrawny,* and such easy skipping words as *melody, merrily, prettily, harmony, fantasy* match sense with sound, other words are not so onomatopœic. A *strangely striped strip of satin* is far too emphatic in sound for the sense, and a *terribly powerful Florida hurricane* is not nearly emphatic enough. Yet to alter the spirit of an original poetic thought for the sake of metre or euphony is unprofessional conduct. So the art of accommodating sense to sound without impairing the original thought has to be learned by example and experiment. Under-emphasis or over-emphasis in a word can be controlled by playing other words off against it, and carefully choosing its position in a line, and making the necessary adjustments to neighbouring lines until the ear at last feels satisfied. It is an axiom among poets that if one trusts whole-heartedly to poetic magic, one will be sure to solve any merely verbal problem or else discover that the verbal problem is hiding an imprecision in poetic thought.

I say magic, since the act of composition occurs in a sort of trance, distinguishable from dream only because the critical faculties are not dormant, but on the contrary, more acute than normally. Often a rugger player is congratulated on having played the smartest game of his life, but regrets that he cannot remember a single incident after the first five minutes, when he got kicked on the head. It is much the same with a poet when he completes a true poem. But often he wakes from the trance too soon and is tempted to solve the remaining problems intellectually. Few self-styled poets have experienced the trance; but all who have, know that to work out a line by an exercise of reason, rather than by a deep-seated belief in miracle, is highly unprofessional conduct. If a trance has been interrupted, it is just too bad. The poem should be left unfinished, in the hope that suddenly, out of the blue, days or months later, it may start stirring again at the back of the mind, when the remaining problems will solve themselves without difficulty.

Donne's chief failing as a love-poet was his readiness to continue the inspired beginning with a witty development. For instance:

> Goe, and catche a falling starre,
>   Get with child a mandrake roote . . .

Here Donne paused, apparently remembered Villon's *neiges d'antan*, and went on:

>   Tell me, where all past yeares are . . .

And then consciously searched for a rhyme to *roote*. But he had not the least idea where the poem was taking him, except into a discussion of impossibility. So he continued in quite a different key:

>   Or who cleft the Divels foot,
> Teach me to heare Mermaides singing,
> Or to keep off envies stinging . . .

He paused again and apparently remembered Shakespeare's:

>   Blow, blow thou winter wind,
>   Thou art not so unkind
>   As man's ingratitude . . .

and Dante's remarks about the bitterness of having to seek advancement from haughty patrons. So he ended the verse with the quite irrelevant:

>   And finde
>   What winde
> Serves to advance an honest minde.

Again he opened magnificently:

>   I wonder by my troth, what thou, and I
>   Did, till we lov'd? were we not wean'd till then?
>   But suck'd on countrey pleasures, childishly?

Here inspiration faded and he resorted to artifice:

>   Or snorted we in the seaven sleepers' den?
>   T'was so; But this, all pleasures fancies bee.
>   If ever any beauty I did see,
>   Which I desir'd, and got, t'was but a dreame of thee.

Donne is adept at keeping the ball in the air, but he deceives us here by changing the ball. Coleridge often does the same thing, for example when he fakes a sequel to the inspired opening passage of *Christabel*—but he handles the ball so clumsily that we are seldom deceived.

It is unprofessional conduct to say: "When next I write a poem I shall use the sonnet form"—because the theme is by definition unforeseeable, and theme chooses metre. A poet should not be conscious of the metrical pattern of a poem he is writing until the first three or four lines have appeared; he may even find himself in the eleventh line of fourteen before realizing that a sonnet is on the way. Besides, metre is only a frame; the atmospheres of two sonnets can be so different that they will not be recognized as having the same form except by a careful count of lines and feet. Theme chooses metre; what is more, theme decides what rhythmic variations should be made on metre. The theory that all poems must be equally rich in sound is an un-English one, borrowed from Virgil. Rainbow-like passages are delightful every now and then, but they match a rare mood of opulence and exaltation which soon fatigues. The riches of *Paradise Lost* fatigue, and even oppress, all but musicians. Rainbows should make their appearances only when the moment has come to disclose the riches of the heart, or soul, or imagination; they testify to passing storms and are short-lived.

Another professional principle is that *mimesis* should be regarded as vulgar. By mimesis I mean such *tours de force* as Virgil's:

Quadrupedante putrem sonitu quatit ungula campum,

and Tennyson's:

> *The moan of doves in immemorial elms,*
> *And murmuring of innumerable bees.*

To these I should add the Homeric.

> *Autis epeita pedonde cylindeto laäs anaides,*

the shameless stone of Sisyphus bounding downhill, if I did not think that this was high-spirited verbal comedy, proclaiming disbelief in the whole theory of divine punishment.

Pope's translation of the Sisyphus passage, by the way, runs:

> *With many a weary sigh, and many a groan,*
> *Up the high hill he heaves a huge round stone . . .*

though the corresponding lines in the *Odyssey* do not mimic Sisyphus's breathlessness. And Pope's concluding couplet is wretchedly incompetent:

> *The huge round stone, resulting with a bound*
> *Thunders impetuous down and smokes along the ground.*

The false internal rhymes of *round* and *bound* and the half-rhymes *down* and *ground* effectively act as brakes on the stone's merry progress. As Blake said in one of his Public Addresses: "I do not condemn Pope or Dryden because they did not understand imagination, but because they did not understand verse."

One of the most difficult problems is how to use natural speech rhythms as variations on a metrical norm. And here we meet with the heresy of free verse. Until the time of Blake and his oratorical cadences, it was generally agreed that the reader should never be allowed to lose his sense of metrical norm. But Blake, finding the contemporary technique of poetry too cramping, burst it wide open and wrote something that was neither poetry nor prose. Whitman did much the same, though for different reasons: he epitomizes the restless American habit, first noted in the eighteenth century, of moving adventurously west across the trackless prairie, scratch-farming as one goes, instead of clinging to some pleasant Pennsylvanian farm, improving crops and stock by careful husbandry, and building a homestead for one's children and grandchildren. All who, like Whitman, choose to dispense with a rhythmical norm are welcome to explore the new country which he opened up, but it now wears rather a dismal look. Robert Frost's poems, which combine traditional metres with intensely personal rhythms, show the advantage of staying put and patiently working at the problem.[2]

A dogma has recently been planted in English schools that the King James version of the Bible is poetry. It is not. The polishing of the English translation was, of course, admirably done by a team of capable University scholars, trained in the

[2] Mr. Eliot has written about free verse: "It is not defined by non-existence of metre, since even the worst verse can be scanned." This is to beg the question. In so far as verse can be scanned, it is not freed of metre. He has also written:

> But the most interesting verse which has yet been written in our language has been done [sic] either by taking a very simple form, like the iambic pentameter, and constantly withdrawing from it, or taking no form at all, and continually approximating to a very simple one. It is this contrast between fixity and flux, this unperceived evasion of monotony, which is the very life of verse.

Interesting to some, embarrassing to others, like a jaunt in a car after mixing a little water with the fuel to make it go by fits and starts. I was never interested in that sort of experiment; I expect verse to be verse, and prose to be prose.

oratorical art. Sometimes they even included a perfectly metrical line:

How art thou fallen from Heaven, O Lucifer, son of the morning!

And:

Come down and sit in the dust; O virgin daughter of Babylon, Sit on the ground. . . .

But one might as well call *The Times* leaders poetry, because they are written by skilled journalists and because they contain a high proportion of blank-verse lines, sometimes as much as 30 per cent.

Ben Jonson told Drummond of Hawthornden that "for not keeping of accent"—that is to say, allowing his readers to lose the sense of material norm—"Donne deserved hanging." Jonson had also said that Donne was "the first poet in the world in some things," and that he had a few of his early poems by heart. It is difficult to reconcile these statements. But Jonson seems to be referring to the *Satyres*, where Donne at times deliberately changes the metre—as when a competitor in a walking race shamelessly bends his knees and breaks into a short run:

> . . . *So in immaculate clothes, and Symetrie*
> *Perfect as circles, with such nicetie*
> *As a young Preacher at his first time goes*
> *To preach, he enters, and a Lady, which owes*
> *Him not so much as good will, he arrests,*
> *And unto her protests, protests, protests;*
> *So much as at Rome would serve to have throwne*
> *Ten Cardinalls into the Inquisition;*
> *And whispers by Jesu, so often, that A*
> *Pursevant would have ravish'd him away*
> *For saying of our Ladies psalter. But 'tis fit*
> *That they each other plague, they merit it . . .*

In the same satire, Donne also makes the units of sense play havoc with the units of metre:

> . . . *No, no, Thou which since yesterday hast beene*
> *Almost about the whole world, hast thou seene,*
> *O Sunne, in all thy journey, Vanitie,*
> *Such as swells the bladder of our court? I*
> *Thinke he which made your waxen garden, and*
> *Transported it from Italy to stand*
> *With us, at London, flouts our Presence, for*
> *Just such gay painted things, which no sappe, nor*
> *Tast have in them, ours are; And naturall*
> *Some of the stocks are, their fruits, bastard all.*

But let me speak up for Donne. There are, of course, certain familiar proprieties in English poetry. Accent must be kept, which means, as I have shown, that however the metrical norm may be varied, it should stay recognizable—one must not write lines that go off into another metre altogether. Rhyme must be kept within certain decent limits, and the consonantal part of rhyme must be regarded as more important than the vowel. It is, for instance, indecent to rhyme *charm* with *calm*, or (*pace* W. H. Auden) *bore* with *mother-in-law*; though *love* and *prove*, *all* and *usual*, *fly* and *extremity* are traditionally countenanced. Three-syllable rhymes are indecent, so are mixed metaphors; and what Corinna called "sowing with the sack" —namely overornamentation of every kind. Again: an even level of language should be kept: one must decide to what period each poem belongs and not relapse to an earlier, or anticipate a more modern, diction. Thus it is indecent to address *you* and *thee* in the same verse to the same person— even if Pope and Marvell are quoted in justification. And, most important, there should be no discrepancy between the sound and the sense of a poem. It would be difficult, for instance, to quarrel on technical grounds with a simple iambic stanza such as this:

> *Mother is dead; my heart to pieces torn,*
> *I hear my kinsmen weep—*
> *Uncle, niece, nephew, cousin, who convey her*
> *Unto her last long sleep.*

But turn this into dactyls, and the effect is ludicrous:

> *Mother is dead and my heart is in pieces,*
> *Hark how the friends of the family weep!*
> *Cousins and uncles and nephews and nieces*
> *Accompany her to her last long sleep.*

These are elementary rules, a few chosen at random from what I may call the Common Law of English Verse. But, in English satire, all rules can be deliberately broken. Byron's satiric comment on Keats's death, for example:

> *Strange that the soul, that very fiery particle,*
> *Should let itself be snuffed out by an article. . . .*

is emphasised by the deliberate use of the three-syllabled rhyme.

And comically inexact rhyme is the strength of Siegfried

Sassoon's squib, written in the palmy days of George V, which he has generously allowed me to resurrect:

> Because the Duke is Duke of York,
> The Duke of York has shot a huge rhinoceros;
> Let's hope the Prince of Wales will take a walk
> Through Africa, and make the Empire talk
> By shooting an enormous hippopotamus,
> And let us also hope that Lord Lascelles
> Will shoot all beasts from gryphons to gazelles
> And show the world what sterling stuff we've got in us.

The word *satire* is not derived, as most people suppose, from the witty, prick-eared satyrs of the early Greek comedy, but from the Latin phrase *satura lanx*, or "full platter." Latin satire was a burlesque performance at a harvest festival, in which full-fed countrymen would improvise obscene topical jokes to a recurrent dance tune—as the islanders of Majorca still do to the *copeo*, at their annual pig-killing. The harvest atmosphere was free and easy; anything went. Urban satire, as Horace, or Juvenal, or Persius wrote it, was quite a different affair: Greek in origin, and bound by the same rules as epic or pastoral verse. Samuel Butler's *Hudibras* is fescennine; so are Donne's satires. Donne, in fact, did not deserve hanging if he failed to keep his accent in the satires; he could plead privilege.

Pope, who modelled himself as a satirist on Horace, thought fit to regularize Donne's lines:

> Thou, who since yesterday hast roll'd o'er all
> The busy, idle blockheads of the ball,
> Hast thou, oh Sun! beheld an emptier sort,
> Than such as swell this bladder of a court? . . .
>
> Thus finish'd and corrected to a hair,
> They march, to prate their hour before the fair.
> So first to preach a white-glov'd chaplain goes,
> With band of lily, and with cheek of rose,
> Sweeter than Sharon, in immac'late trim,
> Neatness itself impertinent with him. . . .

The difference between these two versions is that Donne's is readable, and Pope's is not; the regularity of the metre defeats its object after the first fifty couplets. Its readers remain unmoved; they sigh, and fall gently asleep. And this suggests another subject.

The Irish and early Welsh bards had made a discovery,

which the Greeks and Romans had never made, and which reached England very late; namely, that regular verse, though a wonderful aid to memory, is soporific unless frequent changes occur in the metre; and that though, say, Virgil's *Æneid* or Homer's *Iliad* may contain numerous poems, the verse which links these poems together, because written in the same metre, robs them of their force. What jeweller would display a pearl, unless perhaps a black one, in mother-of-pearl setting? The Irish bards, while vellum was prohibitively dear, recorded their chronologies, their treatises on geography, husbandry, and so on, in mnemonic rhyme. Yet their tales (of which they had to know nine hundred or more) were prose; and these the poet told in his own way, to keep them fresh, and individual, and up to date; until he reached a dramatic climax, and this was a traditional poem, which he had to know by heart.

Mother-of-pearl, though a noble material for cutting and engraving, is not pearl. The greater part of every long poem, even Spenser's *Faerie Queene*, is necessarily mother-of-pearl. Ben Jonson hinted at this in his *Discoveries*. He wrote:

> Even one alone verse sometimes makes a perfect poem as when Aeneas hangs up and consecrates the Armes of *Abas* with this inscription:

> *Aeneas haec de Danais victoribus arma . . .*

and calls it a *Poeme* or *Carmen*.

This drawing of attention to the poems included in a long work written in set stanzas—as Dante enthusiasts point to *The Death of Ugolino* and similar pearls—suggests that the rest is not up to sample. And how can it be, if the same metre is insisted on throughout?

In blank verse drama one can easily mark off the poems from the roughage. Not only is blank verse capable of almost infinite variations, but prose is allowed to supply comic relief of passages which further the plot. Shakespeare, for instance, makes Trinculo and Stephano in *The Tempest* speak familiar quay-side prose, which Caliban answers in poems. But it is manifestly impossible that a long narrative poem which contains genealogy, description of scenery, battles, love-passages, laments and so on, can be reduced to a single metre without dilution of the poetic content. Long poems are like old French or Spanish tapestries: the design and colour and needlework may be charming but there is no sharpness of detail, no personal characterization, no difference in quality or colour between foreground and background.

Are there any anthropologists present? If so, they may recall the giant yam of Abulam. At Abulam in New Guinea, yams for ordinary eating are planted and tended by the women, but every planting season a tense competition arises among the men: who can grow the yam of the year. This is a purely ritualistic yam, like the Harvest Festival marrow in an English village. The winning exhibit is said to be of approximately the size and shape of a bull-hippopotamus (discounting its head and legs) and perfectly inedible. It provides, in fact, an emblem of the literary epic, which was still being cultivated in Victorian days. With the passing of this Epic, followed by the formal Elegy, and the Ode addressed to heedless nightingales, rocking-chairs, abstractions, and noblemen, of what does poetry now consist? It is reduced, at last, to practical poems, namely the lyrical or dramatic highlights of the poet's experiences with the Goddess in her various disguises. The prose setting is withheld; and, because of this, professional standards demand that it should either explain itself fully, or present a note, as schoolchildren do who arrive late or without some necessary part of their school equipment.

Before closing, I must tell you about a girl who is reading English here under Professor X. I asked her: "What poems do you enjoy most?" and she answered with dignity: "Poems are not meant to be enjoyed; they are meant to be analysed." I hope you do not think that I subscribe to this heresy.

GEORGE SAINTSBURY

"The Mothers"

[The student should compare Graves' inspired mythology with Saintsbury's more conventional but hardly less energetically formulated scholarship. Upon close inspection Saintsbury's mortal "Mothers" are remarkably similar to Graves' divinities. Anglo-Saxon, Latin and Greek, medieval hymnology, and native influence (Welsh and Irish) are the ancestors of English prosody. Saintsbury sees the same mixture but in different proportions; he dismisses Celtic influence, which Graves holds crucial, as relatively unimportant.

[The matter of Saintsbury's prejudices and quirky style crops up, as well as what Wellek and Warren call his "strange empiricism." Saintsbury irritates with his John Bullish chauvinism (his attitude toward Celtic influence is parochial and British) and his aggressive, no-nonsense approach. But his empiricism saves him from foolish legalism and theoretical inconsistency; his chauvinism grows out of an overwhelming love of poetry.]

AMONG the influences, conscious or unconscious, actual or possible, which must or may have acted upon an Englishman desirous of writing English verse in the twelfth century, the antecedent prosodies of the languages with which he was acquainted, or which had in this or that way worked upon the language he was using, must, of course, hold a great place, and for our purpose almost the greatest. They may be said to be five in number—(A) Anglo-Saxon, (B) Latin (with a faint possibility of Greek), (C) French, (D) Scandinavian, and (E) Celtic. The part played by the first three is certain and

Reprinted from A History of English Prosody, Volume I. Macmillan and Co. Ltd., 1906, All rights reserved. Used by permission of the publisher.

all-important; that of the last two much smaller, and in any
direct fashion rather problematical, but scarcely to be quite
neglected.

A.   Anglo-Saxon

The assignment of the first place among these to Anglo-
Saxon[1] is not merely conventional, nor is it in any sense per-
fidious. It is true that some of the most serious errors (as they
seem to the present writer) which have ever crept into the discussion of English prosody, have come from a too obstinate
determination to serve that prosody heir, at all costs and in
all points, to Anglo-Saxon. It is also true that, as I think we
shall see, what has been by an engaging absurdity called "the
rhythm of the foreigner" has in the main superseded the
rhythm of this by no means aboriginal native. But, in the first
place, the language which supplies the main stuff and substance of all English speech, and which supplied all but an
infinitesimal proportion of it at the time when our enquiries
proper begin, cannot but have a prerogative position. And, as
we shall see, Anglo-Saxon supplied much more than the materials; it supplied an invaluable *differentiating* element from
"the rhythm of the foreigner" in perhaps the most important
of all points, the point which has given English poetry most
of its predominant and incomparable beauty.

As is pretty generally known, Anglo-Saxon prosody, though
in one sense by no means simple, is in another simplicity itself.
With rare and late exceptions, the whole body of Anglo-Saxon
verse reduces itself to a single form which was practically identical in principle in all the cognate languages—English, German, and Scandinavian. The staple line of this verse consists
of two halves or sections, each containing two "long,"
"strong," "stressed," "accented" syllables, these same syllables

[1] In the remarks which follow, the laws assigned to Anglo-Saxon verse
are drawn up so as to exhibit not the writer's private opinions, but the
consensus of the best modern scholars. The comments are those of one
who does not pretend to professional Anglo-Saxon "scholarship" himself, but who has read all printed Anglo-Saxon poetry carefully. They
are those of one who has read Middle English and Modern English
verse as to the manner born. Although it is sometimes thought illiberal
to lay stress on this advantage, I believe it to be all-important. The
Welsh critic who, the other day, observed that a Welsh postman could
correct the work on Welsh prosody of the best Celtic scholar in
France, may have shown something of the proverbial "cenfigenous-
ness" of his race in expression; but I fancy he was right in fact.

being, to the extent of three out of the four, alliterated. At the first casting of the eye on a page of Anglo-Saxon poetry no common *resemblances* except these seem to emerge. But we see on some pages an altogether extraordinary *difference* in the lengths of the lines or, in other words, of the number of "short," "weak," "unstressed," "unaccented" syllables which are allowed to group themselves round the pivots or posts of the rhythm. Yet attempts have been made, not without fair success, to divide the sections or half-lines into groups or types of rhythm, more or less capable of being represented by the ordinary marks of metrical scansion.[2]

These, however, though in the sections, or in parts of them, something like our rhythm-bars may be seen, never for long together, and very seldom even as individual wholes, give us rhythm corresponding to ours. The difference between a passage of Langland and a passage of Chaucer appears everywhere, and of course even more strikingly, between a passage of any Anglo-Saxon poet and one of any modern. A sort of monotone or hum, generally of what we call trochaic type, less frequently of what we call dactylic or anapæstic, will indeed disengage itself for the attentive reader. But nothing more, look where he will and school his ear as carefully as he may, in Caedmon and Cynewulf, in *Beowulf* and *Byrhtnoth*, everywhere and in everything. The sharp and uncompromising section, the accents, the alliteration—these are all that the poet has to trust to in the way of rules *sine queis non*. But before long the said careful reader becomes aware that there is a "lucky license," which is as a rule, and much more also; and that this license—itself by no means merely licentious—concerns the allowance of unaccented and unalliterated syllables. The range of it is so great that on a single page-opening, taken at random, you may find the lines varying from nine to fifteen syllables, and, seeking a little farther, come to a variation between eight and twenty-one. Such contrasts are of course exceptional, but the contrast as such, and its principles such as they are, are the rule—the fourth rule after a fashion, as we have said. Middle pause, so strong as to be more than pause

---

[2] The standard authority on the subject is, of course, E. Sievers, *Altgermanische Metrik*, Halle, 1893. Herr Sievers, with others many and reverend, would make the correspondence of groups much more exact than it used to be thought, and it is urged that some combinations of syllables *never* occur. If so, so much the better for the theory of the present book, which can, however, do without it. For an excellent summary account see Mr. W. P. Ker, *The Dark Age*, Edinburgh, 1904, p. 228 *sq.*

only, alliteration, accent, and substitution of equivalenced groups instead of rigid syllabic uniformity—these are the four pillars of the structure of Anglo-Saxon prosody.

B. Latin

There should be very little reasonable doubt that no preceptist example in the prosody of Early Middle English had half the force of that of Latin. That Latin was the "Grammatica"[3]—the pattern literary language—of all nations in the Middle Ages admits of no question. That it was practically the only language in which these nations had finished literary examples before them admits of as little. But in regard to English, there is the important additional fact that the first Englishman who attained a distinct literary position had composed a treatise in versification which, according to his lights, embodied the traditional ideas of Latin prosody in so far as they were received and receivable by the time. Bede's Ars Metrica was certainly the main, and not improbably the only, treatise on the subject that any Englishman of fair education was likely to know for some five hundred years after the date of its composition. And it reflected—through Victorinus, Audax, Mallius Theodorus, and others, as far back, at least, as Terentianus Maurus—ideas derived from the best classical times, mingled with others derived from times which, in the common estimate, are not so good.

Any reader of this treatise, however, and any student of the subject, with or without a treatise to assist him, but availing himself of the actual Latin poetry at his disposal, must have been, whether he chose to admit it or not, puzzled, and, unless he was a person of extraordinary genius, might have been misled, by the fact that this Latin poetry presented examples of verse constructed on two almost wholly different systems. There was, on the one hand, the system of "classical" prosody, of which the best examples, from Virgil to Claudian, were perfectly well known to even the darkest of the "Dark" ages. Although a thorough and experimental acquaintance with this is not so common as it would have been fifty or even thirty years ago, it cannot be necessary, in the introductory matter of a book like the present, to give a minute account of it to any probable reader. Derived—directly and as a matter of acquiescent learning and deliberate imitation derived—from

[3] Cf. Dante, De Vulgari Eloquio.

Greek, it presented a series of orderly arrangements in certain
prosodic forms, of syllables, the greater number of which by
far were definitely accounted beforehand as "long" or "short";
while of the rest almost all in Latin, as compared with a somewhat smaller proportion in Greek, had their length or shortness determined for them by the circumstances of their
position—by the number or character of the consonants which
followed the particular vowel in its actual collocation.

The units thus classified beforehand were to be arranged in
certain schemes of metrical adjustment. Some of these, such
as the Alcaic and Sapphic, admitted, in Latin, of no variation,
except by elision—the technical disappearance or occultation
of a final syllable, under certain fixed rules, before the initial
one of the next word. The number of syllables in a line was
here always the same; the order of long and short syllables—
in other words, the arrangement in "feet"—was invariable likewise. Others, such as the hexameter and some forms of the
iambic trimeter, were arranged on a principle of greater li-
cence. Taking, generally but not in detail, the equivalence of
one long syllable to two short as granted, "feet"—collocations
of one long and a short, of one short and a long, of a long and
two shorts, of two longs, of three shorts, and of two shorts and
a long—might, on conditions more or less rigid, be substituted for each other. But these licenses were in every case
curbed by rules, not so much arbitrary as deduced from the
necessities of keeping the general character of the line; and
in no case, save in the comparatively rare one of a "common"
syllable, or in virtue of those changes of position which were
themselves rigidly defined, might the intrinsic quality-quantity
of a syllable, the character of the prosodic integer, be tampered
with.

Such were the laws of the severer muses of Latin—examples of which, as has been said, were before every writer of any
education from the first civilisation of the outlying European
peoples to the period at which our book properly begins. But
every such writer in every such nation had before him, at the
same time, examples, in some cases even better known to him,
of poetry written in the same language, but governed by an
entirely different system of versification. In Italy itself the
Graeco-Roman prosody had been merely superimposed upon
one based on quite different principles. Not merely were the
collocations of longs and shorts in the so-called "Saturnian"
metres (and perhaps in others) arranged on much simpler and
less elaborately varied principles, but the inviolability of in-

trinsic quantity (which had already in Greek been much less[4] than in literary Latin) was of extremely little account. The stress or slur of the voice—the lilt of the accompanying music —were allowed to make long short and short long with almost entire complaisance; and to some slight extent this liberty was allowed to encroach on regular metres, such as the iambic, which approached nearest to the popular forms.

The results of this, revived and in turn imposed on "metre" in a fashion which does not directly concern us, our man of 1200 was constantly hearing in the services of the Church, and, if he was a reading man, often meeting in manuscript specimens of sacred and profane verse. The lowest term to which the line could be cut down—the syllable—had an extraordinary promiscuity of values, determined apparently by accent, by musical setting or suggestion, and by many other things, besides or contrary to the original prosodic quantification; but the next superior unit, the "foot," was in quite a different position. It was clearly upon it that the scansion depended; you could take with it either no liberties at all, or liberties in the older forms strongly determined by the laws of equivalence. And this establishment and consecration of the foot communicated an unmistakable rhythmical swing. Further, in this later prosody there was present something which was not usual in Classical nor, save late and rarely, present in Anglo-Saxon prosody—that is to say, Rhyme. And it could not require any remarkable acuteness to decide (whether consciously or unconsciously) that this rhyme in the first place bound and clenched the rhythm, emphasised and ensured its recurrence, in a very convenient fashion; in the second, that it accompanied line and rhythm with an added music no less agreeable than convenient. The exact origin and progress of the rhythmical reversion and the rhyme-innovation are very speculative questions.

When, by the results of the vast extension of the later Roman Republic and the earlier Roman Empire, Rome became the political and literary centre of the Western world, the Latin language necessarily became the at least secondary speech of education and means of conversation to nations whose languages differed indeed very much from each other, but differed in most, if not in all cases, even more from Latin.

---

[4] I know that some excellent scholars demur to this. But for me the well-known *locus* of Martial (ix. [11] 12) settles the question, and I see no reason to limit it to proper names.

All, beyond question, learnt the great examples of Roman poetry; all naturally endeavoured to imitate them; all, as a matter of inevitable consequence, found the gravest innovations
necessary. It may have looked at first as if mere chaos and barbarism would be the result; as a matter of fact the earliest result that we possess is very nearly chaotic, and is quite bar-
baric. The hexameters of Commodian, an African bishop of
the earliest fourth century, are among the greatest curiosities
of literature.[5] By entirely neglecting the classical qualities of
the words and syllables used, they can be got into batches of
spondees and dactyls which are numerically satisfactory. But
this neglect of quantity, whether intrinsic or positional, as well
as the other neglect of such laws as that of elision, is an absolute necessity. With the right quantities, and observing the
right laws, Commodian's lines become mere ruinous heaps,
destitute not only of any metre, but of any rhythm, mere
handfuls not so much of prose as of possible materials of prose.
And when the severer metres were attempted in this fashion,
something not unlike the same result continued to be produced for more than another thousand years.

But Order, if not the first law of earth, as it is said to be of
Heaven, never takes very long to establish itself even here below; and it was quite impossible that nations which were teem-
ing with poetry, and which were naturally tempted to express
themselves poetically in what they could not help regarding
as the noblest of tongues—the tongue of their rulers, the
tongue, before long, of the dominant religion, the only tongue
that enabled a man to conceal or reveal his thoughts wherever
he was—should content themselves with the mere "pidgin"-
metre of the African bishop. It is not the business of this book
to attempt a conjectural—there can probably never be a certain—reconstruction of the steps of method, and the selection of material, which led to the rhythmical Latin prosody
of the Middle Ages—one of the most exquisitely artificial-
natural of all prosodic systems, and one lending itself, with a
divine indifference, to poetry and to doggerel. As observed
experimentally throughout the productions of a thousand
years, of which the hymns of the Latin Church are the noblest, and the "Goliardic" poems most amusing exam-

[5] Here is one:—

Respuis infelix bonum disciplinae caelestis,

where the propriety of the quantification as far as the cæsura sets off
the anarchy which follows it.

ples, it has two main characteristics, both of which must have
presented themselves to the more or less distinct and distinguishing consciousness of a fairly educated person in any European country during the twelfth century, while both were
kept by the services of the Church in the ears, if not exactly in
the minds, of the most uneducated. The first of these was the
great phenomenon of rhyme; the other was a modification,
very difficult to express in scientific terminology, but exceedingly easy to seize, and not very difficult to reproduce in practice, of the exact quantitative measures of classical poetry, selected, in the first place, with a mainly instinctive but extraordinarily felicitous eclecticism, and modified, in the second,
after a fashion showing nothing short of inspiration.[6]

The exact origin of rhyme is another of those points which
Fate, or Logic, or, if anybody pleases, Pusillanimity, dispenses
us from attacking. The more probable, though it is certainly
not the favourite, opinion seems to be that rhyme, of which
symptoms, if not full examples, are found in the early poetry
of most parts of the world, and which is not absent from formal Greek and Latin verse itself, was kept out of this formal
poetry by the simple fact that its main function of "time-
beating"—of marking, emphasising, and accompanying the
poetic division—was in these cases made superfluous by the
extreme accomplishment of the metrical system. It stands
equally to reason that, when it makes its appearance, this formal accomplishment should in turn be revised, as in any case
it must evidently have been, owing to the different intonation,
or rather intonations, natural to the new models.[7]

These intonations themselves must have had most to do
with the selection of the metres to be rhythmed, and the particular alterations applied in the process of rhythmicising. But
Church music and Church service, on the one hand, and the
aggregation of students from all parts of Europe in the centres
of study on the other, seem to have effected a sort of common
measure of prosodic values;[8] and while it is notorious that the
exact nationality of most of the comic, bacchic, and amatory

---

[6] Among the innumerable but here irrelevant points of interest may be
noted the way in which different nations suited accentual Latin poetry
to their own accent. See this, which many must have dimly thought,
well and I think first expressed, in Mr. Ker's *Dark Ages*, p. 202 sq. I
believe he had been led to notice it first, as I had myself, by Baudel-
aire's poem, *Franciscae meae laudes*, modern as that is.
[7] See note above.
[8] Again with exceptions.

poetry of the two centuries just referred to is extremely dubi-
ous, it is not really possible to discern any difference corresponding to the known nationality of the authors of the great
hymns. It would probably be impossible to effect, and would
certainly be very dangerous to attempt, too many mediate gen-
eralisations in reference to the alterations preferred. The commonest feet (putting aside the combinations of four or even
five syllables admitted by ancient prosody), in that prosody
itself, had been iamb, trochee, and spondee among dissyllabic,
dactyl, and anapæst among trisyllabic feet. But the spondee,
though by no means, as some have thought, an unknown modern foot (it would be interesting to know how any correct pronunciation of "humdrum" or "randan" can make either anything but a spondee), is not common[9] in the modern tongues,
and in mediæval Latin, at any rate, the trochee and the
anapæst have a greater relative prominence than in ancient.
The systems, or schemes of arrangement, were exceedingly numerous, and sometimes of such complication that, without
musical accompaniment, they have an air of non-naturalness.
But the most ancient and the most popular are simple enough,
such as the universally used and extremely effective adjustment of acatalectic and catalectic trochaic dimeters—

> Pone luctum, Magdalena,
> Et serena lacrimas,

which is for some purposes no doubt better arranged in one
"fifteener"; as its shortened variety of catalectic and brachycatalectic which gives the still more popular *thirteener*—

> **Meum mihi est propositum in taberna mori;**

as the galloping dactylic tetrameter—

> *Fumus et mulier et stillicidia.*

But both in these and in almost all others there are noticeable
two, perhaps three, things. The first is that syllabic uniformity
is more strictly observed than ever—so much so that even
elision is distinctly eschewed. The second is that these comparatively or wholly rigid syllabic lengths are cut up into feet
as rigid. The third is that in the selection of the syllables that
make up these feet, classical quantity is ignored in degrees

[9] Milton, however, was certainly fond of it, and so were others, as we
shall see.

which may seem to vary, but which in all probability are reducible to one single norm—that of an elastic, but by no means indefinitely elastic, pronunciation.

In other words, and not to dwell on a subject which, intensely interesting as it is, is not our subject, the supposed educated Englishman of 1100-1200, looking at his Ovid, and at any poems that happened to be then written in accent-Latin, would find that in both cases the movement of the verse was separable into definite and the same units, but that tho parts which composed these were apparently selected on quit different principles. He would (or he might) notice that the rhythm of such a line as

Miraque res, media subito tenus exstitit alvo

(*Met.* xiii. 893) was, as far as the first six words are concerned, identical with that of

Cur mundus militat sub vana gloria

(always supposing that this poem was, as it may have been, written by 1200). But if he was a really observant person he would also observe that Ovid never uses, for such a rhythmical or metrical effect, such combinations of syllables as cur mundus or sub vana, and that while militat actually does, and gloria in a different case may often do, such duty with him, he would carefully abstain from beginning the next word to militat with a consonant, or making gloria an oblique case. The observer would, also, at least possibly observe that in his own pronunciation and intonation these refinements were rather superfluous. What practical conclusions he might draw will be matter of future consideration for us.

B2. Greek(?)

If anybody at the same time had had any Greek before him (which is improbable, but not quite impossible),[10] he would have found the same state of things prevailing in a more aggravated dichotomy. *Classical* Greek literature would have presented itself to him with an initial and continuing superiority of freedom, in respect of common quantity of syllables and of "equivalent" adjustment of combined feet, but with a system on the whole as regular. *Modern* Greek literature would have shown the process which was going on in Latin,

[10] In the *Dark* Ages we find a good deal of rather "pidgin" Greek; less in the early *Middle*.

repeated, anticipated, or paralleled (for the facts are extremely hard to decide upon), in a way systematically similar, but very inferior in actual result. There is not the slightest reason (such as is sometimes alleged as due to the prejudice arising from familiarity with classical models) why the hexameters of Tzetzes, the iambics of Theodorus Prodromus, and the accentual fifteeners of Manasses, should not be at least as attractive and acceptable as the carolling and chanting hexameters of Bernard of Morlaix, the solemn iambics of a hundred hymn-writers, and the tripping and laughing thirteeners of Mapes, or whosoever may have stood for "Golias." They are, in fact, not merely not acceptable, but ineffably disgusting. And though no such phrase can be applied to the Greek hymns at their best, yet they seldom rise to the splendour and the "cry" of the Latin—thereby exactly reversing classical experience. From the point of view of mere prosody, however, this does not matter. The help or the hindrance provided by Greek would have been, in rare and doubtful cases, exactly the same as that provided by Latin in cases innumerable and indubitable. The student, or the listener, or the reader would have been provided with schemes, forms, practices, sometimes of a rigid, and always of a carefully adjusted character.

C. French and Provençal[11]

The third prosody, French, with which in some examples, at least, he had many chances, and at most some certainty, of being familiar, presented qualities not new or different, but differently combined and adjusted. There was rhyme, either perfect or imperfect (assonance), which distinguished it sharply from Anglo-Saxon; and there was also a recurrent and diffused rhythm which distinguished it therefrom at least as strongly. There was—as distinguishing it from at least the classical form of Latin, and still more remarkably from all forms of Anglo-Saxon—an almost, if not quite, universal refusal to admit any inequality or equivalence of syllables in the line. Number of syllables seemed to count alone. But there was, superadded to this, a sharp cæsura such as had existed in the classical, but did not always exist in the later, Latin, and which corresponded to the "sections" of Anglo-Saxon; and there was an arrangement, not quite to be paralleled in either

---

[11] The habit, common in linguistic scholars, of sharply separating Northern and Southern French is not literary.

of these languages, that of buckling, by similarity of rhyme or assonance, a large—sometimes a very large—number of lines into a sort of largest integer (the *laisse* or *tirade*), corresponding to the smaller stanza-integers which were found in Latin verses and poems of the modern type. Furthermore, in French (and in its southern sister, Provençal, perhaps still more) there was a fancy for elaborating lyrical forms of great intricacy, making the Sapphics and Alcaics of the ancients quite simple things in comparison, and for the device of the *refrain*, so natural to uncivilised poetry, and so charming, where rightly used, in poetry civilised as well as uncivilised.

D. Scandinavian

This prosody certainly had influence on the later Anglo-Saxon verse, especially in the famous *Rhyming Poem*, and from political and ethnological causes must have exercised a good deal (perhaps unconsciously and indirectly) on at least the northern parts of England. Its basis had originally been identical with that of Anglo-Saxon, or very closely allied to it. But it had even earlier proved susceptible to the attraction of rhyme, which Anglo-Saxon resisted with such curious stoutness; it was more definitely metrical in its rhythm, more regular, and much more inclined to the stanza, which in Anglo-Saxon we hardly find save, thanks to its refrain, in *Deor*. And before very long it settled itself into the artificial forms of what is called, by a very misleading and objectionable, but now almost accredited title, "*Court*-Poetry."

E. Celtic

Last, and least known to the present writer, but fortunately of least probable effect, come the prosodies of the "Celtic fringe." Irish and, still more, Welsh poetry is famous for the extreme intricacy of its verse-laws, but scholars now roundly declare that the oldest Irish we have is based upon accentual Latin. And though it would seem that the famous Welsh triad or triplet may be autochthonous, the more elaborate forms, the "four-and-twenty measures," probably owe their origin to the genius of the race and language, no doubt, but to that genius working upon Latin suggestions. If any formal influence was exercised on Middle English (there can be no reasonable doubt that some of the *matter* of Layamon and others comes from Celtic sources), it must have been chiefly in the suggestion of intricate stanza arrangements, and especially in the in-

ternal rhymes quaintly interwoven, where, however, an awkward reminder of Latin again comes in.[12]

Let us then briefly resume the influences which were at the
disposal of a student of English prosody (had such a man
existed), though it is not to be supposed that even one such
student did exist, cir. 1150-1200; which at least must or may
have insensibly worked upon almost every practitioner of English verse at the time. He had the débris of Anglo-Saxon
prosody, presenting a scheme which, whether at one time the
"stuffings," the unaccented makeweights of its sections, were
subject to any system of equivalence or not, had undoubtedly,
in the majority of its examples, ceased to regard the constitu-
tion of these makeweights with any prudish or precisian
scrupulosity. The principles of this prosody were, in the first
place, the selection of certain strong syllables as pivots or
pillars; and, in the second, the requirement that these pivots or
pillars should put on an outward garment of phonetic similarity, either by vowel incipience generally, or by the incipience
of certain consonants in particular. There was, for a third
requirement, the necessity of a sharp pause in the middle of
the verse (or, as may be preferred, between the constituents
of each pair of verses), and there may have been internal
pauses within the division thus made. The verse or couplet
thus effected did not necessarily or even commonly submit itself to any system of rhythm recognisable in the other prosodies, but in a certain number—perhaps a very large number
—of cases there was an approximation to the trochaic movement; that is to say, to the rhythm which has an initial arsis,
length, stress, accent, or what not, descends from this to a
thesis, shortness, slur, etc., and ascends again at the beginning
of a new "foot" with the same alternation.

Further, he might, at least, notice that the practice of
poetry in these measures had sensibly died down, and that
it had to a great extent passed into the composition of rhythmical prose, on the same principles slightly relaxed.

On the other hand he had, in the quantitative Latin of his
reading, a system which, while it agreed with Anglo-Saxon
to some extent in the admission of equivalence, differed from
it in every other conceivable manner and feature, and provided

[12] We will not here discuss the vexed question whether rhyme was
given by Celtic to Latin or by Latin to Celtic. I have very little doubt
about it; but here it does not matter, for the Englishman of 1200 was
certain to get *his* notions of rhyme from Latin or French, not from
Irish or Welsh.

a definite metrical rhythm. He had, in the accentual Latin of his reading and hearing, one which, less complaisant as to equivalence, adjusted itself much more easily and satisfactorily to his own language and habits of speech. In French and in Provençal (if, as he easily might from political connections, he knew any) he had a prosody corresponding to this last, but even more rigidly syllabic—syllabic, indeed, first of all, but relieving itself by a very free indulgence in elaborate stanzas of different lengths of line. He found something like these staves or stanzas in Scandinavian and Celtic, if he happened to know anything about them. And in all the living poetries, even in the later remains of moribund Anglo-Saxon, much more in accentual Latin, French, Provençal, Scandinavian, and Celtic, he found—Rhyme.

Such were the gifts, the examples, the patterns with which "the Mothers" provided him. The whole gist and bent of this work is to set forth exactly what he and his descendants have done with them.

ROBERT BRIDGES

A Letter To A Musician On English Prosody

[Robert Bridges had a lifelong interest in the principles
of English versification. He experimented with meters of his
own invention; his scholarship on prosody has permanent
value. No student should fail to consult his Milton's Prosody
(1901, 1921): the most complete analysis of iambic structure
ever undertaken. His knowledge was not only derived from a
formidable command of Latin and Greek, musical theory, and
the exhaustive analysis of examples, but also from insights
gained as a master craftsman in English verse.

[Bridges sees clear differences among the various systems of
meter. The principal systems are three: quantitative, syllabic,
and stress. A confusion in terminology blurs the brilliant clarity
of this essay: what Bridges names "syllabic verse" is more ac-
curately described as syllable-stress verse.

[Bridges' classical bias leads him to an unwarranted scepticism about syllable-stress verse, the traditional metric of English poetry. Bridges finds the syllabic system a "wretched skeleton" on which to hang a prosody; yet despite the poverty of
this system, its lack of precise rules and its rhetorical freedom,
Bridges observes "the extreme beauty to which verse has attained under the syllabic system."]

My dear—, when lately you asked me to recommend you a
book on English Prosody, and I said that I was unable to do so,
I had some scruples of conscience, because, as a matter of fact,
I have never myself read any of the treatises, though I have
looked into many of them, and from that, and from the report
of students and reviewers, I think that I know pretty well the
nature of their contents; so that your further inquiries come to

Reprinted from Collected Essays Papers &c of Robert Bridges, Vol. II.
Used by permission of The Clarendon Press Oxford.

me as a challenge to explain myself, which if I could not do, I should be in a contemptible position. I embrace the opportunity the more willingly because you are a musician. If my notions are reasonable you will understand them; if you do not, you may conclude that they are not worthy of your attention.

Preliminary

It is impossible, however one might desire it, to set out with satisfactory definitions of Prosody and Poetic rhythm, for the latter term especially is difficult to fix: and it will be best to examine perfected poetry and see what it is that we have to deal with.

If we take verses by Virgil, Dante or Milton, who were all of them artistic geniuses, we find that their elaborate rhythms are a compound, arrived at by a conflict between two separate factors, which we may call the Speech-rhythm and the Metric rhythm. Take an example from Virgil,

Fluminaque antíquos subterlabentia muros.[1]

I have no doubt that I enjoy this rhythm as Virgil intended it, for I read it in measured longs and shorts, and I find that the speech-accent on antíquos, contradicting the metrical ictus, enhances the beauty, and joins on smoothly to the long level subterlabentia, with its two little gliding syllables at the end in quiet motion against the solid muros. There is no room for difference of opinion; and the same phenomenon meets us everywhere. The poetic rhythm derives its beauty from the conflict between a (prosodial) metre, which makes us more or less expect a certain regular rhythm of accent corresponding with the typical metric structure, and, on the other hand, a speech-rhythm which gives it all manner of variety by overriding it. In the above instance, though the essence of the metre is the sequence of long and short syllables, we yet regard the hexameter as a typically falling rhythm, i.e. with its main accents on the initial syllables of the constituent feet, which would give ántiquós; and the beauty of Virgil's line contains the contradiction or dislocation of those accents.

Moreover, if we were unacquainted with hexameter verse (i.e. with the prosody), the line quoted would seem a line of

[1] The line scans: Flu mi na|quean ti|quos sub|ter la|ben ti a|mu ros, (Ed. note)

prose, in prose-rhythm, and it would be in itself no less beautiful than it is. Only the knowledge that it is an hexameter adds
to our satisfaction; the definition of the value of the syllables
and the recognition of the verse-form give us pleasure, and
especially because it is one of many varieties of a most skillfully invented form, which by their accumulation make pleasing poems. But this reflection may also convince us of the
subjective nature of the quality of poetic rhythm, and consequently how it must defy exhaustive analysis, although it may
allow of the analytical separation of its components.

And since we can imagine that the hexameter had never
been invented, and yet that these words might still have been
written, it will follow that poetic rhythm may be regarded as
common speech-rhythm subjected to certain definitions and
limitations: and the laws of these will no doubt be the
prosody.

Let us for the moment suppose that there is no such thing
as prosody, and inquire into the elements or factors of speech-
rhythm.

The Vocal Factors of Speech-Rhythm

Now if you read English verse aloud, your main endeavor is
to express the rhythm. You know what you mean by this, and
you are aware whether you are successful or not.

Supposing that you express the rhythm as you wish, you
will find that you have freely used the only three means which
are at your disposal. First, you will have distinguished some
syllables by their comparative length and brevity. Secondly,
you will have varied the pitch of your voice. Thirdly, you will
have varied the strength of your voice, enforcing some syllables with greater loudness; and you will have freely combined
these different components of rhythm. There is nothing else
that you can do towards expressing the rhythm, except that
(and especially in elaborately written verse) you will have relied a great deal on pauses or silences of suitable duration.
These pauses are essential to good reading, but they are not
essential to our present consideration. First there are the
metric pauses, which merely isolate balancing sections of verse-
rhythm. Then there are the grammatical pauses or stops:
these are interruptions of the metric rhythm, which are either
condoned for the sake of the sense, or are observed to indicate
and separate the ever-varying sections of the speech-rhythm

(being thus to speech-rhythm what metric pauses are to the metre). Now the grammatical pause is a physical necessity, as the breath-place, and it must of course be a true "rest" of actual time-value. But its time-value in poetry is indefinite, and it has therefore no rhythmical significance except as the sign of the break in the grammar. If these pauses be all excluded, you will find so few true *intra-rhythmical* pauses left, *i.e.* time-rests within a section of rhythm and essential to its expression, that we may consider them as belonging to a more advanced treatment of the subject, and confine ourselves to the active varieties of vocal effect, namely, QUANTITY, PITCH, and LOUDNESS.[2]

Of these three you will find on examination that the first, that is difference of quantity, is the only one which will give rhythm without the aid of either of the others. It is well to make this quite clear, and musical examples are the simplest.

Let us, to begin with, take an example where all three are present, the slow movement of an orchestral symphony. When this is performed by the orchestra we hear different time-values of the notes, their differences of pitch, and actual enforcements of loudness, and all of these seem to be essential to the rhythmic effect.

But now if we take the same *Andante* and perform it on the choir-organ, the conditions of which preclude the differences of loud and soft, we find that, though the effect is generally poorer than in the orchestral performance, yet the rhythm is unaffected. We have here then an example of an elaborate rhythm expressed without variations of loudness.

[2] LOUDNESS. I use this word and not "stress," because, though some authorities still maintain that stress is only loudness, I need the word stress to indicate a condition which is much more elaborate, and induced very variously. (a) I should admit that loudness may give stress, but (b) I hold that it is more frequently and more effectually given by tonal accent, in which case it is (for our purpose) included under Pitch. (c) It is also sometimes determined by Quantity, and (d) sometimes by Position; as in the last place of our decasyllabic verses where that lacks true accentual stress. When therefore I confine my third voice-effect to loudness, and pretend that my classification is exhaustive, I leave a small flaw in my demonstration: but you will perceive that it does not materially invalidate the argument, because position is the only condition which escapes; and that plainly belongs to a much more elaborate scale of treatment, wherein metres would be analyzed and the effects of the combinations of the different factors would also be shown. For instance, a concurrence of length, high pitch, loudness, and position gives an overwhelming stress, and all possible combinations among all four of them may occur, and the first three of them are all very variable in degree. It is no wonder that it is difficult to define *stress*.

Now to exclude Pitch. The commonest example that I can think of is the monotoning of the prayers in a cathedral service. Here varieties of pitch are of course absent, but you may generally detect the quantities to be complicated by some variation of loudness. In proportion, however, as monotoning is well done the sound is level in force. Perhaps you will ask, where is the rhythm? I was once induced to establish a choir in a country church, and among my first tasks I had to train the boys in choral monotone. They were naturally without any notion of educated speech-rhythms. But there is no difficulty in teaching boys anything that you yourself understand; they can imitate anything, and love to do it. I had therefore only to offer the correct rhythms to their ears, and they adopted them at once. When we had got the vowels and consonants right, both to spare my own voice, and also because I preferred a model which could not suggest stress to them, I made the organ set the rhythms, and pulling out the great diapason I beat on it the syllables of the Lord's Prayer for the boys to pick up. This was of course nothing but boo, boo, boo, only the boos were of different durations: yet the rhythm was so distinct, it was so evident that the organ was saying the Lord's Prayer, that I was at first rather shocked, and it seemed that I was doing something profane; for it was comic to the boys as well as to me; but the absurdity soon wore off. Now here was rhythm without loudness or pitch.

If you should still ask what I mean by saying that this was rhythm, you need to extend your notion of speech-rhythm to include every recognizable motion of speech in time. The Lord's Prayer is not in poetic rhythm, but if it had been, then the organ would have expressed it even more plainly, and there is no line to be drawn in speech-rhythms between those that are proper verse-rhythms and those that are only possible in prose: there is really no good speech-rhythm which might not be transferred from prose into a poetry that had a sufficiently elaborated prosody, with this proviso only, that it must be a short member; for good prose constructs and combines its rhythms so that in their extension they do not make or suggest verse.

Since we see, then, that rhythm may be expressed by quantity alone, we have to examine whether either *pitch* or *loudness* are sufficient in themselves to give rhythm.

Let us first take Pitch. A common hymn-tune of equal notes would seem to be the most promising example, and to fulfill the conditions, but it does not. It is a melody, and that implies rhythm, but in so far as it has rhythm it is dependent on its *metre*, which exists only by virtue of certain pauses or rests which its subdivision into short sections determines. Now, given these sections, they discover initial and other stresses which are enforced by the words or the metre or the harmony, or by all three, and without these aids and interpretations the structure is arhythmic, and it can be read in many different ways.

It remains only to consider Loudness, which may here be described as accent without pitch or quantity. Now if we take a succession of perfectly equal notes, differing only in that some of them (any that you may choose) are louder than the others, the experiment will suggest only the simple skeletons of the most monotonous rhythms, and if one of these declare itself, such as a succession of threes or fours, you will probably be unconsciously led to reinforce it with some device of quantitive phrasing. To compare such a result with the experiment of beating the Lord's Prayer on the organ is to compare something too elementary to be of any value with something that is too complex and extensive to define.

The Office of Prosody

My examples will have sufficiently illustrated my meaning; your conviction will depend on your own consideration of the matter. On the supposition that you agree we can take an important step, and say that, looking at the question from the point of view of speech-rhythm, it would seem that it is the addition of Prosody to speech-rhythm which determines it to be poetic rhythm or verse. What, then, exactly is Prosody? Our English word is not carried over from the Greek word, with its uncertain and various meaning, but it must have come with the French word through the scholastic Latin; and like the French term it primarily denotes the rules for the treatment of syllables in verse, whether they are to be considered as long or short, accented or unaccented, elideable or not, etc., etc. The syllables, which are *the units* of rhythmic speech, are by nature of so indefinite a quality and capable of such different vocal expression, that apart from the desire which every artist must feel to have his work consistent in itself, his appeal to an audience would convince him that there is no chance of his elaborate rhythms being rightly interpreted unless his treatment of syllables is understood. Rules must therefore arise and be agreed upon for the treatment of syllables, and this is the first indispensable office of Prosody.

Then, the syllables being fixed, their commonest combinations (which are practically commensurate with word-units) are defined and named; and these are called *feet*. And after this the third step of Prosody is to prescribe metres, that is to register the main systems of feet which poets have invented to make verses and stanzas. Thus the Alcaic stanza is—

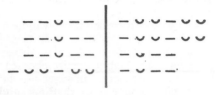

and in tabulating metres Prosody is at once involved in rhythm, for we may say generally that every metre has a typical accentual rhythm of its own—which was presumably the motive of its invention—though it may be in some cases difficult to fix on one to the exclusion of all others; certainly (to take easy examples) we may regard the hexameter as a typically falling rhythm, and the iambic as a rising rhythm. The force of this prosodial rhythm will vary in different metres, and with different readers; but one thing stands out very prominently, namely, that in the essential scheme of the Greek metre which I have tabulated above it is the quantities only that are prescribed and fixed, while the accents or stresses are not prescribed, so that any speech-rhythm which had a corresponding sequence of those quantities would fit the scheme;[3] whereas, if the metre had been an accentual scheme, that is, if the syllabic signs had been indeterminate with respect to quantity (instead of being longs and shorts), but marked with prescribed accents in certain places, then the quantities would have been free, and any speech-rhythm with a corresponding sequence of accents would have fitted the form, independently of the length or shortness of any one particular accented or unaccented syllable. There could thus be two quite distinct systems of Prosody, according as the metres were ruled by one or other of these different factors of speech-rhythm.

THREE KINDS OF PROSODY

Now the history of European verse shows us three distinct systems of Prosody, which can be named:—

[3] Not always making good verse; but the details of that are omitted as not affecting the argument: their varieties often cancel each other.

1. The Quantitive system
2. The Syllabic system
3. The Stress system

I will give a short account of each of these.

1. The system of the Greeks was scientifically founded on quantity, because they knew that to be the only one of the three distinctions of spoken syllables which will give rhythm by itself. But the speech-quantities of their syllables being as indeterminate as ours are, the Greeks devised a convention by which their syllables were separated into two classes, one of long syllables, the other of short, the long being twice the duration of the short, as a minim to a crotchet; and this artificial distinction of the syllables was the foundation of their Prosody. The convention was absolutely enforced, even in their prose oratory, and their verse cannot be understood unless it is strictly observed. For the result which they obtained was this: the quantities gave such marked and definite rhythms, that these held their own in spite of the various speech-accents which overlaid them. The Latins copying their method arrived at a like result.

2. The syllabic system, which has prevailed in various developments throughout Europe from the decay of the Greek system up to the present time, had no more scientific basis than the imitation of the Latin poetry by writers who did not understand it. But I believe that in such matters the final cause is the efficient cause, and that it was therefore the possibility of the results which we have witnessed that led them on their pathless experiments. Criticism discovers two weaknesses in the system: one, the absence of any definite prosodial principle, the other, which follows from the first, the tendency for different and incompatible principles to assert themselves, indiscriminately overriding each other's authority, until the house is so divided against itself that it falls into anarchy.

I will shortly illustrate one or two points. First, my statement that this syllabic system arose from writing quantitive verse without the quantities. The octosyllabic church-hymns give a good example, and for all that I know they may have actually been the first step. The earliest of these hymns were composed in correct iambic metre, e.g. (fourth century):—

> Splendor paternae gloriae
> De luce lucem proferens
> Lux lucis et fons luminis
> Dies dierum illuminans.

Compare with this what writers wrote who did not know the classic rules, e.g.:—

1. Ad coenam Agni prouidi
    Et stolis albis candidi
    Post transitum maris rubri
    Christo canamus principi.

2. Ne grauis somnus irruat
    Nec hostis nos surripiat
    Nec caro illi consentiens
    Nos tibi reos statuat.

Such stanzas virtually contain the whole of European syllabic Prosody;[4] though as a matter of fact the rule of elision, which these writers often neglected, was preserved. Since these hymns were intended to be sung to tunes that were generally of equal notes with tendency to alternate accent, the quantities did not signify, and there was a *tendency to alternate stress*, which came to be the norm and bane of syllabic verse;[5] and this leads to another somewhat curious observation, namely, that these writers of non-quantitive iambics were withheld from the natural tendency to write merely in alternate stress to suit their tunes (see ex. 2, above) by their familiarity with the free rhythms of the older well-loved hymns;[6] and since those broken rhythms had been originally occasioned by the unalterable overruling features of the language, they were almost as difficult to avoid as they were easy to imitate. It is pretty certain that the frequency of inversion of the first foot in all English syllabic (iambic) verse is an unbroken tradition from the Latin; the convenience of allowing a disyllable at the beginning of the line being conveyed and encouraged by precedent.

The "prosody" of European syllabic verse may be roughly set out as follows:—

[4] My necessary brevity confines me to consideration of the disyllabic metres; but this is justified by their overruling historical importance, and their overwhelming preponderance in European syllabic verse.
[5] In the absence of a philosophic grammar of rhythm one can only offer opinions as guesses, but it would seem to me that alternate stress can only be of rhythmic value in poetry as the firmest basis for the freest elaboration. One's memory hardly reaches back to the time when it could satisfy one. The force of it always remains as one of the most powerful resources of effect, but its unrelieved monotony is to an educated ear more likely to madden than to lull. (See Remark, No. XII, below.)
[6] And '*Turcos oppressi et barbaras gentes excussi*' is in this category.

(1) There must be so many syllables in the verse.
(2) Any extra syllables must be accounted for by elision.
(3) Any syllable may be long or short.
(4) There is a tendency to alternate stress.

This is honestly the wretched skeleton[7] (indeed, in Milton's perfected "iambics" we may add that any syllable may be accented or unaccented), and no amount of development can rebuild its hybrid construction.[8] For our present consideration of the rules of Prosody the bare skeleton will serve; but to the description we may add that the history of its development shows that it determined its metrical forms mainly by rhyme, and that "stress," there being nothing of equal force to oppose it, gradually predominated, invading and practically ruling syllabic verse long before it was openly recognized, or any hint was given of formulating its principles, or constructing a Prosody of it, the principles of which are irreconcilable with the syllabic system, and which I will now describe.

3. *Stress-Prosody.* In this system the natural accentual speech-rhythms come to the front, and are the determining factor of the verse, overruling the syllabic determination. These speech-rhythms were always present; they constituted in the classical verse the main variety of effects within the different metres, but they were *counterpointed*, so to speak, on a quantitive rhythm, that is, on a framework of strict (unaccented) time, which not only imposed necessary limitations but, certainly in Latin, to a great extent determined their forms. In the syllabic Prosody, in which the prosodial rules were so much relaxed, these speech-rhythms came in the best writers to be

_____

[7] Try the experiment of supplying lacunae. Suppose four syllables to be missing from the middles respectively of a Greek iambic, a Latin hexameter, and an English blank verse. In the two former cases the prosodial limitations exclude many desirable words; in the syllabic scheme almost any words will fit.

[8] I would not wish to seem to underestimate the extreme beauty to which verse has attained under the syllabic system. Shakespeare and Milton have passages of blank verse as fine as poetry can be. I would make three remarks here. (1) A free and simple basis (such as the syllabic system has) probably offers the best opportunity for elaboration. (2) It is probable that no verse has ever been subject to such various elaboration as the European syllabic verse; the question is rather whether any further development on the same lines is possible. (3) On the simplest syllabic scheme it is impossible in English to write two verses exactly alike and equivalent, because of the infinite variety of the syllabic unit and its combinations: and these natural and subtle differences of value, though common to all systems of prosody, are perhaps of greater rhythmical effect in the syllabic than in the quantitive system.

of first importance, and in Milton (for example) we can see that they are only withheld from absolute authority and liberty by the observance of a conservative syllabic fiction, which is so featureless that it needs to be explained why Milton should have thought it of any value. For all Milton's free-speech rhythms, which are the characteristic beauty of his verse, and by their boldness make his originality as a rhythmist, are confined by a strict syllabic limitation, viz. that the syllables which compose them must still keep the first two rules of the syllabic Prosody, and be resoluble into so many "iambs." But these so-called iambs are themselves now degraded to nothing, for the disyllabic unit which still preserves that old name has no definition: it has lost its quantities, nor are its lost quantities always indicated by accent or stress; its disyllabic quality, too, is resoluble by the old law of Latin elision (which Milton extended to liquids, reducing Chaucer's practice to certain fixed rules) into trisyllabic forms, so that *either* or *both* of the syllables of the fictive iamb may be long or short, accented or unaccented, while the whole may be a trisyllabic foot of many varieties. Yet in his carefully composed later poetry Milton kept strictly to the syllabic rules, and never allowed himself any rhythm which could not be prosodially interpreted in this fictitious fashion—"counted on the fingers." Now the stress-system merely casts off this fiction of Milton's, and it dismisses it the more readily because no one except one or two scholars has ever understood it.

Stress being admitted to rule, it follows that the stress-rhythms are, up to a certain point, identical with modern music, wherein every bar is an accent followed by its complement: and there is no rhythm of modern music which is not also a possible and proper rhythm of stress-prosody; and the recognition of pure stress-prosody was no doubt mainly influenced by the successes of contemporary music. But poetry is not bound, as our music is, to have equal bars; so that its rhythmic field is indefinitely wider. To understand the speech-rhythms of poetry a musician must realize from what an enormous field of rhythm he is excluded by his rule of equal bars. Musicians, however, do not nowadays need to be informed of this; for, having executed all the motions that their chains allowed them, they are already beginning to regret their bonds, and tax their ingenuity to escape from them, as the frequent syncopations and change of time-signature in their music testify.

What rules this new stress-prosody will set to govern its

rhythms one cannot foresee, and there is as yet no recognized Prosody of stress-verse. I have experimented with it, and tried to determine what those rules must be; and there is little doubt that the perfected Prosody will pay great attention to the quantitive value of syllables, though not on the classical system.[9] Here, however, I wish only to differentiate that system from the others, and what I have said shows this conclusion:

SUMMARY

1. In the Greek system the Prosody is quantitive.
2. In the syllabic system it is "syllabic" (as described).
3. In the stress-system it is accentual.

And while in the classical Prosody the quantities were the main prosodial basis, first ordered and laid down, with the speech-rhythms counterpointed upon it, in the stress-system, on the other hand, it is the speech-rhythms which are the basis, and their quantitive syllables will be so ordered as to enforce them, and their varieties will be practically similar to the varieties of modern music with its minims, crotchets, quavers, dotted notes, etc., etc.

These things being so, it would seem to me indispensable that any treatise on Prosody should recognize these three different systems: indeed, a Prosody which does not recognize them is to me unintelligible. Before my few final remarks you will expect me to say something about rime.

RIME

Rules for rime are strictly a part of Prosody within my definition of the term, but they call for no discussion here.

---

[9] Indifference to quantity is the strangest phenomenon in English verse. Our language contains syllables as long as syllables can be, and others as short as syllables can be, and yet the two extremes are very commonly treated as rhythmically equivalent. A sort of rhythmical patter of stress is set up, and MISPRONUNCIATION IS RELIED ON to overcome any 'false quantities.' *This was taught me at school,* e.g. the Greek word γλῠκὖς was pronounced as a spondee of the heaviest class accented strongly on the first syllable, and then had to be read in such a verse as this (corresponding to the *tıa* of the line quoted from Virgil)—

τοῦτ' ἄρα δεύτατον εἶπεν ἔπος, ὅτε οἱ γλυκὺς ὕπνος.

It is really difficult to get an average classical scholar, who has been educated as I was, to see that there is any absurdity here. On the other hand, an average educated lady will not believe that the scholars can be guilty of an absurdity so manifest. (See Remark V, below)

It is, however, well to understand the relation in which rhyme scientifically stands to poetry. The main thing in poetry must be the ideas which the words carry; its most important factors are the aesthetic and intellectual form, and the quality of the diction in which the ideas are conveyed; with none of these things are we concerned, but supposing these at their best, with the rhythms suitable and the Prosody also sufficient, the poet will still find that his material is often insurmountably refractory in the matter of syllabic euphony. His wish is that the sounds should always be beautiful or agreeable, and this is impossible, for language was not invented with this aim, and it almost always falls short of what is desirable (the history of English accidence is a disgrace to the aesthetic faculties of the nation); there is, in fact, a constant irremedial deficiency in this merely phonetic beauty, and it is reasonable that extraneous artifices should have been devised to supply it. Alliteration, assonance, and rhyme are all contrivances of this sort; they are in their nature beautifications of the language independent of the ideas, and of the rhythm, and of the diction, and intended to supply by their artificial correspondences the want of natural beauty in the garment of language. But it must not be overlooked that they were also well nigh necessitated by the unscientific character of the syllabic Prosody, which having in ignorance discarded the scientific Prosody of the poetry which it imitated, had to devise new rules for itself experimentally as it grew up, and eagerly seized on such external artifices of speech to dress out its wavering forms, just as an architecture which has lost its living traditions of fine form will seek to face itself with superficial ornament. Alliteration in early English Poetry was a main feature of structure. It has perished as a metrical scheme, but it is freely used in all poetry, and it is so natural to language that it finds a place in the commonest as well as in the most elaborated speech of all kinds. Rime has had a long reign, and still flourishes, and it is in English one of the chief metrical factors. Like a low-born upstart it has even sought to establish its kinship with the ancient family of rhythm by incorporating the aristocratic *h* and *y* into its name. As it distinguishes verses that have no other distinction, its disposition determines stanza-forms, etc.; and for this reason it usurps a prominence for which it is ill-suited. Dryden, indeed, and others have ridiculed the notion of "unrimed" verse in English; and their opinion is a fair consequence on the poverty of their Prosody. Milton's later poems were an attempt so to strengthen English Prosody as to render it independent of rime. In my opinion he saw exactly what was needed, and it would have been strange if he had not seen. Rime is so trammelling, its effects so cloying, and its worthiest resources are so quickly exhausted,[10] and often of such conspicuous artificiality, that a Prosody which was good enough to do without it would immediately discard it, in spite of its almost unparalleled achievements.

REMARKS

I. If these three systems are to be treated of together as one system, it is necessary to find a common-measure of them, and the science of rhythm is at present inadequate to the task.

II. The confusing of them is so universal as to have acquired a sort of authority; and the confusion has discredited the whole subject.

III. The main source of error is the wrong way in which classical scholars read classical verse, and the teaching of their misinterpretations in our schools. Classical poetry being on a quantitive system of longs and shorts, it must be read, not as we read our syllabic verse, but in longs and shorts as it was composed, and if it is not so read it is misunderstood. If it is read in longs and shorts, then the quantitive rhythms appear, and the speech-accents give no difficulty.

IV. To give one all-convincing example of what classical scholars actually do, by treating the different systems as equivalent, the hexameter will serve. This, as Professor Mackail once complained to me, is read by them as AN ACCENTUAL RHYTHM IN THE TRIPLE TIME OF MODERN MUSIC, that is, made up of tribrachs and trochees all stressed on the first syllable. It is of course patent that if the hexameter were in a time of modern music it would be a duple and not a triple time; but it has absolutely nothing in common with the stress-rhythms of modern music.

V. A difficulty is naturally felt in the unlikelihood that such a consensus of learned opinion, from the confident multiscience of Goethe to the equally confident fastidiousness of Matthew Arnold, should be open to such a monstrous reproach of elementary incompetence. But the explanation is not difficult, if the whole blunder is perceived as the misrepresentation of quantity by accent. English people all think that an accent (or stress) makes a syllable long, whereas many

---

[10] If you observe the rimes to Knight in Spenser's *Faery Queene*, you will find the poem considerably damaged thereby.

of our words are accented as independently of their quantities as the Greek words were, e.g. *magistrate*, *prolific*: and all our pyrrhic words (= ◡◡) like *habit*, *very*, *silly*, *solid*, *scurry*, are accented, like the Latin, on the first syllable, and some very strongly, and this of course absolutely explodes the vulgar notion that accented syllables can be reckoned always as long: besides, you may see that this *accent in some cases actually shortens the syllable* further, as in the word *báttle*; for in the older form *battail*, in which the first syllable had not this decided accent, you will not pronounce it so short, but immediately that you strengthen its accent, as in our *battle* (= bắt'l) the *t* closes up the *a* much more quickly and perceptibly shortens it.

VI. To call Milton's blank verse "iambic," as he himself called it, is reasonable enough, and in the absence of a modern terminology[11] it serves well to distinguish it from the hexametric epic verse, and it describes its disyllabic basis, and suggests its rising rhythm (which may rightly be considered as the typical iambic stress, such as we see in Catullus's carefully accentual verse, "Phaséllus ílle quém vidétis hóspites," etc.): moreover, our disyllabic verse is the direct descendant of and substitute for the classic iambic. But a scientific treatise on Prosody cannot afford to use analogical terms.

VII. I should confidently guess that the five-foot metres of our blank verse, etc., came from the Sapphic line.[12] This was always familiar and was very early reduced by musical settings to an accentual scheme, which still obtains in common settings of decasyllabic "iambic" lines in church hymns, and occurs frequently in all our blank verse. I open Wordsworth at hazard in *The Borderers* and find—

> Here at my breast and ask me where I bought it.
> I love her though I dare not call her daughter.
> Oh the poor tenant of that ragged homestead.
> Justice had been most cruelly defrauded.

These lines would all be quite comfortable in the notorious *Needy Knife-Grinder*, which was a skit on the accentual Sapphic, though it is often taken seriously. . . .

---

[11] The absence of terminology is evidence of the unscientific character of the system as I have described it.
[12] The scheme of the Sapphic line was:

$$-◡\ -◡\ -◡◡\ -◡\ -◡$$

(Ed. note)

XI. The use of the Greek quantitive terminology in explaining syllabic or stress-verse implies that the terms are equivalent in the different systems, or requires that they should be plainly differentiated. It is demonstrable that they are not equivalent, and if they are differentiated the absurdity of applying the Greek notions to English poetry is patent. Try the inverse experiment of writing Greek verse with the "syllabic" definition of the classic feet.

XII. The syllabic system attained its results by learned elaboration; and in blank verse this elaboration evolved so many forms of the line (as we see in Milton) that almost any prose, which maintained a fair sprinkling of alternate accents, could be read as blank verse; the puerile degradation of the haphazard decasyllabic rhythm satisfied the verse-maker, and equally beguiled the writer of prose, who sought after rhythmical effect. A clergyman once sympathetically confessed to me that he was himself by nature something of a poet, and that the conviction had on one occasion been strangely forced upon him. For after preaching his first sermon his rector said to him in the vestry, "Do you know that your sermon was all in blank verse?" "And, by George, it was" (he said with some pride); "I looked at it, and it was!" This man had the usual long classical training, and was a fellow of his college.

XIII. To judge from one or two examples I should be tempted to say that the qualification of an English prosodist might be (1) the educated misunderstanding of Greek and Latin verse; (2) a smattering of modern musical rhythm. His method (1) to satisfy himself in the choice of a few barrel-organ rhythms, and (2) to exert his ingenuity in finding them everywhere. The result is not likely to be recommendable to a student.

TREATISE ON METRE / EZRA POUND 103

The question is extremely simple. Part of what a musician

EZRA POUND

Treatise On Metre

[The occasion for Pound's "Treatise" is similar to that of
Bridges' "Letter": the insensitivity, the legalism, and the
deafness evinced by scholars. Pound's name-calling is characteristically in excess of his subject; the polemical vigor, however, carries this essay along and gives Pound's sensible
remarks power and plausibility.

[Most intriguing is Pound's definition of rhythm: "Rhythm
is a form cut into time." A poet reveals a sense of rhythm in
his proper handling of syllabic weights and durations. No book
of rules, no grammar of procedure can ever substitute for a
musical ear. A poet achieves a prosody, a style of rhythm, by
the inspired manipulation of aural "shapes in time."]

I

I heard a fair lady sigh: "I wish someone would write a
good treatise on prosody."

As she had been a famous actress of Ibsen, this was not simple dilettantism, but the sincere wish for something whereof
the lack had been inconvenient. Apart from Dante's De Vulgari Eloquio I have encountered only one treatise on metric
which has the slightest value. It is Italian and out of print, and
has no sort of celebrity.

The confusion in the public mind has a very simple cause:
the desire to get something for nothing or to learn an art
without labour.

Fortunately or unfortunately, people CAN write stuff that
passes for poetry, before they have studied music.

The question is extremely simple. Part of what a musician HAS to know is employed in writing with words; there are no special "laws" or "differences" in respect to *that part*. There is a great laxity or vagueness permitted the poet in regard to *pitch*. He may be as great a poet as Mr. Yeats and still think he doesn't know one note from another.

Mr. Yeats probably would distinguish between a *g* and a *b flat*, but he is happy to think that he doesn't, and he would certainly be incapable of whistling a simple melody in tune.

Nevertheless before writing a lyric he is apt to "get a chune[1] in his head."

He is very sensitive to a limited gamut of rhythms.

Rhythm is a form cut into TIME, as a design is determined SPACE.

A melody is a rhythm in which the pitch of each element is fixed by the composer.
(Pitch: the number of vibrations per second.)

I said to a brilliant composer[2] and pupil of Kodaly
: These people can't make a melody, they can't make a melody four bars long.
He roared in reply: Four bars, they can't make one TWO bars long!

Music is so badly taught that I don't suggest every intending poet should bury himself in a conservatory. The "Laurencie et Lavignac Encyclopédie de la Musique et Dictionnaire du Conservatoire"[3] has however an excellent section on greek metric, better than one is likely to find in use in the greek language department of your university.

In making a line of verse (and thence building the lines into passages) you have certain primal elements:
That is to say, you have the various "articulate sounds" of the language, of its alphabet, that is, and the various groups of letters in syllables.

These syllables have differing weights and durations
    A. original weights and durations
    B. weights and durations that seem naturally imposed on them by the other syllable groups around them.

---

[1] ch, neo-celtic for *t*.
[2] Tibor Serly.
[3] Pub. Delagrave. Paris.

Those are the medium wherewith the poet cuts his design in TIME.

If he hasn't a sense of time and of the different qualities of sound, this design will be clumsy and uninteresting just as a bad draughtsman's drawing will be without distinction.

The bad draughtsman is bad because he does not perceive space and spatial relations, and cannot therefore deal with them.

The writer of bad verse is a bore because he does not perceive time and time relations, and cannot therefore delimit them in an interesting manner, by means of longer and shorter, heavier and lighter syllables, and the varying qualities of sound inseparable from the words of his speech.

He expects his faculty to descend from heaven?
He expects to train and control that faculty without the labour that even a mediocre musician expends on qualifying to play fourth tin horn in an orchestra, and the result is often, and quite justly, disesteemed by serious members of his profession.

Symmetry or strophic forms naturally HAPPENED in lyric poetry when a man was singing a long poem to a short melody which he had to use over and over. There is no particular voodoo or sacrosanctity about symmetry. It is one of many devices, expedient sometimes, advantageous sometimes for certain effects.

It is hard to tell whether music has suffered more by being taught than has verse-writing from having no teachers. Music in the past century of shame and human degradation slumped in large quantities down into a soggy mass of tone.

In general we may say that the deliquescence of instruction in any art proceeds in this manner.

I. A master invents a gadget, or procedure to perform a particular function, or a limited set of functions.

Pupils adopt the gadget. Most of them use it less skilfully than the master. The next genius may improve it, or he may cast it aside for something more suited to his own aims.

II. Then comes the paste-headed pedagogue or theorist and proclaims the gadget a law, or rule.

III. Then a bureaucracy is endowed, and the pin-headed secretariat attacks every new genius and every form of inventiveness for not obeying the law, and for perceiving something the secretariat does not.

The great savants ignore, quite often, the idiocies of the ruck of the teaching profession. Friedrich Richter can proclaim that the rules of counterpoint and harmony have nothing to do with composition, Sauzay can throw up his hands and say that when Bach composed he appears to have done so by a series of "procedures" whereof the secret escapes us, the hard sense of the one, and not altogether pathetic despair of the other have no appreciable effect on the ten thousand calves led up for the yearly stuffing.

Most arts attain their effects by using a fixed element and a variable.
From the empiric angle: verse usually has some element roughly fixed and some other that varies, but which element is to be fixed and which vary, and to what degree, is the affair of the author.
Some poets have chosen the bump, as the boundary. Some have chosen to mark out their course with repetition of consonants; some with similar terminations of words. All this is a matter of detail. You can make a purely empiric list of successful manoeuvres, you can compile a catalogue of your favourite poems. But you cannot hand out a receipt for making a Mozartian melody on the basis of take a crotchet, then a quaver, then a semi-quaver, etc. . . . .
You don't ask an art instructor to give you a recipe for making a Leonardo da Vinci drawing.
Hence the extreme boredom caused by the usual professorial documentation or the aspiring thesis on prosody.

The answer is:

LISTEN to the sound that it makes.

II

The reader who has understood the first part of this chapter has no need of reading the second. Nothing is more boring than an account of errors one has not committed.
Rhythm is a form cut into time.

. . .

The perception that the mind, either of an individual or a nation can decay, and give off all the displeasing vapours of decomposition has unfortunately gone into desuetude. Dante's hell was of those who had lost the increment of intelligence with the capital. Shakespeare, already refining the tough old catholic concept, refers to ignorance merely as darkness.

From the time Thos. Jefferson jotted down an amateur's notes on what seemed to be the current practice of english versi-fication, the general knowledge, especially among hacks, ap-pears to have diminished to zero, and to have passed into infinite negative. I suppose the known maxima occurred in the North American Review during Col. Harvey's intumes-cence. During that era when the directing minds and charac-ters in America had reached a cellarage only to be gazed at across the barriers of libel law, the said editorial bureau rebuked some alliterative verse on the grounds that a consonant had been repeated despite Tennyson's warning.

A parallel occurs in a recent professorial censure of Mr. Binyon's Inferno, the censor being, apparently, in utter igno-rance of the nature of Italian syllabic verse, which is composed of various syllabic groups, and not merely strung along with a swat on syllables 2, 4, 6, 8, 10 of each line.

You would not expect to create a Mozartian melody or a Bach theme by the process of bumping alternate notes, or by merely alternating quavers and crotchets.

Great obfuscation spread from the failure to dissociate heavy accent and duration.
Other professors failed to comprehend the "regularity" of classic hexameter.
So called dactylic hexameter does NOT start from ONE type of verse.
There are, mathematically, 64 basic general forms of it; of which 20 or 30 were probably found to be of most general use, and several of which would probably have been stunts or rarities.

But this takes no count either of shifting caesura (pause at some point in the line), nor does it count any of the various shadings.

It ought to be clear that the variety starting FROM a colony of 64 different general rhythm shapes, or architypes, will be vastly more compendious, will naturally accommodate a vastly greater amount of real speech, than will a set of vari-ants starting from a single type of line, whether measured by duration or by the alternating heaviness of syllables,

specifically:
ti tum ti tum ti tum ti tum ti tum

from which every departure is treated as an exception.

The legal number of syllables in a classic hexameter varied from 12 to 18.

When the greek dramatists developed or proceeded from anterior greek prosody, they arrived at chorus forms which are to all extents "free," though a superstructure of nomenclature has been gummed on to them by analysers whom neither Aeschylus nor Euripides would ever have bothered to read.

These nomenclatures were probably invented by people who had never LISTENED to verse, and who probably wouldn't have been able to distinguish Dante's movement from Milton's had they heard it read out aloud.

I believe Shakespeare's "blank verse" runs from 10 to 17 syllables, but have no intention of trying to count it again, or make a census.

None of these professorial pint pots has anything to do with the question.
Homer did not start by thinking which of the 64 permitted formulae was to be used in his next verse.

THE STROPHE

The reason for strophic form has already been stated. The mediaeval tune, obviously, demanded an approximately even number of syllables in each strophe, but as the duration of the notes was not strictly marked, the tune itself was probably subject to variation within limits. These limits were in each case established by the auditive precision of the troubadour himself.

In Flaubert's phrase: "Pige moi le type!" Find me the guy that will set out with 64 general matrices for rhythm and having nothing to say, or more especially nothing germane or kindred to the original urge which created those matrices, and who will therewith utter eternal minstrelsy, or keep the reader awake.

As in the case of Prof. Wubb or whatever his name was, the ignorant of one generation set out to make laws, and gullible children next try to obey them.

III

The populace loved the man who said "Look into thine owne hearte and write" or approved Uc St Circ, or whoever it was who recorded: "He made songs because he had a will to make songs and not because love moved him thereto. And nobody paid much attention to either him or his poetry."

All of which is an infinite remove from the superstition that poetry isn't an art, or that prosody isn't an art WITH LAWS.

But like the laws of any art they are not laws to be learnt by rule of thumb. "La sculpture n'est pas pour les jeunes hommes" said Brancusi. Hokusai and Chaucer have borne similar witness.

Pretended treatises giving recipes for metric are as silly as would be a book giving you measurements for producing a masterpiece à la Botticelli.

Proportion, laws of proportion. Pier della Francesca having thought longer, knew more than painters who have not taken the trouble.

A B C of Reading

"La section d'or"[4] certainly helped master architects. But you learn painting by eye, not by algebra. Prosody and melody are attained by the listening ear, not by an index of nomenclatures, or by learning that such and such a foot is called spondee. Give your draughtsman sixty-four stencils of "Botticelli's most usual curves"? And he will make you a masterpiece?

Beyond which we will never recover the art of writing to be sung until we begin to pay some attention to the sequence, or scale, or vowels in the line, and of the vowels terminating the group of lines in a series.

[4] Traditions of architectural proportion.

Part Two

THEORIES OF METER

OTTO JESPERSEN

Notes On Metre[1]

[Otto Jespersen might well be the greatest philologist of modern times. No other writer on the subject of language has displayed such vast knowledge, theoretical insight, and logical clarity. Most importantly, Jespersen possessed genuine sensitivity to literature: revealed by his listening ear for the subtleties of verse and a graceful English prose style.

[In this relatively brief and nearly unknown essay, Jespersen makes a number of crucial discoveries. He establishes the principles of English meter on a demonstrably accurate structural basis; he recognizes meter as a Gestalt phenomenon; he sees metrics as descriptive science rather than proscriptive regulation. His formulation of the principle of relative stress remains, sixty-five years later, the best explanation of metrical effect in English.]

1. The iambic pentameter may without any exaggeration be termed the most important metre of all in the literatures of the North-European world. Since Chaucer used it in its rimed form (the heroic line) and especially since Marlowe made it popular in the drama in its unrimed form (blank verse), it has been employed by Shakespeare, Milton, Dryden, Pope, Thomson, Cowper, Wordsworth, Byron, Shelley, Tennyson, by Lessing, Goethe, and Schiller, as well as by numerous Scandinavian poets, in a great many of their most important works.

Reprinted from Linguistica (Copenhagen: Levin & Munksgaard, 1933); and from The Selected Writings of Otto Jespersen (London: George Allen & Unwin, Ltd, 1962). Used by permission of the copyright owners, George Allen & Unwin, Ltd

[1] Read in Danish in the "Kgl. danske videnskabernes selskab" on the 16. Nov. 1900, printed as "Den psykologiske grund til nogle metriske fænomener" in Oversigt 1900 p. 487. Here translated with a few rearrangements and many omissions, chiefly with regard to Danish and German examples and the refutation of the views of the Danish metrist E. v. d. Recke.

I shall here try to analyse some peculiarities of this metre, but my remarks are directly applicable to other metres as well and indirectly should bear on the whole metrical science, which, if I am right in the theories advanced below, would seem to require a fundamental revision of its principles, system of notation, and nomenclature.

According to the traditional notation the metre mentioned above consists of five iambi with or without an eleventh weak syllable:

$$\cup - \mid \ \cup - \mid \ \cup \ - \ \mid \ \ \cup - \mid \ \cup \ - \ \mid \ (\cup)$$

Her eyes, | her haire, | her cheeke, | her gate, | her voice   (1)*
Give ev' | ry man | thine ear', | but few | they voyce: (2)
Take each | mans cen | sure, but | reserve | thy
    judg' | ment.[2]   (3)
Ein un | nütz Le | ben ist | ein früh | er Tod.   (4)
Zufrie | den wär | ich, wenn | mein Volk | mich rühm | te. (5)

2. But pretty often we find deviations from this scheme, a "trochee" being substituted for an "iambus." This phenomenon, which may be called briefly inversion, is especially frequent in the first foot, as in

$$- \ \cup \ \cup \ - \ \cup \ - \ \cup \ - \ \ \ \cup \ - \ \cup$$

Told by | an id | iot, full | of sound | and fu | ry.   (1)
Even two "trochees" may be found in the same line, as in

$$- \ \cup \ \ \ \cup \ - \ \ - \ \ \cup \ \cup \ - \ \ \cup \ - \ \cup$$

Tyrants | themselves | wept when | it was | report | ed.   (2)
Ihn freu | et der | Besitz; | ihn krönt | der Sieg (*ihn*
    emphatic)   (3)

Why, now, are such inversions allowed? How is it that the listener's sense of rhythm is not offended by the fact that once or even twice in the same line he hears the very opposite movement of the one he expected, a "trochee" instead of an "iambus"? He expects a certain pattern, a regular alternation in one particular way of ten syllables, and his disappointment at encountering one trochee can be mathematically expressed as affecting two tenths of the whole line; in the case of two trochees his disappointment is one of four tenths or two fifths; and yet he has nothing like the feeling of displeasure or disharmony which would seize him if in a so-called "hexameter" like

[2] The places from which quotations are taken will be indicated at the end of the paper. Quotations from Shakespeare are given in the spelling of the 1623 folio, except that sometimes an apostrophe is substituted for a mute e, and that the modern distinction of u and v, and of i and j is carried through.

Strongly it bears us along in swelling and limitless billows
—an "anapaest" were substituted for a "dactylus":

It is strong, bears us along in swelling and limitless billows;
or if in
Jack is a poor widow's heir, but he lives as a drone in a bee-
hive—
we substituted an "amphibrach":

Behold a poor widow's heir, but he lives as a drone in a bee-
hive.

Naturally science cannot rest contented by calling deviations
"poetical licences" or by saying that the whole thing depends
on individual fancy or habit: as poets in many countries, however different their verse is in various other respects, follow
very nearly the same rules, and to a great extent followed these
before they were established by theorists, there must be some
common basis for these rules, and it will be our task to find
out what that basis is.

3. The permissibility of a trochee in an iambic metre is very
often justified by the assertion that purely iambic lines following one another without intermission would be intolerably
monotonous and that therefore a trochee here and there serves
to introduce the pleasing effect of variety.[8] But there are several objections to this view. In the first place even a long series of perfectly regular lines are not disagreeably monotonous
if written by a real poet. In one of Shakespeare's finest scenes
we find in the first hundred lines not more than four inversions (As you like it II. 7); it can hardly be those four lines
which make the whole scene so pleasing to the ear. In Valborg's speech in Oehlenschläger's Axel og Valborg III. 69 we
have 28 beautiful lines without a single deviation from the
iambic scheme.

Secondly, if harmony were due to such irregularities, it
would be natural to expect the same effect from similar deviations in trochaic and other metres. The reader of Longfellow's
Hiawatha will no doubt feel its metre as much more monotonous than the five-foot iambus, yet here no deviations would
be tolerated; an iambus in a trochaic metre is an unwelcome
intruder, while a trochee in an iambic line is hailed as a
friendly guest.

[8] "Their attractiveness may be due precisely to the fact that the accent
of the first foot comes as a surprise to the reader," Sonnenschein,
Rhythm 105.

Thirdly, the theory gives no explanation of the fact that the use of trochees is subject to some limitations; if the only purpose were to relieve monotony, one would expect trochees to be equally welcome everywhere in iambic verses, but that is very far from being the case. True, the rare occurrence of trochees in the fifth foot is explained by saying that deviations from the ordinary pattern are always best tolerated in the beginning of the verse, because then there is still time to return to the regular movement. But if this were the only reason, we should expect trochees to tend to decrease as we approached the end of the line, the second foot presenting more instances than the third, and the third than the fourth; but this again does not tally with the actual facts, for the second foot has fewer inversions than any other foot except the fifth. König gives the following numbers for Shakespeare:

> first foot more than 3000,
> second foot only   34,
> third foot more than   500,
> fourth foot more than 400.

(*Der Vers in Shakespeares Dramen*. Strassburg 1888, Quellen und Forschungen 61, p. 79, cf. 77. Only "worttrochäen" are here numbered, not "satztrochäen.")

4. If we are to arrive at a real understanding of the metre in question and of modern metre in general, it will be necessary to revise many of the current ideas which may be traced back to ancient metrists, and to look at the facts as they present themselves to the unsophisticated ears of modern poets and modern readers. The chief fallacies that it is to my mind important to get rid of, are the following:

(1) *The fallacy of longs and shorts.* Modern verses are based primarily not on length (duration), but on stress (intensity). In analysing them we should therefore avoid such signs as — and ⌣ , and further get rid of such terms as iambus ⌣ — , trochee — ⌣ , dactylus — ⌣ ⌣ , anapaest ⌣ ⌣ — , pyrrhic ⌣ ⌣ , choriamb — ⌣ ⌣ — , etc. To speak of an iambus and interpret the term is a foot consisting of one weak and one strong syllable is not quite so harmless a thing as to speak of consuls and mean something different from the old Roman consules. It is not merely a question of nomenclature: the old names will tend to make us take over more than the terms of the old metrists.—There are other

misleading terms: what some call "arsis" is by others termed "thesis," and inversely.

(2) *The fallacy of the foot*, i.e. the analysis of a line as consisting of parts divided off by means of perpendicular straight lines ◡ — | ◡ — | ◡ — | etc. Such signs of separation can only delude the reader into "scanning" lines with artificial pauses between the feet—often in the middle of words and in other most unnatural places. On the other hand a natural pause, occasioned by a break in the meaning, may be found in the middle of a foot as well as between metrical feet. It is also often arbitrary where we put the division-mark: Are we to scan Tennyson's line

> The de | light of | happy | laughter—or
> The delight | of hap | py laugh | ter?

The line mentioned above (1, 1) is analysed by E. K. (now Sir Edmund) Chambers in his Warwick ed. of Macbeth as having "the stress inverted in every foot" and a dactylus in the first:

> Tóld by an | i díot, | fúll of | sóund and | fúry.

Some metrists (Bayfield among them) even incline to treat such lines as 1.3 as "trochaic" with an anacrusis:

> Take | each mans | censure, | but re | serve thy | judg'ment.

In such cases it would almost seem as if the vertical stroke were used as the bar in music, to indicate where the strong note or stress begins, though most metrists would deny the legitimacy of that analogy.

We shall see below that the abolition of the fallacy of the foot will assist us in understanding the chief irregularities of blank verse.

(3) *The fallacy of two grades.* The ancients recognized only longs and shorts though there are really many gradations of length of syllables. In the same way most of the moderns, while recognizing that stress is the most important thing in modern metres, speak of two grades only, calling everything weak that is not strong. But in reality there are infinite gradations of stress, from the most penetrating scream to the faintest whisper; but in most instances it will be sufficient for our purposes to recognize four degrees which we may simply designate by the first four numbers:

> 4 strong
> 3 half-strong
> 2 half-weak
> 1 weak.

It is not always easy to apply these numbers to actually occurring syllables, and it is particularly difficult in many instances to distinguish between 3 and 2. Unfortunately we have no means of measuring stress objectively by instruments; we have nothing to go by except our ears; but then it is a kind of consolation that the poets themselves, whose lines we try to analyse, have been guided by nothing else but *their* ears—and after all, the human ear is a wonderfully delicate apparatus.

5. Verse rhythm is based on the same alternation between stronger and weaker syllables as that found in natural everyday speech. Even in the most prosaic speech, which is in no way dictated by artistic feeling, this alternation is not completely irregular: everywhere we observe a natural tendency towards making a weak syllable follow after a strong one and inversely. Rhythm very often makes itself felt in spite of what might be expected from the natural (logical or emotional) value of the words. Thus syllables which ought seemingly to be strong are weakened if occurring between strong syllables, and naturally weak syllables gain in strength if placed between weak syllables. *Uphill* is 24 in *to walk uphill*, but 42 in *an uphill walk*. *Good-natured* is 44, but becomes 43 or 42 in *a goodnatured man*. The last syllable of *afternoon* is strong (4) in *this afternoon*, but weaker (2 or 3) in *afternoon tea*. *Back* is weaker in *he came back tired* than in *he came back with sore feet*, etc.

Illustrations of this principle are found in the following verse lines in which the middle one of the three italicized syllables is weakened, giving 434 (or 424) instead of 444:

But *poore old* man, thou prun'st a rotten tree.   (1)
The course of *true love never* did run smooth.   (2)
Oh that this *too too solid* flesh would melt.   (3)
You are my ghests: do me no *foule play, friends*.   (4)
The *still sad* music of humanity.   (5)
A *long street climbs* to one *tall-*tower'd mill.   (6)
Doch sein geschwungner *Arm traf* ihre Brust (*ihre* emphatic).   (7)

6. Of two successive weak syllables that one is the relatively stronger which is the further removed from the strongly stressed syllable; consequently we have the formula 412 in *happily, gossiping, lexicon, apricot, Socrates*, etc., and the inverse 214 (or 314) in *condescend, supersede, disinter*; 2141 in *collocation, expectation, intermixture*, 21412 in *conversational, international, regularity*.

The effect of surroundings is seen clearly in the following line, where *when one* is 23 after the strong *know*, and 32 before the strong *lives*:

I know when one is dead, and when one lives. (1)

Other examples (*I, and, when*—now "weak," now "strong" without regard to meaning) are found in the passage analysed below in 24. *It is* according to circumstances may be 12 or 21, and the same is true of *into* in Shakespeare and other poets. *Is* is "strong," i.e. 2 between two weak syllables (1) in

A thing of beauty is a joy for ever—

and any page of poetry affords examples of the same phenomenon.

7. Our ear does not really perceive stress relations with any degree of certainty except when the syllables concerned are contiguous. If two syllables are separated by a series of other syllables, it is extremely difficult even for the expert to tell which of them is the stronger, as one will feel when comparing the syllables of such a long word as *incomprehensibility*: *bil* is the strongest, *hen* is stronger than both *pre* and *si*, but what is the relation between *hen* and *com*? or between *in* and *ty*? Another similar word is *irresponsibility*, only here the first syllable is stronger than the second. What is decisive when words have to be used in verse is everywhere the surroundings: the metrical value of a syllable depends on what comes before and what follows after it.

Even more important is the fact that we have to do with *relative degrees of force only*: a sequence of syllables, a verse line may produce exactly the same metrical impression whether I pronounce it so softly that it can scarcely be heard at two feet's distance, or shout it so loudly that it can be distinctly perceived by everyone in a large theatre; but the strongest syllables in the former case may have been weaker than the very weakest ones in the latter case.

8. This leads us to another important principle: the effect of a *pause*: If I hear a syllable after a pause it is absolutely impossible for me to know whether it is meant by the speaker as a strong or as a weak syllable: I have nothing to compare it with till I hear what follows. And it is extremely difficult to say with any degree of certainty what is the reciprocal relation between two syllables separated by a not too short pause.

9. Let us now try to apply these principles to the "iambic pentameter." The pattern expected by the hearer is a sequence

of ten syllables (which may be followed by an eleventh, weak
syllable), arranged in such a way that the syllables occupying
the even places are raised by their force above the surround-
ing syllables. It is not possible to say that the scheme is

    1 4   1 4   1 4   1 4   1 4   (1),

for this is a rare and not particularly admired form, as in

  Her eyes, her haire, her cheeke, her gate, her voice.   (1)
  Of hairs, or straws, or dirt, or grubs, or worms.   (2)

Lines of that type were pretty numerous in the earliest days
of blank verse, in Gorboduc and in Peele. But it was soon felt
that it was much more satisfactory to make the difference in
force between the strong and the weak elements of the line
less than that between 1 and 4 and at the same time less uni-
form, for the only thing required by the ear is an upward and
a downward movement, a rise and a fall, an ascent and a descent, at fixed places, whereas it is of no importance whatever
how great is the ascent or the descent. It is therefore possible
to arrange the scheme in this way, denoting the odd syllables
by a and the even ones by b:

$$a \diagup b \diagdown a \diagup b \diagdown a \diagup b \diagdown a \diagup b \diagdown a \diagup b (\diagdown a) \frown$$

or, if we denote relative strength by a capital,

  aBaBaBaBaB(a).

10. It is the relative stress that counts. This is shown conclusively when we find that a syllable with stress-degree 2
counts as strong between two 1s, though it is in reality weaker
than another with degree 3 which fills a weak place in the
same line because it happens to stand between two 4s. This
is, for instance, the case in

      The course of true love never did run smooth (1):
did (2) occupies a strong place though no sensible reader
would make it as strong as love, which counts as weak in the
verse.

In consequence of this relativity it is possible on the one
hand to find lines with many weak syllables, e.g.

            It is a nipping and an eager ayre. (2)
Here is and and on account of the surroundings are made
into 2s; the line contains not a single long consonant and only
two long vowels.

On the other hand there are lines with many strong and
long syllables, such as

And ten low words oft creep in one dull line.   (3)

The long day wanes: the slow moon climbs: the deep
Moans round with many voices.   (4)
Thoughts blacke, hands apt, drugges fit, and time agreeing. (5)
Day, night, houre, tide, time, worke, and play.   (6)
Rocks, caves, lakes, fens, bogs, dens, and shades of death. (7)

In lines like the last two, however, the pauses make the
regular alternation of 3 and 4 difficult or even impossible.

With inversion in the beginning we have Browning's dread-
fully heavy

Spark-like mid unearthed slope-side fibree-roots (8).

A comparison of such extremes of light and heavy lines
shows conclusively that *quantity as such has no essential importance in the building up of blank verse.*

The principle of relativity allows an abundance of variety;
there are many possible harmonious and easy-flowing verses,
with five, or four, or three really strong syllables (degree 4);
and the variety can be further increased by means of pauses,
which may be found between the lines or at almost any place
in the lines themselves, whether between or in the middle of
so-called feet.

So much for the normal "iambic pentameter."

11. Let us now analyse a line with inversion, e.g.

Peace, children, peace! the king doth love you well. (1)

The stress numbers for the first four syllables are 4314 (or
possibly 4214, though 3 seems more likely than 2 for the second syllable). Here the ear is not disappointed in the first syllable: after the pause preceding the line one does not know what
general level to expect: a syllable which objectively is pretty
strong might turn out to be a relatively weak introduction to
something still stronger. A mathematician might feel tempted
to express this in the following way: the proportion between
the 0 of the pause and the 4 of a strong syllable is the same
as between 0 and the 1 of a weak syllable.

It is therefore not till this strong syllable is followed by one
that is weaker instead of stronger that the ear experiences a
disappointment and feels a deviation from the regular pattern.
But the transition from the second to the third syllable is a
descent in strict conformity with the pattern; and in the same
way there is perfect regularity in the relation between the third
and the (strong) fourth, and indeed in the whole of the rest
of the line. The scheme accordingly is the following:

$$a \searrow b \searrow a \nearrow b \searrow a \nearrow b \searrow a \nearrow b \searrow a \nearrow b,$$

which should be compared with the scheme given above, § 9, as normal.

This amounts to saying that while according to the traditional way of notation one would think that the departure from the norm concerned two-tenths (one-fifth) of the line if one heard a "trochee" instead of an "iambus," the ear is really disappointed at one only out of ten places. The deviation from the norm is thus reduced to one-tenth—or even less than that, because the descent is only a small one. The greater the descent, the greater will also be the dissatisfaction, but in the example analysed the descent was only from 4 to 3. A beginning 4114 is comparatively poor, but 4314 or 4214 does not sound badly, for from the second syllable (or from the transition to the third) one has the feeling that everything is all right and the movement is the usual one. In the case of two inversions in the same line we have in two places (not in four!) disappointments, each of them amounting to less than one-tenth, and so far separated from the other that they do not act jointly on the ear.

12. We shall now collect some classified examples which tend to show that poets have instinctively followed this hitherto never formulated principle.

A. First we have instances in which the three syllables concerned belong to the same word. Such words, of the stress-formula 431 or 421, are very frequent in Danish and German; I have therefore been able to find a great many lines like the following:

Sandhedens kilder i dets bund udstrømme.   (1)
Staldbroder! hav tålmodighed med Axel.   (2)
Granvoxne Valborg!—Elskelige svend!   (3)
Kraftvolles mark war seiner söhn' und enkel.   (4)
Unedel sind die waffen eines weibes.   (5)
Hilfreiche götter vom Olympus rufen.   (6)

In English, on the other hand, words of this type are comparatively rare, and in Elizabethan times there was a strong tendency to shift the stress rhythmically so as to have 412 instead of 431 or 421, thus in torchbearer, quicksilver, bedfellow, etc. (references in my Modern Engl. Gr. I 5.45). Cf. also the treatment of berry in gooseberry, blackberry, and of kerchief in handkerchief. But we have 431 in

Sleek-headed men, and such as sleepe a-nights.   (7)
Grim-visag'd warre hath smooth'd his wrinkled front.   (8)
All-seeing heaven, what a world is this?   (9)

13. B. The first two syllables form one word.

Doomesday is neere, dye all, dye merrily.   (1)
Welcome, Sir Walter Blunt, and would to God . . .   (2)
England did never owe so sweet a hope.   (3)
Something that hath a reference to my state.   (4)
Nothing that I respect, my gracious lord.   (5)
Ofspring of Heav'n and Earth, and all Earths Lord.   (6)
Noontide repast, or Afternoons repose.   (7)

This is frequent in Danish:

Valborg skal vorde Axel Thordsøns brud.   (8)
Alting er muligt for et trofast hjerte.   (9)

14. C. The first word is one syllable, the second two or
more.

Urge neither charity nor shame to me.   (1)
Dye neyther mother, wife, nor Englands queene!   (2)
Peace, master marquesse, you are malapert.   (3)
Peace, children, peace! the king doth love you well. (4)
First, madam, I intreate true peace of you.   (5)

Danish and German examples:

Tak, høje fader, for din miskundhed!   (6)
Spar dine ord! Jeg kender ikke frygt.   (7)
Den bære kronen som er kronen voxen.   (8)
Frei atmen macht das leben nicht allein.   (9)
Sie rettet weder hoffnung, weder furcht.   (10)

In cases like the following one may hesitate which of the
first two syllables to make 4 and which 3:

Young, valiant, wise, and (no doubt) right royal.   (11)
Friends, Romans, countrymen, lend me your ears.   (12)
Foule wrinkled witch, what mak'st thou in my sight? (13)
Ros, rygte, folkesnak i sold den ta'er.   (14)
Rat, mässigung und weisheit und geduld.   (15)

15. D. Two monosyllables.
Here there will naturally be a great many cases in which the
correct distribution of stresses is not self-evident: one reader
will stress the first and another the second word. I think however that in the following lines most readers will agree with
me in stressing 4314 or 4214 (or 5314):

Long may'st thou live, to wayle thy childrens death. (1)
Greefe fils the roome up of my absent childe.   (2)
God will revenge it. Come, lords, will you go.   (3)
Their woes are parcell'd, mine is generall.   (4)
Sweet are the uses of adversitie.   (5)

Lye there what hidden womans feare there will.   (6)
Cours'd one another downe his innocent nose.   (7)
Knap var det sagt, sa stod for dem den tykke.   (8)
Klog mand foragter ej sin stærke fjende.   (9)
Dank habt ihr stets. Doch nicht den reinen dank.   (10)
Wohl dem, der seiner väter gern gedenkt.   (11)

In the middle of a line:

As it is wonne with blood, *lost be it* so.   (12)
Den nordiske natur. *Alt skal du* skue.   (13)
So kehr zurück! *Thu, was dein* Herz dich heisst.   (14)

16. While in the lines examined so far a natural reading
will stress the second syllable more than the third, it must be
admitted that there are many lines in which the words themselves do not demand this way of stressing. Nevertheless the
possibility exists that the poet had it in his mind, and expert
elocutionists will often unconsciously give a stronger stress to
the second syllable just to minimize the deviation from the
scheme and avoid the unpleasant effect of the sequence 4114.
I think this is quite natural in cases like the following, in which
a proper name or another important word calls for an emphatic
enunciation which makes the second syllable stronger than it
might have been in easy-going prose:

Clarence still breathes; *Edward* still lives and raignes. (1)
Never came poyson from so sweet a place.   (2)
Never hung poyson on a fowler toade.   (3)
Tyrants themselves wept when it was reported.   (4)
Hakon er konge, Valborg er en mø.   (5)
Himlen er ej sa bla som disse blomster.   (6)

Even in a line like:
Cowards dye many times before their deaths   (7)

an actor may feel inclined to express his contempt and to point
the contrast to the following words "The valiant never taste of
death but once" by giving special stress (53 or 54) to *cowards*
and by extra stress on *many* to weigh down *die* to something
comparatively insignificant, which is all the more natural as
the idea of death has been mentioned in the preceding lines,
while *cowards* is a new idea: new ideas are well known to at-
tract strong stress. It is worth noting how often the figure is
used as a rhetorical device to emphasize a contrast, in exclama-
tions and in personal apostrophe (cf. König, p. 78). It is
particularly apt for this use because a forcible attack of the
voice after a pause will immediately catch the attention, before
the verse settles down in its usual even course.

17. In spite of all this there will remain some instances in which the second syllable cannot easily be made stronger than the third. Metrics is no exact science aiming at finding out natural laws that are valid everywhere. All we can say is that by arranging syllables in such and such a way the poet will produce a pleasing effect; but of course a poet is free to sacrifice euphony if other things appear more important to him— not to mention the possibility that he is momentarily unable to hit upon anything more felicitous.

18. In all the cases dealt with in the preceding paragraphs there was a pause immediately before the strong syllable which had taken the place of a weak. The pause is often, but of course not everywhere indicated by a full stop or other punctuation mark. A natural explanation of the varying frequency of inversion at different places in the line (see above 3) is found in the fact that a pause is not equally natural at all places. In the vast majority of cases inversion is found at the very beginning of a line, because the end of the preceding line is more often than not marked by a break in the thought and, even where this is not the case, a reciter or actor will often make a pause between two lines. Not quite so frequently comes a pause and inversion in the middle of a line, after the second or third "foot." It is necessarily rarer after the first foot, because a division of the line into two such unequal parts (2 + 8 syllables) is not natural: the two syllables are awkwardly isolated and cut off from organic cohesion with the rest. This is even more true of a pause after the eighth syllable: a strong syllable here will not leave us time enough to regain the natural swing of the verse before the line is ended. In such a case as

> It is his Highnesse pleasure, that the Queene
> Appeare in person here in Court. Silence! (1)

it would not even be unnatural to shout out the two last syllables as 44 or 45.

19. In yet another way a pause may play an important role in the verse. If we analyse the following lines in the usual way we find that the syllables here italicized form trochees where we should expect iambs, and if we read them without stopping they are felt to be inharmonious:

> Like to a step-*dame*, or a dowager.   (1)
> Lye at the proud *foote* of a conqueror.   (2)
> As wilde-geese, *that* the creeping fowler eye.   (3)
> And let the soule *forth that* adoreth thee.   (4)
> To bear the file's *tooth and* the hammer's tap.   (5)
> John of the Black *Bands with* the upright spear.   (6)

A snow-*flake, and* a scanty couch of snow
Crusted the grass-*walk and* the garden-mould.   (7)
Den, der er blind*født* e*ller* blind fra barndom.   (8)
Nu, det var smukt *gjort, det* var vel gjort, godt gjort.   (9)
Denn ihr allein *wisst, was* uns frommen kann.   (10)

If, on the other hand, we read these lines with the pause
required (or allowed) by the meaning, the ear will not be
offended in the least. The line is in perfect order, because in
the first place *dame* with its 3 is heard together with *step* (4)
and thus shows a descent in the right place, and secondly or
with its 2 is heard in close connexion with a (1), so that we
have the required descent between these two syllables.
Graphically:

Like to | a step- | dame, or | a dow | ager
...... | iamb | trochee | iamb | ...
...... 1   4   3   2   1   4 ......
...... a／b   ＼a(＼)b＼   a／b ......

The descent marked in parenthesis between *dame* and or is
not heard, and is thus non-existent. Similarly in the other examples.[4]

20. The phenomena dealt with here (in 12 ff. and 19) are
singularly fit to demonstrate the shortcomings of traditional
metrics (cf. above 4). In the first case (inversion after a pause)
we had a "trochee," whose second syllable acts in connexion
with the first syllable of the following foot, as if the latter had
been the second syllable of an iambus. In the second case (19)
we had a "trochee" whose first syllable as a matter of fact will
be perceived in the verse as if it were the first part of an
iambus, and whose second syllable is similarly playing the role
of the latter part of an iambus, and yet it is impossible to call
these two successive iambic syllables a real iambus. In both
cases the ear thus protests against the paper idea of a "foot."
In the former case the perpendicular line | is made to sep-
arate the two syllables whose mutual relation is really of great
rhythmic importance and which accordingly ought to go together. In the latter case two similar straight lines join together
syllables which are not to be heard together, and whose relation to one another is therefore of no consequence, while the
syllables that have to be weighed against one another are by

---

[4] A corresponding interpretation of the metre of Shakespeare's *Lucrece*
1611 and 1612 is found in A. P. van Dam, *W. Shakespeare, Prosody
and Text*, Leyden 1900, p. 206.

the same means separated as if they did not concern one another. Could anything be more absurd?

21. The irregularities in lines like

And they shall be one Flesh, one Heart, one Soule. (1)
The wretched annimall heav'd forth such groanes   (2)

might be explained by means of a pause after *be* and *animal*: *shall be* is 12, and *one flesh* 34, and similarly *animal* is 412 and *heav'd forth* 34, but the irregular ascent between 2 and 3 is concealed by the pause: 1 / 2 (/) 3 / 4 or a / b (/) a / b.

This explanation does not, however, hold good for numerous groups of a similar structure, e.g.

In the sweet pangs of it remember me.   (3)
And the frcc maides that weave their thred with bones. (4)
In the deepe bosome of the ocean buried.   ·   (5)
But the queenes kindred and night-walking heralds. (6)
Of the young prince your sonne: send straight for him. (7)
I will feede fat the ancient grudge I beare him.   (8)
As his wise mother wrought in his behalfe.   (9)
Of a strange nature is the sute you follow.   (10)
Whose homes are the dim caves of human thought. (11)
The ploughman lost his sweat, and the greene corne. (12)
Did I deserve no more then a fooles head?   (13)

This figure is frequent in English verse, but not in other languages. I incline to read it with 1234 and thus to say that the ascent is normal between the first and the second as well as between the third and the fourth syllable, so that there is only the one small anomaly of a slight ascent instead of a descent between the second and the third syllable. It is worth noting how frequently this figure contains an adjective (stressed 3) before a substantive (stressed 4); *fool's* before *head* is equivalent to an adjective.

Some metrists here speak of a double iambus (⌣ ⌣ ‒ ‒). Robert Bridges (*Milton's Prosody*, 1894, p. 56) calls it "a foot of two unstressed short syllables preceding a foot composed of two heavy syllables" and says, "Whatever the account of it is, it is pleasant to the ear even in the smoothest verse, and is so, no doubt, by a kind of compensation in it."

22. The role of a pause which covers and hides away metrical irregularities is seen also in the case of extra-metrical syllables. In Shakespeare these are particularly frequent where a line is distributed between two speakers. The pause makes us forget how far we had come: one speaker's words are heard

as the regular beginning, and the next speaker's as the regular ending of a verse, and we do not feel that we have been treated to too much, though this would not pass equally unnoticed if there had been no break. Examples may be found in any book on Shakespeare's verse. An interesting use of an extra-metrical syllable is made in King Lear IV. 1. 72

(Let the superfluous . . . man . . . that will not see,)

Because he do's not feele, feele your power quickly:
the second *feel*, which is necessary for the meaning, is heard as a kind of echo of the first and therefore enters into its place in the line. . . .

* * * * * * * * * * * * *

25. We have not yet offered an answer to the question raised in 2: why is a trochee among iambs easier to tolerate than inversely an iamb among trochees? But the answer is not difficult on the principles we have followed throughout. Take some trochaic lines, e.g.

> Tell me not, in mournful numbers,
> Life is but an empty dream—

and substitute for the second line something like

> A life's but an empty dream,—or
> To live's but an empty dream.

The rhythm is completely spoilt. Or try instead of

> Then the little Hiawatha
> Learned of every bird its language—

to say:

> The sweet little Hiawatha
> Acquired every sound and language.

(*Every* of course in two syllables as in Longfellow).
In such cases with 14 instead of 41 we have the disagreeable clash of two strong syllables, further, we have two disappointments per line. It is true that if we pronounced the first strong syllable weaker than the second, thus made the whole 1341, we should have only one disappointment: a $/$ b $/$ a $\setminus$ b instead of the regular a $\setminus$ b $/$ a $\setminus$ b; but it will be extremely hard to find examples of the sequence 34 as regularly occurring in any of the cognate languages. We shall see in the next paragraph the reason why 34 is not found within one and the same word; and when a word of the formula 14 is placed before a strongly stressed word, it is not generally reduced to 13, as the ordinary tendency in such cases is rather to substitute for it 31 or 21, see many examples from English in my *Mod. E. Gr.* I 156 ff.: "The other upon Saturn's bended neck" (Keats), "Protracted among endless solitudes" (Words-

worth), "a spirit *without* spot" (Shelley), "in *forlorn* servitude" (Wordsworth). Danish examples see *Modersmålets fonetik* 139. The disinclination to "invert" in trochaic rhythms is thus seen to be deeply rooted in linguistic habits and in the phonetic structure of our languages.

26. What is the essential difference between a rising and a falling rhythm? (or, in the old terms, between an "iambic" or "anapaestic" rhythm on the one hand and a "trochaic" or "dactylic" rhythm on the other?) Some writers minimize this difference and say that they are virtually identical, as the "anacrusis" has no real importance; instead of the sequence 14 14 14 . . . (◡ − ǀ◡−ǀ◡−ǀ. . .) they would write 1 41 41 41 . . . ,(◡ǀ−◡ǀ−◡ǀ−. . .) According to them the initial weak syllable is just as unimportant as an up-beat (auftakt, mesure d'attaque) is in music.

But is such an up-beat (a note before the first bar begins) really unimportant in music? I have taken a number of music books at random and counted the pieces in which such an up-beat occurs; I found that it was less frequent in pieces with a slow movement (largo, grave, adagio, andante) than in those with a quick movement (allegro, allegretto, rondo, presto, prestissimo, vivace):

	Beethoven	Schubert	Schumann	Sum
Slow				
with up-beat	5	1	5	11
without up-beat	17	7	7	31
Quick				
with up-beat	31	14	12	57
without up-beat	19	11	10	10

This agrees with the general impression of verse rhythms: a sequence didúm didúm didúm . . . tends to move more rapidly than dúmda dúmda dúmda . . . I think this depends on a deeply rooted psychological tendency: there is a universal inclination to hurry up to a summit, but once the top is reached one may linger in the descent. This is shown linguistically within each syllable: consonants before the summit of sonority (which in most cases is a vowel) are nearly always short, while consonants after the summit are very often long; cp. thus the two *n*'s of *nun*, the two *t*'s of *tot*, the two *m*'s of *member*. Words of the type 43 with long second syllable are frequent: *football, folklore, cornfield, therefore*, while corresponding

words with 34 are rare: they tend to become 24 or even 14:
throughout, therein, austere, naïve, Louise, forgive—with
more or less distinct shortening of the vowel.

In this connexion it is perhaps also worth calling attention
to the following fact. As a stressed syllable tends, other things
being equal, to be pronounced with higher pitch than weak
syllables, a purely "iambic" line will tend towards a higher
tone at the end, but according to general phonetic laws this
is a sign that something more is to be expected. Consequently
it is in iambic verses easy to knit line to line in natural continuation.[5] Inversely the typical pitch movement of a "trochaic" line is towards a descent, which in each line acts as
an indication of finality, of finish. If a continuation is wanted,
the poet is therefore often obliged to repeat something—a feature which is highly characteristic of such a poem as
Hiawatha, where each page offers examples like the following:

> *Should you ask me, whence these stories?*
> *Whence these legends and traditions,*
> *With the odours of the forest,*
> *With the dew and damp of meadows,*
> *With the curling smoke of wigwams,*
> *With the rushing of great rivers,*
> *With their frequent repetitions,* (N.B.)
> *And their wild reverberations,*
> *As of thunder in the mountains?*
> *I should answer, I should tell you,*
> *From the . . . etc. (From the 6 times.)*
> *Should you ask where Nawadaha*
> *Found these songs, so wild and wayward,*
> *Found these legends and traditions,*
> *I should answer, I should tell you*
> *In the . . . (In the 4 times) . . .*[6]

These, then, seem to be the distinctive features of the
two types of metre: rapidity, ease of going on from line to line
without a break on the one hand,—and on the other slow-
ness, heaviness, a feeling of finality at the end of each line,
hence sometimes fatiguing repetitions. Tennyson utilized this
contrast in a masterly way in *The Lady of Shalott*, where the
greater part of the poem is rising, but where a falling rhythm

[5] Two rimed lines in succession will, however, produce the impression
of finish—a feature that is often found in the Elizabethan drama, more
particularly when a scene or a speech ends with a sententious saying.
[6] These two things, a trochaic metre and constant repetition, are found
together in Finnish popular poetry, which Longfellow imitated.

winds up the whole in the description of her sad swan-song:

> Heard a carol, mournful, holy,
> Chanted loudly, chanted lowly,
> Till her blood was frozen slowly,
> And her eyes were darkened wholly,
>   Turned to tower'd Camelot.

REFERENCES FOR THE LINES QUOTED.

Sh = Shakespeare. The titles of plays indicated as in A. Schmidt's Shakespeare-Lexicon. Numbers of act, scene, and line as in the Globe edition.

PL = Milton's *Paradise Lost*, as in Beeching's reprint of the original edition of 1667.

Ø = Øhlenschläger, *Axel og Valborg*, number of page according to A. Boysen's edition of *Poetiske skrifter i udvalg*, III. 1896.

P-M = Paludan-Müller, *Adam Homo*. Anden deel, 1849.

H = Hertz, *Kong Renés datter*. 7de opl. 1893.

G = Goethe, *Iphigenie auf Tauris*. Number of act and line according to Sämtliche werke XI in Cotta's Bibl. d. weltlitt.

1. 1. Tro. I. 1. 54. — 2, 3. Hml. I. 3. 68, 69. — 4. G I. 115. — 5. G I. 226.

2. 1. Mcb. V. 5. 27. — 2. R3 I. 3. 185. — 3. G I. 27.

5. 1 As II. 3. 63. — 2. Mids. I. 1. 134. — 3. Hml. I. 2. 129. — 4. Lr. III. 7. 31. — 5. Wordsw. Tint. Abb. — 6. Tennyson, En. Arden 5. — 7. G III. 317.

6. 1. Lr. V. 3. 260.

9. 1. Tro. I. 1. 54. — 2. Pope.

10. 1. Mids. I. 1. 134. — 2. Hml. I. 4. 2. — 3. Pope Ess. Crit. 347. — 4. Tennyson Ulysses. — 5. Pope. — 6. Rom. III. 5. 178. — 7. PL II. 621. — 8. The Ring and the Book I. 6.

11. 1. R3 II. 2. 17.

12. 1. P-M 21. — 2. Ø 8. — 3. Ø 23. — 4. G I. 329. — 5. G I. 483. — 6. G III. 242. — 7. Cæs. I. 2. 193. — 8. R3 I. 1. 9. — 9. ib. II. 1. 82.

13. 1. H4A IV. 1. 134. — 2. ib. IV. 3. 31. — 3. ib. V. 2. 68. — 4. As I. 3. 129. — 5. R3 I. 3. 295. — 6. PL IX. 273. — 7. ib. IX. 403. — 8. Ø 7. — 9. Ø 21.

14. 1. R3 I. 3. 274. — 2. ib. I. 3. 209. — 3. ib. I. 3. 255. — 4. ib. II. 2. 17. — 5. ib. II. 1. 62. — 6. Ø 17. — 7. H 95. — 8 Ø. Hakon Jarl. — 9. G I. 106. — 10. G III. 71. — 11. R3 I. 2. 245. — 12. Cæs. III. 2. 78. — 13. R3 I. 3. 164. — 14. P-M 40. — 15. G I. 332.

15. 1. R 3 I. 3. 204. — 2. John III. 4. 93. — 3. R3 II. 1. 138. — 4. ib. II. 2. 81. — 5. As II. 1. 12. — 6. ib. I. 3. 121. — 7. ib. II. 1. 39. — 8. P-M 12. — 9. Ø 27. — 10. G I. 93. — 11. G I. 351. — 12. R3 I. 3. 272. — 13. Ø 8. — 14. G I. 463.

16. 1. R3 I. 1. 161. — 2. ib. I. 2. 148. — 3. ib. I. 2. 149. — 4. ib. I. 3. 185. — 5. Ø 15. — 6. Ø 8.

18. 1. Wint. III. 1. 10.

19. 1. Mids. I. 1. 5. — 2. John V. 7. 113. — 3. Mids. III. 2. 20. — 4. R3 I. 2. 177. — 5. The Ring and the Book I. 14. — 6. ib. I. 47. — 7. ib. I. 608—9.

21. 1. PL VIII. 499. — 2. As II. 1. 36. — 3. Tw. II. 4. 16. — 4. ib. II. 4. 46. — 5. R3 I. 1. 4. — 6. ib. I. 1. 72. — 7. ib. II. 2. 97. — 8. Merch. I. 3. 48. — 9. ib. I. 3. 73. — 10. ib. IV. 1. 177. — 11. Shelley Prom. I. 659. — 12. Mids. II. 1. 94. — 13. Merch. II. 9. 59.

22. Hml V. 2. 352. — ib. IV. 7. 80.

23. 1. Lr. V. 3. 317. — 2. Rom. III. 5. 178. — 3. R3 III. 4. 11.

YVOR WINTERS

The Audible Reading Of Poetry

[Winters "rediscovers" the principle of relative stress. Both
his scansions as well as his concept of the correct "audible
reading of poetry" seem to me unexceptionable. Winters states
his case with more bluntness than tact; however, I prefer
Winters' honest prejudices to the posturings of incense burn-
ers. And the general theory of meter that Winters advocates
has never, to my knowledge, been convincingly controverted.

[Winters selects the poems of the Elizabethan songwriters
for special metrical attention, noting the effects achieved by
substitution and "springing." It is unfortunate that Winters
shows no interest in the relationship between words and music,
or in the influence music had on the later Elizabethan lyric.
A history of English metric that would take into account the
relevant developments in musical rhythms might shed more
light than futile debates between rival prosodists. The Elizabethan songbooks offer a starting point for such a history.]

MY TITLE may seem to have in it something of the jargon of
the modern Educationist; if so, I am sorry, but I mean to
indicate something more than the reading of poetry aloud.
I mean to indicate the reading of poetry not merely for the
sensual ear, but for the mind's ear as well; yet the mind's ear
can be trained only by way of the other, and the matter,
practically considered, comes inescapably back to the reading
of poetry aloud.

It is also important to learn to read prose aloud, and to
hear the prose when one reads it silently. Melville, Gibbon,
or Samuel Johnson about equally will be lost on us if we do

Reprinted from The Function of Criticism: Problems and Exercises
by Yvor Winters. By permission of the publisher, Alan Swallow.
Copyright 1957 by Yvor Winters.

not so hear it. Yet the readers are numerous who hear nothing when they read silently and who are helpless in their efforts to read aloud: some of them have defective sensibilities; some have merely never been trained; some have been trained by one or another of our psychological educationalists to read in this fashion in order that they may read more rapidly. That they can read more rapidly without hearing, I believe there is no doubt, especially if the matter with which they are dealing is trivial. The trouble is that the activity cannot properly be called reading. Such "readers" are barbarians; literature is closed to them, in spite of the fact that they may think otherwise. The scholar who appears to have read everything has commonly understood very little, and his failure to hear is one of the reasons.

My subject may seem a bit precious and tenuous, but it is neither; it is a matter of the utmost importance to the proper understanding of poetry, a matter fully as important as the philosophical speculation and learned paraphrasing of the New Critics, of whom I am sometimes reputed to be one. It is a matter of which there is almost no understanding at the present time.

Poetry, as nearly as I can understand it, is a statement in words about a human experience, whether the experience be real or hypothetical, major or minor; but it is a statement of a particular kind. Words are symbols for concepts, and the philosopher or scientist endeavors as far as may be to use them with reference to nothing save their conceptual content. Most words, however, connote feelings and perceptions, and the poet, like the writer of imaginative prose, endeavors to use them with reference not only to their denotations but to their connotations as well. Such writers endeavor to communicate not only concepts, arranged, presumably, either in rational order or in an order apprehensible by the rational mind, but the feeling or emotion which the rational content ought properly to arouse. The poet differs from the writer of any kind of prose in that he writes in metrical language. Any good prose is rhythmical up to a certain point: even purely expository prose should be rhythmical to the point that audible obstructions are minimized and meanings are emphasized; the prose of such a writer as Melville is far more elaborately rhythmical than this. But a rhythm which is not controlled by a definite measure will be relatively loose and lacking in subtlety. Poetry and music are based upon definite measure; in this they differ from all other forms of composition.

Rhythm and meter, it should be observed, are quite distinct from each other, in spite of the fact that many critics (myself among them) sometimes use the two words as if they meant the same thing. Meter is the arithmetical norm, the purely theoretic structure of the line; rhythm is controlled departure from that norm. The iambic pentameter norm, for example, proceeds as follows:

One *two*, one *two*, one *two*, one *two*, one *two*.

Yet no other line in the language corresponds exactly to the line just given; and to achieve another as regular one will have to resort to the same repetitive structure with a new pair of syllables. Every other line will depart from this one for these reasons: no two syllables ever have the same degree of accent—that is, so far as versification is concerned there is no such thing as an inherently accented or unaccented syllable, but syllables which count technically as accented can be recognized as such only with reference to the other syllable or syllables within the same foot; secondly, although quantity or syllable-length has no part in the measure, it is, like accent, infinitely variable and it affects the rhythm; and thirdly, feet of other types may be substituted for iambic feet, at least within reason. As I have said, rhythm results from the proper control and manipulation of these sources of variation.

Now rhythm is in a measure expressive of emotion. If the poet, then, is endeavoring to make a statement in which rational understanding and emotion are properly related to each other, metrical language will be of the greatest advantage to him, for it will provide him with a means of qualifying his emotion more precisely than he could otherwise do, of adjusting it more finely to the rational understanding which gives rise to it. The rational and emotional contents of the poem thus exist simultaneously, from moment to moment, in the poem; they are not distinct, but are separable only by analysis; the poet is not writing in language which was first conceptual and then emotionalized, nor in prose which has been metered; he is writing in poetical language. And the rhythm of the poem permeates the entire poem as pervasively as blood permeates the human body: remove it and you have a corpse. It is for this reason that the audible reading of poetry is quite as important as the philosophical understanding of poetry; without audible reading, and adequate audible reading, you simply do not have poetry.

We are thus confronted with the question of what constitutes adequate audible reading. From what I have just said, it should be obvious that adequate audible reading will be reading in which the rhythm of the poem is rendered intact, without the sacrifice of any other element. But what variety of reading will best achieve this end, and what are some of the problems which arise in connection with it?

Since I am defending an unpopular cause, I shall not scruple to avail myself of eminent support. In looking over the *Selected Writings* of Paul Valéry recently issued by New Directions, I found Valéry writing as follows:

> ... in studying a piece of poetry one intends to recite, one should not take as source or point of departure ordinary conversation and common parlance, in order to rise from this level of prose to the desired poetic tone: but, on the contrary, I thought one should take song as a base, and should put oneself in the state of a singer; adjust one's voice to the plenitude of musical sound, and from there descend to the somewhat less resonant state suitable to verse. This, it seemed to me, was the only way to preserve the musical essence of poems. Above all, the voice must be placed quite away from prose, and the text studied from the point of view of necessary attack, modulation, sustained tone, little by little, lowering this musical disposition, which in the beginning one has exaggerated, to bring it down to the proportions of poetry. . . . above all do not be in a hurry to arrive at the meaning. Approach it without effort and, as it were, insensibly. And only in or by means of the music attain to tenderness or to violence. . . . Remain in this pure musical state until such time as the meaning, appearing little by little, can no longer mar the musical form. You will introduce it at the end as the supreme nuance that will transfigure the passage without altering it.[1]

This appears to be a plea for a restrained but formal chant, in which a sustained tone and movement will serve as an impersonal but definite base for subtle variation. It is only by such a reading, for example, that *Le Cimetière Marin* can be rendered; it is only by a man who so read that such a poem could have been written.

A poem in the very nature of the case is a formal statement; and the reading of a poem is thus a formal occasion. A poem is not conversation; neither is it drama. Conversation is in general the least premeditated and least rhythmical of human utterance; and it depends very heavily upon intonations and even gestures and facial expressions which are not at the disposal of the poet. Dramatic speech is merely more or less

[1] Extracts from "A Discourse on the Declamation of Verse," by Paul Valéry, translated by Louise Varese. *Paul Valéry, Selected Writings*, New Directions, 1950.

formalized conversation. Dramatic poetry, of course, presents a special problem, and one with which I shall not at present concern myself, though it is closer to the kind of poetry with which I am dealing than it is to dramatic prose, and I agree with Valéry that it is commonly botched by the actors. I have never witnessed a performance of Shakespeare without more of pain than of profit or of pleasure. I have been repeatedly reminded of a story told by W. B. Yeats of the great Shakespearian actor of whom it was said that he read Shakespeare so beautifully that no one could tell it was poetry. In general I think the world would be well enough off without actors; they appear to be capable of any of three feats—of making the grossly vulgar appear acceptably mediocre; of making the acceptably mediocre appear what it is; and of making the distinguished appear acceptably mediocre. In any event, they cannot read poetry, for they try to make it appear to be something else, something, in brief, which they themselves can understand.

A poem calls for a formal reading, partly because the poem itself is of its own nature a formal statement, and partly because only such a reading will render the rhythm with precision. Furthermore, it is only with a formal tone as a basis that variations of tone within the poem can be rendered with precision: without such a formal tone to unify the poem, the poem becomes merely a loose assortment of details. The situation here is precisely analogous to that which I have described elsewhere[2] with regard to rhythm and meter: the firmer the metric structure, the more precise can be the rhythmic variations, and the greater the effect obtainable with a very slight variation; whereas if the structure is loose the variations lack significance.

A formal reading which avoids dramatic declamation will necessarily take on something of the nature of a chant. This kind of reading itself has dangers, however, for the reader may carry the procedure so far as to appear precious, and worse, he may deform syllables in the interests of what he considers musical intonation, much as a musical composer will draw syllables out or hurry over them in setting a poem to music. I never heard the late W. B. Yeats read aloud, but I have been told that he was guilty of both of these vices: if it is true that he was guilty of them, one has some reason to sus-

[2] The Influence of Meter on Poetic Convention, in *Primitivism and Decadence*, the essay on John Crowe Ransom, Section IX, in *The Anatomy of Nonsense*, both reprinted in *In Defense of Reason*.

pect that he never properly heard his own poems, a fact which
may have been responsible for a number of curious rhythmical
mishaps which are scattered through his works. A poem
should, on the contrary, be conceived as having a movement
of its own, an autonomous movement, which should be rendered as purely and as impersonally as possible. The reader
has no more right to revise the rhythms in the interest of
what he considers an effective presentation than he has a
right to revise any other aspects of the language. The poem,
once set in motion, should appear to move of its own mo-
mentum.

A more or less recent poet who went farther than any other
has gone in deforming the inherent rhythmic elements in our
language and so rendering the structure of his poems inde-
cipherable is Gerard Manley Hopkins. Hopkins held a theory
of dramatic or declamatory reading, and I suspect from a few
passages in his prose that he combined this with a theory of
musical intonation. Hopkins was an eccentric and extremely
egoistic man, and he worked in isolation. He apparently failed
to realize that his own dramatic and musical deformations of
language were not based on universal principles but were
purely private. As a result one can often be only dumfounded
when he indicates his intentions by metrical signs, and one
can often be only baffled when he fails to do so. In *Spelt from
Sibyl's Leaves*, for example, Hopkins uses an extremely long
line, which, if it is read with normal accentuation, produces
the effect of a loosely irregular but still readable verse. He
does not provide us with many accent marks until he is about
halfway through the poem; from there on he provides marks
in abundance, frequently with strange results. The last two
lines will serve as illustration:

But thése two; wáre of a wórld where bút these / twó tell,
        each off the óther; of a rack
Where, selfwrung, selfstrung, sheathe- and shelterless, /
        thoúghts agáinst thoughts ín groans grínd.

We have here a kind of bad writing which is purely the result
of bad reading; and even the best reading, if superimposed
upon what the poet offers, can salvage the poem but very
imperfectly.

In T. S. Eliot's reading of *The Waste Land*, as we have it
on the recordings issued by The Library of Congress, we have
another kind of dramatic reading, and conceivably a relation-

ship between the way of reading and the way of writing. In those portions which exhibit a more or less definite rhythmic structure—for example, in *Death by Water*—Eliot reads more or less in the fashion which I am recommending, with a minimum of dramatic improvement on the text, and with a maximum of attention to movement. But in those portions of the poem—and they are the greater part of it—in which the rhythm does not cohere, in which the poem tends to fall apart in sandy fragments, Eliot reads dramatically; he does this with a good deal of skill, but most of what he puts into his voice is not in the poem—he descends to the practice of the actor who is salvaging a weak text. It would be interesting to know whether Eliot devised this mode of reading in order to rescue a weak poem, or whether the weak poem resulted in part from his having come gradually to employ such a mode of reading, so that he tended to see in his text as he was composing it something which he was not actually getting down on paper. This latter procedure in any event probably accounts for a good deal of the unrealized poetry of our time. For example, Randall Jarrell's reading of his poem *Lady Bates*, in The Library of Congress series, is very dramatic, very emotional, and very bad: I am unable to hear it without the conviction that Jarrell felt his emotions about his subject so readily and so uncritically that he did not trouble himself to write the poem. The poem itself is formless and dull.

The dependence upon superimposed rhythms or other effects which we get in a grotesque form in some of Hopkins and in a more skillful form in Eliot's reading of *The Waste Land* can lead to an astonishing degree of imperception on the part of critics (which is merely an impressive way of saying on the part of readers). In the volume entitled *Gerard Manley Hopkins*, by the Kenyon Critics, Mr. Harold Whitehall informs us that from about the year 1300 English poetry has become less and less amenable to being read aloud, because less and less rhythmical. And in another volume on Hopkins, edited by Norman Weyand, S. J., and written by a group of Jesuits, a volume entitled *Immortal Diamond*, Walter J. Ong arrives at similar conclusions. Both of these writers believe that there is no real rhythm without heavy stress; both believe that meter is based on declamatory rather than mechanical stress. Ong gives us no clue as to how we are to recognize our stressed syllables, and he fails to explain how Hopkins arrived at any of the stresses which he marked. Whitehall gives us his own system of stressing Hopkins, but it is quite as arbitrary as that of Hopkins, and when Whitehall's marked passages are finished we are left with no means of proceeding. Ong, convinced that there is no fine rhythm without heavy and obvious stress, is oblivious of the sensitivity of Sidney and the post-Sidneyan metrists, and equally of the structural principles of their verse; and his concept of reading aloud is indicated by the following passage: "If the poem calls for shouting, the shouting need not be kept imaginary for fear the beat of the rhythm will go. Shout, declaim, and you will only have thrust this rhythm home. So, too, if the shout should need to die to a whisper . . ." This clerical type of rendition strikes me as about equally impractical, insensitive, and indecorous.

Nevertheless, rhetorical stress has a certain relationship to the structure of meter, but it is not the relationship sought by Hopkins. As I have already said, the language does not divide itself evenly into accented and unaccented syllables, but there is almost infinite variation in degrees of accent. For this reason, the basic rule of English scansion is this: that the accented syllable can be determined only in relationship to the other syllable or syllables within the same foot. The accented syllable of a given foot, as we shall eventually see, may be one of the lightest syllables in its line. But with this rule as a reservation, we may go on to say that poetic meter must be constructed out of the inherent (or mechanical) accentual materials of the language, so that the accented syllable of a foot will be naturally heavier than the unaccented; and if the poet desires to indicate a rhetorical stress he should do it by a metrical stress, or if he is using two syllables either of which might receive heavier stress than the other, then the rhetorical stress should fall where the reader as a result of the previously established pattern will expect the metrical stress.

Keats neglects these considerations in the first line of his last sonnet. The inexpert reader who endeavors to render this line conversationally or dramatically will read it as if he were a sociable lady addressing another sociable lady at a party:

Bright star,   would *I* were steadfast   as *thou* art,

and the rhythm is destroyed along with the possibility of a proper rhyme. The fault, however, lies largely with Keats. It is natural to stress the two contrasting pronouns somewhat, although one need not carry the stress all the way to the ridiculous. Furthermore, on the first pronoun the metrical stress indicates the rhetorical, so that the two are not in conflict. If we consider the words *Would I* in isolation, we shall see that so far as their mechanical properties are concerned, either can be stressed at the expense of the other; however, in this line the stressing of *would* would result in an inverted foot in the second position, and although inversion is possible in this position, it is difficult and generally unlikely, so that we naturally expect the stress to fall on *I*, which likewise is the natural recipient of the rhetorical stress. If we employ the four words *Would I were steadfast* in isolation, the stress may fall variously according to our meaning. If we are implying a contrast between steadfastness and our lack of it, the heaviest stress falls on *would;* if we are implying a contrast between steadfastness and another particular quality, a light stress falls on *would* and a heavy on *stead-;* if we are implying a contrast between our own lack of steadfastness and the steadfastness of another, the heavy stress falls on *I*, as in the actual line, but if, as in this line, the comparison is completed, an actual stress should fall on the second pronoun; but since this pronoun also is coupled with a verb which is mechanically its equal and on the basis of its inherent nature could as well take the accent, and since the foot ends the line, and a rhymed line at that, the accent must fall on *art*. This blunder by Keats could scarcely have occurred as a result of his reading poetry in a dramatic fashion, for he understood the structure of English poetry very well, and had he read the line dramatically he would have noticed the error. It probably occurred as a result of his reading with a somewhat mechanical scansion, so that he failed to observe that the meaning was struggling with the meter. One can read it, of course, by means of a more or less evasive glide, but it constitutes an unhappy moment.

One can observe a related difficulty in the sixth line of Wordsworth's sonnet *Upon Westminster Bridge:*

Ships, towers, domes, theatres, and temples lie.

The first four words of this line are coördinate in grammatical function and in importance, and in ordinary prose the first four syllables would be indistinguishable to the ear in the matter of accent. The average reader, if asked to mark the scansion of this poem, will indicate two spondees at the beginning of the line, but the first two feet are not spondaic— in spite of everything they are iambic. The truly spondaic foot is extremely rare in English; presently I shall have occasion to illustrate it, but for the present I shall merely describe it. It can occur as a variant in iambic verse, only if the accented

syllables in the iambic feet are heavily accented and the unaccented are very light, and only if the cesural pause is heavily
marked; and these conditions must prevail not merely in the
line in question, but throughout much of the poem. The true
spondee is a violent aberration—it is a form of what Hopkins
calls sprung rhythm—and it is possible only where the rhythm
is heavy and obvious. It can be found at least as early as
Barnabe Googe and as late as the songbooks of John Dowland,
and within these limits it may conceivably be found in as many
as thirty poems, but I think it will be difficult to find it
elsewhere except in the work of Gerard Hopkins, although
something approaching it occurs occasionally in Henry
Vaughan. In this sonnet by Wordsworth an extremely smooth
iambic movement has been established in the first five lines,
so effectively established that it dominates the sixth line, and
almost any reader who is aware of rhythm at all will be forced
to impose a very light iambic emphasis on the first two feet
of the sixth line; to do otherwise will bring the poem apart
in ruins. This can be done; but the difficulty indicates a defect
in the poem, and a defect again which probably stems from
faulty reading on the part of the poet. The difficulty is en-
hanced by the length of the syllables (a length increased by
the commas) and by the all but insufferable series of dentals.

The relationship of rhetorical stress to metrical stress, and
hence to reading, would appear, then, to be real, although the
relationship can obviously be abused. Perhaps I should conclude the matter by offering these rules for poet and reader
alike: (1) There should be no conflict between rhetorical
stress and metrical stress, but insofar as it is possible the metrical stress should point the meaning; (2) where the mechanical potentialities of the language indicate the possibility of a
stress in either of two directions, the grammatical structure
should be so definite that a certain rhetorical stress will be unmistakable and will force the metrical interpretation in the
right direction; and (3) the reader should deal with rhetorical
stresses with the utmost restraint—he should indicate them as
far as the occasion requires, but he should not become enthu-
siastic, undignified, or unmetrical about them. They are not to
be superimposed upon the basic rhythm, nor can the basic
rhythm be constructed from them.

I would like next to illustrate the importance of reading,
by illustrating certain very marked differences in rhythm
which may occur within the limits of the iambic pentameter
line. English verse is predominantly iambic in structure, and

although this fact has irritated certain poets and stirred them
to curious experiments, the fact that so vast a number of eminent poets have found the iambic movement more useful than
any other must have some kind of explanation. In the anapestic or dactylic foot the accented syllable must be definitely
heavy or the identity of the foot and of the line will disappear,
and this necessity makes for monotony and a jingling obviousness:

> I sprang to the stirrup, and Joris, and he;
> I galloped, Dirck galloped, we galloped all three. . . .

The unequivocally trochaic line tends to exhibit some of the
same heaviness (as in *Hiawatha*, for example) although the
reason for this is less clear. The seven-syllable tetrameter line
may be described as trochaic, with a monosyllabic foot in the
last position, or as iambic with a monosyllabic foot in the first
position; since it is frequently used as a variant on iambic
tetrameter, the second classification would seem the better.
When this line is used throughout a poem, the poem will be
short, or else will become monotonous: the accents again are
usually heavy most of the time, and although the meter may
be used in a short poem for the purpose of obtaining a didactic or semi-songlike effect, it appears to have few other uses.
The iambic movement, however, appears to be natural to the
language; it asserts itself easily, and the poet does not have to
hammer his accents out to maintain it. This situation allows
the poet to vary the degrees of his accents widely, to vary his
cesuras, and to employ substitution with a certain freedom.
Contrary to the views of Mr. Whitehall and of Father Ong,
this type of meter lends itself very well to audible reading,
but one must first know how to read. And when well written
and well read it is far more flexible and perceptive than any
other kind of English verse thus far devised.

My first example is by Barnabe Googe and was written early
in the reign of Elizabeth, before the advent of Spenser and
Sidney:

> Give money me, take friendship who so list,
> For friends are gone, come once adversity,
> When money yet remaineth safe in chest
> That quickly can thee bring from misery;
> Fair face show friends, when riches do abound,
> Come time of proof, farewell they must away;
> Believe me well, they are not to be found,

If God but send thee once a lowering day.
Gold never starts aside, but in distress,
Finds ways enough to ease thine heaviness.

This poem has certain characteristics which one would expect
to find in a period in which the pentameter line was new,
when the misunderstandings of Wyatt had been only recently
overcome: first of all there are no inverted feet and no trisyllabic feet; secondly the accented syllables are almost all heavy
and of nearly the same weight—there are only two feet in the
poem in which the accented syllables are noticeably light;
thirdly the cesuras are all heavily marked, and in six of the
ten lines they fall at the end of the second foot. The poem
shows only one type of metrical variation; that is, the use of
spondaic feet (or what I have elsewhere called syllabic sprung
meter). The introduction of this variation into the newly acquired iambic pentameter line is Googe's principle contribution to the technique of English verse, and it is a contribution
of no mean importance. There are two spondees at the beginning of line five; there is one at the beginning of six; there is
one at the beginning of nine; and the first foot of the last line
may be read with equal success as a spondee or as an iamb.
All of these spondees can be forced into the iambic pattern,
but they will have to be forced, and the poem will suffer. It is
only in a poem such as this one, in which the rhythm is strongly and obviously marked by a great and regular distinction between accented and unaccented syllables that the true spondee can occur; in a smoother and subtler type of structure,
such as my next example, two syllables of nearly the same degree of accent will be absorbed into the iambic pattern and
will not stand out as approximately equal to each other; furthermore, any attempt to read them as spondees will destroy
the movement of the poem.

My next example is from Shakespeare. Before this sonnet
was written, Sidney and other early experimenters had rendered the line smoother, more varied, and more subtle:

When to the sessions of sweet silent thought
I summon up remembrance of things past,
I sigh the lack of many a thing I sought,
And with old woes new wail my dear time's waste:
Then can I drown an eye unused to flow,
For precious friends, hid in death's dateless night,
And weep afresh love's long-since-cancelled woe,
And moan th'expense of many a vanish'd sight:
Then can I grieve at grievances foregone,

And heavily from woe to woe tell o'er
The sad account of fore-bemoaned moan
Which I new pay as if not paid before.
    But if the while I think on thee, dear friend,
    All losses are restored and sorrows end.

The position of the cesura in this sonnet is less varied than in the poem by Googe; it falls after the second foot in eleven out of fourteen lines; but the cesura is much less noticeable, partly because it is not emphasized by heavy grammatical breaks, and partly because of other qualities of the rhythm. Aside from this difference in cesural value, the most considerable rhythmic difference between this poem and the poem by Googe resides in the fact that there are great differences in the degrees of accent to be found among the syllables which count metrically as accented. It will be remembered that I remarked earlier that the accented syllable can be recognized as such only with reference to the other syllable or syllables within the same foot, for no two syllables bear exactly the same degree of accent: it is this fact which gives the rhythm of the best English verse its extreme sensitivity. But rhythm, in poetry as in music, is controlled variation from an arithmetical norm, and the rhythm ceases to be rhythm, and becomes merely movement, whenever the norm itself is no longer discernible.

I will illustrate what I have been saying by two lines from the sonnet. The scansion of the first line gives us a trochee followed by four iambs. The third foot, however, which is composed of the second syllable of sessions followed by the preposition of (the accented syllable), is very lightly accented. In the following foot, which is composed of sweet, followed by the first syllable of silent, sweet, the unaccented syllable, is more heavily stressed than the accented syllable of the preceding foot, so that we have in effect a series of four degrees of accent within two successive feet. Furthermore, if the reader should suffer from the delusion (a common one) that the second of these feet is really a spondee, let him read it the way he is forced to read the true spondees in the poem by Googe, and he will discover that spondaic rhythm is a very different matter from what he has here, and that the attempt to introduce it into this poem will be disastrous. The same thing occurs in the fourth and fifth feet of line nine:

Then can I grieve at grievances foregone.

It occurs in the first two feet of Bryant's line:

> Where thy pale form was laid with many tears.

It occurs in the last two feet of Ben Jonson's line:

> Drink to me only with thine eyes.

It is, in fact, one of the commonest phenomena in English verse, yet I have seen a good many distinguished scholars and eminent poets interpret it wrongly.

I shall now quote a well known song from John Dowland's *Second Book of Aires*:

> Fine knacks for ladies, cheap, choice, brave and new!
>   Good pennyworths! but money cannot move.
> I keep a fair but for the fair to view;
>   A beggar may be liberal of love.
> Though all my wares be trash, the heart is true.
>
> Great gifts are guiles and look for gifts again;
>   My trifles come as treasures from my mind.
> It is a precious jewel to be plain;
>   Sometimes in shell the Orient's pearls we find.
> Of others take a sheaf, of me a grain.
>
> Within this pack, pins, points, laces, and gloves,
>   And divers toys, fitting a country fair.
> But my heart lives where duty serves and loves,
>   Turtles and twins, court's brood, a heavenly pair.
> Happy the heart that thinks of no removes.

There are sprung, or spondaic, feet in the first, second, sixth, seventh, eleventh, thirteenth, and fourteenth lines of this poem. These feet represent the same kind of variant which we found in Googe, and for the most part we have the same strongly marked difference between accented and unaccented syllables and similarly strong cesural pauses, even in lines in which no spondees occur. Yet whereas the rhythm of Googe is hard, fast, and didactic, the rhythm of this poem is slower, more complicated, and very songlike. The result is partly due to more spondaic variants than we found in Googe, and to spondaic variants in other positions than the initial ones; it is partly due to the introduction at certain points of the type of line which we found in Shakespeare, such as the following:

> It is a precious jewel to be plain.

a line in which the iambic fourth foot, composed of the second syllable of *jewel* and the preposition *to*, is extremely light and short and is followed by a final foot (*be plain*) in which the unaccented syllable is heavier than the accented syllable *to* before it; yet in this last foot the difference between *be* and *plain* is so marked that no one would be tempted to call the foot a spondee.

The author likewise does certain strange and ingenious things with his spondees. The first line, for example, goes as follows:

Fine knacks for ladies, cheap, choice, brave and new!

The first foot is spondaic, the second iambic; the third foot, consisting of the second syllable of *ladies* and of *cheap*, is likewise iambic, but the cesura, reinforced by the comma, in mid-foot, throws the accent onto *cheap* with unusual force, and *cheap* is then followed by the spondaic foot consisting of two syllables which are almost exactly equal to it, and which are likewise set off by commas, so that we have the illusion of a foot consisting of three accented syllables, or an English molossus. The author does something similar but almost more adventurous in the eleventh line, where the heavily iambic foot *this pack* is followed by the heavy spondee *pins, points,* which in turn is followed by the heavily inverted foot, *laces,* with the result that we get four strong accents in sequence, though only one spondee. Technically, this is one of the most brilliant poems in the language. Dowland (or his unknown poet) learned what he could from Googe and improved upon it; and he complicated the method (without destroying it—a difficult feat) by rhythms acquired from the refiners of the intervening period.

I shall now show the use of different types of iambic pentameter rhythm employed in a regular pattern. To do this, I shall employ a song by Campion. The song rhymes in couplets. The metric pattern begins with two lines of what one might call the primitive type, with heavy stresses and heavy cesuras, but with no spondees: in these two lines the first and third feet are inverted, the rest iambic, and the cesura falls after the second foot. The third and fifth lines are evenly iambic and are less heavily stressed, and the cesuras in these lines occur in different positions and are so light as to be all but imperceptible. The fourth and sixth lines are of the same type of iambic movement as the last lines mentioned, but contain seven feet instead of five. There are two stanzas, and the pattern in the two is as nearly identical as the inescapable variations of language permit:

Follow your saint, follow with accents sweet!
Haste you, sad notes, fall at her flying feet!
There, wrapt in cloud of sorrow, pity move,
And tell the ravisher of my soul I perish for her love:
But if she scorns my never ceasing pain,
Then burst with sighing in her sight, and ne'er return again.

All that I sung still to her praise did tend;
Still she was first, still she my songs did end;
Yet she my love and music both doth fly,
The music that her echo is and beauty's sympathy:
Then let my notes pursue her scornful flight!
It shall suffice that they were breathed and died for her delight.

I shall now quote a sonnet by Gerard Hopkins, which is basically iambic pentameter, but which employs every conceivable variant. I have marked and described the scansion of this sonnet in my essay on Hopkins, and at this time I shall make only a few general remarks about the structure. The poem contains iambic feet, trochees, spondees, one molossus (a foot of three accented syllables), monosyllabic feet, trisyllabic feet of one accent each, and one or two feet which must be considered either as containing more than three syllables or else as containing syllables which are extrametrical or elided. The poem is successful as regards structure and rhythm, and it offers a rhythmic departure from the norm about as extreme as anyone is likely to achieve:

No worst, there is none. Pitched past pitch of grief,
More pangs will, schooled at forepangs, wilder wring.
Comforter, where, where is your comforting?
Mary, mother of us, where is your relief?
My cries heave, herds-long; huddle in a main, a chief
Woe, world sorrow; on an age-old anvil wince and sing—
Then lull, then leave off. Fury had shieked "No lingering! Let me be fell: force I must be brief."

O the mind, mind has mountains; cliffs of fall
Frightful, sheer, no-man-fathomed. Hold them cheap
May who ne'er hung there. Nor does long our small
Durance deal with that steep or deep. Here! creep,
Wretch under a comfort serves in a whirlwind: all
Life death does end and each day dies with sleep.

By the use of five short poems I have indicated a number of widely varying rhythms all of which are measured by iambic pentameter. So far as meter and rhythm are concerned all five are masterpieces; and in spite of any faults which may be found in them with regard to other matters, all five are brilliant poems and should be part of the literary experience of any man using the English language. Yet not one of these poems amounts to anything if its rhythm is not rendered with great precision; to read the poem so that its rhythm does not emerge in its totality and in every detail is to reduce the poem to lifeless fragments. You cannot buy expert readings of these poems on disks, as you can buy expert renderings of Bach and Mozart; nor can you go to a concert and hear them—every man is his own performer. It is important, therefore, that one read properly. But to read properly one must understand the principles both of English meter and of English rhythm, and not in a haphazard manner, but precisely; and one must understand the use of one's own voice; and after that one must practice.

I am at a disadvantage in dealing with a subject of this kind before an audience whom I cannot reach with my voice, for I cannot demonstrate, but am forced to try to describe. The nearest thing to a demonstration that I can offer is my reading of my own poems in the Library of Congress series. I do not consider myself a finished performer, nor, I think, are these readings the best of which I am capable. But they are all I can offer, and they will serve to indicate the method in a general way.

I have been told that this method of reading makes all poems sound alike, but this can be true only for those persons to whom all poems sound alike in any event, or for whom essential differences are meaningless. The virtue of the method, on the contrary, is that it gives each poem its precise identity, and no other method will do this. If this precise identity does not interest you, then you are not interested in poetry and you will in all likelihood never discover poetry. Some time ago, when I was defending this method of reading in public, a well-known scholar objected to my theories with a good deal of indignation, and he objected especially to my reading of the Dowland poem which I have quoted in these pages. He said that it was a street song, or peddler's song, and should be rendered as such. I do not know exactly how Elizabethan street songs were rendered, and I do not believe that he knew; but any attempt so to render it would be, I am sure, unfortunate, even if one had the necessary information. The poem is not a street song; it is a poem on love and on the art of poetry and on a relationship between the two, and it is one of the most deeply serious and deeply moving short poems in the Elizabethan period—the peddler is purely metaphorical, and his

part in the poem is both indicated and formulated by the
metrical structure and it should remain formal and no more
than indicated in the reading. If the poet refers by way of metaphor to a cow, the reader is not, I trust, expected to moo. I
refer the reader back to my quotations from Valéry, especially
the last sentence. Of the "meaning" of the poem he says:
"You will introduce it at the end as the supreme nuance that
will transfigure the poem without altering it." By "the end,"
he means the end of the process of studying the poem and
arriving at the proper rendering.

Bad reading and bad (or no) training in metrical theory are
largely to blame, I believe, for the insensitive literary judg-
ments by many critics who in other matters are very brilliant,
and they are to blame also for a fair amount of bad academic
work in literature. At Stanford University, at this writing, we
have over one hundred graduate students in English, and about
half of these are candidates for the doctorate. We are in a
position to select our graduate students very carefully. We
accept none who have not made excellent records here or
elsewhere, and although some come to us from the smaller in-
stitutions (and incidentally some of our best), many come
from places like Yale, Harvard, Chicago, Columbia, Princeton,
and the better state universities. These people have made excellent records in the past, and most of them make excellent
records here; yet almost none can read a line of poetry aloud
so that one can discern the structure, and very few can mark
the scansion from a line of Shakespeare's sonnets. These people are in these respects the products of their teaching, and the
teaching should be improved. Most of our best critics and
many of our best-known poets are not much better off. We
have sunk into amateurism; and as a result we have in our time
the meters of Eliot and of his imitators at the fifth remove,
instead of meters comparable to those of the Elizabethans.
And we have, worse still, a coherent (and fairly vocal) body
of readers so ignorant that they prefer the incompetent to the
expert.

If you answer that there are different kinds of poetry and
hence we have different kinds of reading (this, of course, is the
genteel answer which points to my lack of gentility), I am
bound to reply that you are right: there are inferior kinds of
poetry. By "inferior," I mean inferior in quality, not smaller in
scope. The kind of reading which I defend is equally appropriate to a song by Campion or to an epic by Milton. Any
poem which cannot endure the impersonal illumination of

such a reading or which requires the assistance, whether expert
or clumsy, of shouting, whispering, or other dramatic improvement, is to that extent bad poetry, though it may or may not
be a good scenario for a vaudeville performance.

There will never be a first-rate poet or a first-rate critic who
lacks a first-rate ear; and no one will ever acquire a first-rate ear
without working for it and in the proper manner. Poetry, alas,
like painting and music, is an art—it is not a form of happy
self-indulgence; and to master an art or even understand it,
one has to labor with all of one's mind and with at least a part
of one's body.

W. K. WIMSATT AND MONROE C. BEARDSLEY

The Concept Of Meter: An Exercise In Abstraction

[Wimsatt and Beardsley also acknowledge the principle of relative stress. It should be noted, however, that Jespersen does not restrict the gradations of stress to four levels; he remarks, "But in reality there are infinite gradations of stress, from the most penetrating scream to the faintest whisper; but in most instances it will be sufficient for our purposes to recognize four degrees. . . ." Jespersen abstracts his four levels from the entire range of acoustic phenomena. Meter is generated not by any absolute alternation of scientifically measurable stresses but by an overall pattern, a Gestalt: this pattern need only be approximately maintained to be recognized.

[In the earlier sections of this essay, Wimsatt and Beardsley assert their position vis à vis the musical scanners ("timers") and the linguists. They affirm their belief in the traditional graphic scansion of English meter; they also see the timers and linguists succumbing to the performative heresy. A scansion based on an individual recitation of verse notates a performer's idiosyncrasies; it does not outline exact metrical structure. Wimsatt and Beardsley stress the paradigmatic nature of meter; as an element in poetic structure, it is capable of precise abstraction. "You can write a grammar of the meter. And if you cannot, there is no meter."]

IV

THE METER inheres in the language of the poem, but in what way and at what level? We hold that it inheres in aspects of

Sections IV and V, from Hateful Contraries by W. K. Wimsatt. This essay appeared originally in PMLA, LXXIV, 5 (December 1959), 585-598. Used with permission of the authors and the University of Kentucky Press; copyright © 1965 by the University of Kentucky Press.

the language that can be abstracted with considerable precision, isolated, and even preserved in the appearance of an essence—mummified or dummified. An appropriate example is to hand and does not have to be invented. Back in the 1920's I. A. Richards was much concerned, and properly, to show that the movement or rhythm of poetry was closely inter-dependent with its other kinds of meaning. The movement, he argued, could hardly be said to occur at all except as an aspect of some linguistic meaning. Or at least it had no poetic value except as an aspect of some meaning. It is not quite clear which point Richards was making. But for the sake of his argument he exhibited, in his *Practical Criticism*, a contrivance which he called a "double or dummy"—"with nonsense syllables"—"a purified dummy." The dummy showed several things, perhaps a good deal more than Richards had in mind. For it certainly was not a *pure* dummy. How could it be? It was a linguistic dummy. And so this dummy did have a meter—perhaps even a kind of rhythm. If it did not have a meter, how could it be adduced as showing that movement, or meter, apart from sense did not have poetic value? You can't illustrate the poetic nullity of a certain quality taken pure by annihilating that quality. You do it by purging or purifying, isolating, the quality. And if you can do that, you prove that the quality can be isolated—at least from *certain* other qualities, in this case, the *main lines* of the linguistic meaning. In order to get even this dummy of a meter, Richards had to leave in a good many linguistic features.

> J. Drootan-Sussting Benn
> Mill-down Leduren N.
>   Telamba-taras oderwainto weiring
> Awersey zet bidreen
> Ownd istellester sween. . . .

"If any reader," says Richards, "has any difficulty in scanning these verses, reference to Milton, *On the Morning of Christ's Nativity*, xv, will prove of assistance."[1] There are, indeed, several uncertainties in Richards' composition which correspond to greater certainties in Milton's full linguistic archetype. Still the Milton is not necessary. Let us list some of the things we know about this dummy. The "nonsense syllables" are divided into groups (words). As English readers we find little difficulty pronouncing them. Some of the groups are English words ("Mill," "down,"); others are English syllables, even mor-

[1] *Practical Criticism* (New York, 1935), p. 232.

phemes ("ing," "ey," "een," "er"). The capital initials, the monosyllables, the hyphens, the rhymes, give us very strong indications, absolutely sure indications, where some of the stresses fall. And there are some syllables, notably some final syllables, which are surely unstressed. If we don't inquire too closely how much any given stressed syllable is stressed more than another (and who is to say that we should make that inquiry?), we will indicate the scansion of Richards' dummy somewhat as follows:

> J. Drootan-Sussting Benn
> Mill-down Leduren N.
>   Telamba-taras oderwainto weiring
> Awersey zet bidreen
> Ownd istellester sween. . . .

The main uncertainties will be with the groups "Leduren," "Telamba," "Awersey," "istellester," where there will be a choice or guess in placing the stress. But the choice in no one of the four cases is crucial to the meter. You can choose either way and not destroy the iambics. And Richards' readers who have read this dummy and admired the ingenuity of the argument have certainly all along been giving the dummy the benefit of some implicit scansion.

The dummy does two things for the present argument. It illustrates or strongly suggests the principle that meter may inhere at certain rudimentary levels of linguistic organization, and, more specifically, that the kind of English meter of which we are speaking, so far as it depends on syllabic stress, depends not on any kind of absolute or very strong stress, but merely on a relative degree of stress—on a certain moreness of stress in certain positions. Of this latter we want to say something further before we finish. It is not a principle which is challenged by the linguists—though the exact sense in which they wish to apply it seems doubtful.

Let us now make some general prosodic observations. And first, that to have verses or lines, you have to have certain broader structural features, notably the endings. Milton's line is not only a visual or typographical fact on the page, but a fact of the language. If you try to cut up his pentameters into tetrameters, for example, you find yourself ending in the middle of words or on weak words like "on" or "the." Much English prose is iambic or nearly iambic, but it is only very irregular verse, because if you try to cut it regularly, you get the same awkward and weak result. Lines of verse are syntactic entities, though not necessarily similar or parallel entities. Depending on the degree of parallel, you get different kinds of tension between the fact of the lines and the fact of the overall syntax or movement.

Given the line then or the typographical semblance of a line (the possibility of a line) on the page, let us ask the question how we know we have a meter and know what meter it is. The line may indeed be only a syntactic entity and not metrical in any more precise way—as perhaps it is throughout Robert Bridges' *Testament of Beauty*[2] and in much so-called "free verse." With Mr. Whitehall we can call this a kind of "rhythm," *nonsyllabic, isosyntactic,* so long as the syntactic entities, the phrases or clauses, are "in strictly parallel sequence," as in Hebrew verse and in some "free verse." But this is in fact a very narrow restriction. It rules out all mere cutting of ordinary prose into its phrases or clauses (as in much free verse, and perhaps in Bridges or in parts of Bridges). For again, like Pike's isochronism, phrases and clauses are inevitable, and if they by themselves make a "rhythm" (or a meter), it is impossible not to write in this "rhythm" or meter. To get a meter, some other kind of equality has to be added to the succession of syntactic entities. (Even strictly parallel syntactic entities will be improved metrically by the addition of some more precise kind of equality.) The meter in the sense that it is internal to a given line or that it is something that runs through the series of lines is some kind of more minute recurrence—some exact or approximate number of syllables, with probably some reenforcement of certain syllables, some repeated weighting, what Mr. Whitehall calls a "configurational feature." Here if we take a wide enough look at the world's languages and literatures (at Chinese and classical Greek, as well as the Western vernaculars of our immediate experience), we can talk about pitch and quantity, as well as accent or stress. But for our discussion of English meters, stress is the thing. (Rhyme, assonance, alliteration too are auxiliary "configurational" and metric features—though Mr. Whitehall seems to count them out.)

The important principle of stress or accent in English

[2] Elizabeth Wright, *Metaphor, Sound and Meaning in Bridges' "The Testament of Beauty"* (Philadelphia, 1951), p. 26, says that Bridges' lines are to be timed equally, with the help of pauses at the ends of the lines.

verse is, however, a rather ambiguous thing, for there are in fact two main kinds of stress meter in English: the very old (and recently revived) meter of strong stress with indeterminate or relatively indeterminate number of syllables between the stresses, and the other meter, of the great English art tradition (Chaucer to Tennyson), which is a syllable-stress meter, that is, a meter of counted syllables and of both major and minor stresses.

There are certainly some lines of syllable-stress meter which taken alone could be read also as strong-stress meter (four beats instead of five). To use one of Mr. Frye's examples:

> To bé, or nót to be, thát is the quéstion:
> Whéther 'tis nóbler in the mínd **to súffer**
> The slíngs and árrows of outágeous fórtune . . .

But the precise number of syllables in syllable-stress meter is always somewhat against the strong-stress interpretation. One stress out of five in a pentameter line will inevitably be the weakest; still, because of the numbering of the syllables, and the alternation of the stresses, this fifth too calls out for some recognition.

> To bé, or nót to bé, thát is **the** quéstion.
> With lóss of Éden, tíll one gréater mán . . .

And then we have the matter of the whole passage, the whole act and scene, the whole book, the whole long poem to consider. And Mr. Frye admits that the strong stresses vary in number from eight (the maximum apparently possible within the conditions of the pentameter—a virtuoso feat achieved by Milton) and the scarcely satisfactory three (eked out in musical terms, for a line of Keats by Mr. Frye's assumption of a preliminary "rest"). But the "pentameter" in a long poem by Shakespeare, Milton, Pope, Wordsworth, or Keats is not subject to such fluctuations. The pentameter is always there. It is the meter of the poem. The strong-stress lines of four, of three, of eight, and so on, come and go, playing along with the steady pentameter—and it is a good thing they do come and go, for if every line of *Hamlet* or *Paradise Lost* had the four strong beats which Mr. Frye finds in the opening four or five lines, Mr. Frye would begin to detect something marvelously monotonous; he wouldn't be so happy about his "in-

herent" and "common" four-stress rhythm. One principle of
monotony is enough; it is *the* meter of the poem. In "pentameter" verse it is the iambic pentameter.

A few lines of Chaucer, Shakespeare, Spenser, Pope, Wordsworth, Tennyson, read consecutively, can hardly fail to
establish the meter. What makes it possible for the lighter
stresses to count in syllable-stress meter is the fact that it is
a syllable meter. Following French and classical models, but in
an English way, the poets count their syllables precisely or
almost precisely, ten to a pentameter line, and this measuring
out makes it possible to employ the minor accents along with
the major ones in an alternating motion, up and down. The
precise measurement tilts and juggles the little accents into
place, establishes their occurrence as a regular part of all that
is going on.

Likewise, the clutter of weaker syllables in a strong-stress
meter is against an accurate syllable-stress reading, most often
prevents it entirely. A few lines of *Piers Plowman* or of *Everyman* ought to suffice to show what is what.

> In a somer seson, whan soft was the sonne,
> I shope me in shroudes, as I a shepe were,
> In habits like an heremite, unholy of workes,
> Went wyde in this world, wondres to here.

> Lorde, I wyll in the worlde go renne over all,
> And cruelly out-serche bothe grete and small.
> Every man wyll I beset that lyveth beestly
> Out of Goddes lawes, and dredeth not foly.

This other kind of meter is older in English poetry and may
be more natural to the English tongue, though again it may
not be. Here only the major stresses of the major words count
in the scanning. The gabble of weaker syllables, now more,
now fewer, between the major stresses obscures all the minor
stresses and relieves them of any structural duty. (Sometimes
the major stresses are pointed up by alliteration; they are likely
to fall into groups of two on each side of a caesura.) Thus we
have *Beowulf, Piers Plowman, Everyman,* Spenser's *February
Eclogue,* Coleridge's *Christabel,* the poetry of G. M. Hopkins
(who talks about "sprung rhythm" and "outrides"), the poetry of T. S. Eliot, and many another in our day.[3]

Let us now return and dwell more precisely for a moment

---

[3] Yvor Winters, *The Function of Criticism* (Denver, 1957), pp. 79-
100, 109-23, expresses a view of English meter in general and of Hopkins which we take to be substantially in accord with our own.

on the principle of relative stress. This is a slight but very certain thing in English; it is the indispensable and quite adequate principle for recognizing and scanning verses composed precisely of a given number of English syllables—or more exactly, for seeing if they will scan (for not all sequences of equal numbers of syllables show a measured alternation of accents). This is the main point of our whole essay: simply to reassert the fact of English syllable-stress meter, to vindicate the principle of relative stress as the one principle of stress which in conjunction with syllable counting makes this kind of meter. Mr. Chatman has already quoted the landmark statement about relative stress made by Otto Jespersen in his "Notes on Metre," 1900 (*Linguistica* [Copenhagen, 1933], pp. 272-74), and we need not repeat this. In speaking of this principle let us explain firmly, however, that we do not find it necessary to follow either Jespersen or Trager-Smith in believing in any fixed or countable number of degrees of English stress. We wish in the main to avoid the cumbersome grammar of the new linguists. For all we know, there may be, not four, but five degrees of English stress, or eight.[4] How can one be sure? What one can nearly always be sure of is that a given syllable in a sequence is more or less stressed than the preceding or the following. Or, suppose that there are, as Jespersen and Trager-Smith seem to agree, just four degrees of English stress. The discriminations are not needed for discerning the meter—but only the degrees of more and less. How much more is always irrelevant.

The main thing to observe about the principles of relative stress and counted syllables is that by means of these you can explain the necessary things about English syllable-stress verse. For one thing, quite starkly, you can tell an iambic line from one that is not iambic.

Preserved in Milton's or Shakespeare's name.

When a student misquotes this Popean line in a paper, it is not our perfect memory of the poem but our sense of the meter (and our belief in meter) which tells us he has left out a word. The four-beat theory of the pentameter could not make this discovery.

---

[4] Alexander J. Ellis, "Remarks on Professor Mayor's Two Papers on Rhythm," *Transactions of the Philological Society 1875-1876* (Strasburg, 1877), p. 442, distinguished "nine degrees" of "force" or stress in English and likewise nine degrees of "length," "pitch," "weight," and "silence."

To take another kind of example: let us suppose that Pope had written:

A little advice is a dangerous thing.

Persons who say that the line is one of Pope's four-beat lines will be hard put to explain why it isn't a good line; it still has its four strong beats. Yet nobody can actually say that the revised line is a good Popean line and goes well with the other lines of the *Essay on Criticism*. And all we have changed is the position of one relative accent, which makes it impossible that the syllable "is" should receive a stronger accent than the preceding syllable, and hence impossible that there should be five iambs in the line.

A líttle advíce is a dángerous thíng.

That one shift of accent throws us immediately into the anapestic gallop, and we have a line that belongs in Anstey's *Bath Guide*.

Another kind of example:

Ah, Sunflower, weary of time.

Hardly the Goldsmith or Anstey anapestic gallop. Yet unmistakably an anapestic line. The strong syllables "Ah," and "flow-," coming where they do, create a heavy drag. Nevertheless, "sun" is even stronger, at least stronger than "flow-," a fact which is crucial. A reader can take the two opening syllables as he likes, as iamb, trochee, or spondee (if there is such a thing), and still not defeat the subsequent anapests. The very weak syllables "er" and "y" in two key iambic stress positions make it unthinkable that the line should be read as iambic.

Again: the beginning of the line is a characteristic place, in both iambic and anapestic lines, for the full inversion.

Ruin hath taught me thus to ruminate.
Whether 'tis nobler in the mind to suffer . . .
Softly, in the dusk, a woman is singing to me;
Taking me back down the vista of years, till I see . . .

But:

Hail to thee, blithe spirit!

This is something different. The unquestionably iambic move-

ment following the very strong first syllable[5] might, if we were
desperate, be accounted for by saying that the word "Hail"
breaks into two syllables, "Hay-ul," with a resultant needed
extra weak syllable and the familiar opening pattern of iambic
inversion. But a much more energetic and irrefutable assertion
of the iamb appears in the progressive rise or stress increase
of the three syllables "thee, blithe spirit." (Note well: the
slack of a given foot can be stronger than the stress of the preceding foot.) For a trochaic reading of this line, you would
have to have "thee, blithe," a rhetorical impossibility, making
a nonsensically hopping line.

The notion of an accentual spondee (or "level" foot) in
English would seem to be illusory, for the reason that it is impossible to pronounce any two successive syllables in English
without some rise or fall of stress—and some rise or fall of
stress is all that is needed for a metrical ictus. This fact produces in English iambic meter two kinds of ambiguous situations or metrical choices, that of two weak syllables coming
together, and that of two strong syllables coming together. In
each of these situations, the iambic principle is saved merely
by the fact that certain unhappy choices are impossible.

[5] The problem of "rising" and "falling" meters is one which we are
content to touch lightly. Temporal theorists, working on the analogy
of the musical downbeat, tend of course to make all meters falling.
George R. Stewart, Jr., a moderate timer, makes the following revela-
tory statement: "If a person comes upon a road and walks a few rods
before arriving at the first milestone, he will have to pass five milestones, counting the first, before he has walked four measured miles;
in other words, since the start and the finish must be shown, five
markers are necessary to establish four units. In verse the stresses are
the markers, and the feet are the units. Five stresses can mark off only
four intervals, so that what we ordinarily call a five-foot line might be
more properly described as a four-foot line with a little left over at
beginning and end" (*The Technique of English Verse* [New York,
1930], p. 42). (For Mr. Stewart "rising" and "falling" are qualities
of phrasing, not of meter, p. 37.) Suppose, however, that we are
counting not "measured miles" but precisely milestones—not equal
times but precisely stresses. And suppose that a man walks not a "few
rods" but a full mile before reaching the first milestone. The first
slack syllable of the iambic line is as much a mile as any other slack
syllable. The line begins at the beginning of that syllable. The iambic
line which starts with a strong and then one weak syllable is a more
difficult matter. But many such lines, like the one from Shelley's "Sky-
lark" which we discuss above, can be shown in one way or another to
be in fact iambic. The shape of the phrases is likely to have much to
do with it. Other lines of this sort, such as some in Tennyson's *The
Lady of Shalott*, may in fact be ambiguous—that is, they may be
susceptible of being satisfactorily read either as iambic or as trochaic.

Rocks, caves, lakes, fens, bogs, dens, and shades of death.

Certainly it is impossible to pronounce the first two, the first
three, the first six syllables of this line with a perfectly even
stress. On the other hand, no determinate pattern of stresses
seems dictated. No doubt several are possible and are actually
employed or experienced by various readers of this Miltonic
passage. To us the most plausible seems as follows:

Rocks, cáves, lákes, fens, bógs, dens . . .

The more regularly iambic reading,

Rócks, cáves, lákes, fens . . .

seems forced. The only reading which will clearly defeat the
iambic movement is absurd:

Rócks, cáves, lákes, féns . . .

Two weak syllables together present perhaps the more difficult problem. But all cases will not be equally difficult.

In profuse strains of unpremeditated art.

Here certainly the crucial fact is that "strains" is more stressed
than "-fuse." Only observe that much—come out on the
fourth syllable with an ictus, and the first two syllables can be
stressed any way anybody wants. There are only two possible
ways: "Ín pro-" or "In pró-". The second way, invoking a
kind of Miltonic indult for the disyllable beginning with
"pro-," makes the line more regularly iambic, but it is not
necessary.

Upon the supreme theme of Art and Song . . .

This is the same thing, only pushed ahead to the second and
third feet of the line. The situation of the four syllables here,
two weak and two strong, has been described as a kind of
compensation, a "hovering" of the accent, or as a "double or
ionic foot" (Ransom, *Kenyon Review*, XVIII, 471). And
doubtless some such notion does something to help our ra-
tionalizations. But we may observe also that only the coming
together of the two strong accents makes possible the coming
together of the two weak. "The" and "su-" are so weak only
because "-preme" is so strong; and because "-preme" is so
strong, "theme" has to be yet stronger. (Imagine a group of
persons arguing about themes. One says theme X is good.
Another says theme Y is good. Another says, "Yes, but the

supréme théme is Zeta." Just the reverse of the stress required in the Yeats line.) In a system where the only absolute value, the ictus, consists only in a relationship, we needlessly pursue a too close inquiry into the precise strength of the stronger point in the relationship. A somewhat more difficult, double, example of the two-weak, two-strong pattern is provided by Marvell.

> To a green thought in a green shade.

One may begin by observing that whatever we do with the two pairs of weak syllables, it remains absolutely certain that "thought" is stronger than "green," and that "shade" is stronger than "green." (The relative strength of the two "greens" produces of course the peculiarity of the logico-rhythmic character of the line—the interaction of its sense with its meter. But here we speak precisely of the meter.) "To a," because of its introductory position, presents no difficulty. "In a" is more curious just because of its medial position. Probably a rather marked caesura, in spite of the continuing syntax and the shortness of the line, is created by the head to back juxtaposition of the two ictuses "thought" and "in." This again is part of the peculiar gravity of the line. The most plausible reading seems to us:

> To a green thought in a green shade.

If anybody wants to read:

> To a green thought in a green shade.

arguing for two anapests compensated for by two single-syllable strong feet, there is probably no triumphant way to refute the reading. Still the lack of pause between "green" and the nouns which follow it is against the single-syllable foot. The single-syllable foot occurs in lines that sound like this: "Weave, weave, the sunlight in your hair."

Some of the most perplexing problems confronting the theorist of English meter—no matter to what school he belongs—are those arising in connection with the "dipody" or double-jump single foot (x x x x). This foot was much used by narrative poets of the late Victorian and Edwardian eras and also, because of its accentual difficulties and ambiguities, has been a favorite ground for exercise in several kinds of temporal scansion. Regular or nearly regular instances of the dipody are perhaps easy enough.

I would I were in Shoreham at the setting of the sun.
A recent handbook remarks very sanely: "Although the meter
is duple insofar as there is an alternation between unaccented
and accented syllables, there is also an alternation in the degree
of stress on the accented syllables . . . the result is that the
two-syllable feet tend to group themselves into larger units"
(Laurence Perrine, *Sound and Sense* [New York, 1956],
p. 160). "You will probably find yourself reading it as a four-
beat line." It is a kind of strong-accent meter, with number
of syllables and minor stresses tightened up into a secondary
pattern. An easy enough substitute for the dipody will be of
course the anapest (x x x́). The iamb also (x x́) is available,
and also the single strong-stress syllable, either at the start
of the line, or just after a medial pause.

Brooding o'er the gloom, spins the brown eve-jar.
Thus dipodic meters can occur where no single line has more
than two dipodies, and many lines have only one, and in these
latter the reader may well have a choice just where to place
the dipody. Meters of this sort are very slippery, elusive. One's
first feeling on reading them may be that a strong lilt or swing
is present, though it is hard to say just how it ought to be defined. A recurrent feature may be that the line seems to start
on a strong stress, with falling meter, but then, with the aid
of the agile dipody, swings up midway into a rising meter to
the finish. The number of syllables in the line will vary greatly,
and the principle of relative stress operates with a vengeance—
the weaker syllable of the dipody showing all sorts of relations
to the stresses of the other feet. It is a tricky, virtuoso meter,
very apt in nursery rhymes and in the rakish, barrack-room,
mad-hatter, pirate-galleon narratives of the era to which we
have alluded above. Meredith's pleasant little monstrosity
"Love in the Valley" is a striking instance of the difficulties.
It seems safe to say that no *great* English poems have been
accomplished in any variant of this meter. The theory of meter
which we are defending is, we believe, better fitted to explain
—and reveal the ambiguities of—the dipodic meter than any
other theory. But the illustration and arguing of the point are
perhaps beyond present requirements.

V

IT IS ONE of the hazards of an argument such as this that it is
often on the verge of slipping from questions about something

that seems to be merely and safely a matter of "fact" to questions about value. It is quite possible that some prosodists of the linguistic and musical schools would grant that meter, as we have described it, is a fact, but in the same breath would put it aside as of little consequence, at least when compared to the strong-stress pattern or some principle of equal timing. This was, for instance, the spirit of D. W. Prall's attack on the traditional metric in his *Aesthetic Analysis* (New York, 1936, esp. pp. 117, 130). Such a metric was trivial, "artificial," misleading. Our own difference from some recent writers may partly be reduced to a difference in emphasis, which reflects a different estimate of significance. We maintain not only that meter, in our sense, does occur, but that it is an important feature of verse.

To make out a broad-scale case for this claim might require much space and effort. Fortunately, we can do perhaps all that is necessary at the moment if we work upon an assumption that is now quite widely entertained, or indeed is a commonplace with students of poetry today: that there are tensions between various poetic elements, among them meter and various aspects of sense, and that these tensions are valuable.

One of the good features of Mr. Chatman's *Kenyon* essay is his constant appeal to an idea of "tension" between the full spoken poem and some kind of metrical pattern. "I believe that the beauty of verse often inheres in the tensions developed between the absolute, abstract metrical pattern and the oral actualization of sequences of English sounds" (p. 436). A student in a seminar presided over by one of the present writers was stumped, however, in scanning a line at the blackboard and refused to put the next stress mark anywhere at all. "I don't see how to show the interaction between the meter and the sense." As if by scanning he *could* show the interaction. As if anybody expected him to. As if the meter itself could be the interaction between itself and something else. This interest in tension, or interaction, is excellent. But how can there be a tension without two things to be in tension?

Wóndring upón this wórd, quáking for dréde.
(Clerk's Tale, 1. 358)

Here is a very special relation of phrase to meter. The double inversion, at the start of the line and again after the caesura, gives the two participial verbs a special quiver. But this depends on the fact that there *is* a meter; the inversions otherwise would not be inversions.

You can write a grammar of the meter. And if you cannot, there is no meter. But you cannot write a grammar of the meter's interaction with the sense, any more than you can write a grammar of the arrangement of metaphors. The interactions and the metaphors are the free and individual and unpredictable (though not irrational) parts of the poetry. You can perceive them, and study them, and talk about them, but not write rules for them. The meter, like the grammar and the vocabulary, is subject to rules. It is just as important to observe what meter a poem is written in (especially if it is written in one of the precise meters of the syllable-stress tradition) as it is to observe what language the poem is written in. Before you recognize the meter, you have only a vague apprehension of the much-prized tensions.

Perhaps it needs to be said that there is a difference between deviations from a meter (or "exceptions," as Mr. Ransom calls them) and the constant strain or tension of a meter (as an abstract norm or expectancy) against the concrete or full reality of the poetic utterance. The deviations are a part of the tension, but only an occasional part. The deviations occur only here and there—though some of them, the inverted first foot, the dropping of the first slack syllable, the extra slack syllable internal to the line (elided, or not elided in the anapest)—occur so often as to assume the character of an accepted complication of the norm. But the tension in the wider sense is always there. Here one might discourse on the "promotion" and "suppression" of syllables to which both the linguists and Arnold Stein refer. These are useful terms. There is no line so regular (so *evenly* alternating weak and strong) that it does not show some tension. It is practically impossible to write an English line that will not in some way buck against the meter. Insofar as the line does approximate the condition of complete submission, it is most likely a tame line, a weak line.

And thus: "scanning" a line is not a dramatic, or poetic, reading of a line. Scanning a line is reading it in a special, more or less forced, way, to bring out the meter *and* any definite deviations or substitutions. Scanning will not bring out the other parts of the tension; it will tend to iron them out. On the other hand, a good dramatic, or poetic, reading will tend to bring out the tensions—but note well that in order to do this it must be careful not to override completely and kill the meter. When that is done, the tensions vanish. (Another reason why the meter must be observed is, of course, that if a line is truly metrical, a reading which actually destroys the meter can only be an incorrect reading—by dictionary and rhetorical standards.) A good dramatic reading is a much more delicate, difficult, and rewarding performance than a mere scanning. Yet the scanning has its justification, its use. We would argue that a good dramatic reading is possible only by a person who can also perform a scansion.

"The trouble with conventional metrics," complains Mr. Chatman, "is that because it cannot distinguish between levels of stress and intonation, it often cannot distinguish meaningful from trivial performances" (p. 436). The answer is that metric is not required to do this, though it is needed for it. Mr. Chatman or another reader will have to make his own reading as meaningful as possible, but he will be in a better position to do this if he recognizes the meter. We are speaking all along, if not about a sufficient, yet about a necessary, rule for poetic reading.

If we may insert a brief pedagogic excursus: Schoolteachers nowadays, beginning in grade school and going right up into graduate school, probably try much too hard to prevent their students from a "mechanical" or thumped-out scansion, telling them rather to observe the variations, the tensions—telling them in effect to promote all tensions as much as possible. But the fact is that the tensions and the variations will pretty much take care of themselves if the student lives long enough and provided he is equipped with just one principle (of no precise application) that the variations and tensions are there and ought somehow to be recognized. The variations and tensions tend to assert themselves. The meter, because it is artificial, precisely measured, frail if meticulous, tends to be overridden and, if not actually destroyed (as it cannot be in any correct reading), at least obscured. This you can see if you ask college freshmen to scan a passage of Milton or to write fifteen lines in imitation. The probability is that the student of average gifts, if he has never at any stage of his schoolroom education been required or allowed to whang out the meter, is not aware that it is there and hence has very little notion of what the teacher means by the tensions.

For the word "tension," let us substitute at this point, in a concluding suggestion, the word "interplay"—meaning the interplay of syllable-stress meter with various other features of linguistic organization, but especially with those which are likely to set up other quasi-metric or rhythmic patterns. One of the disadvantages of the old strong-stress meter is doubtless its limited capacity for interplay. The stress pattern of the meter is so nearly the same as the stress pattern of the syntax and logic that there is nothing much for the meter to interplay with. The same must be true for all meters depending on patterns of repeated or parallel syntax—such as the center of the Hebrew Psalms and the free verse of Walt Whitman. Where such meters gain in freedom and direct speech-feeling, they lose in opportunity for precise interplay. Conversely, where syllable-stress meters lose in freedom and naturalness of speech-feeling, they gain in the possibility of precise interplay. Perhaps this suggests a reason why the greatest English poetry (Chaucer, Shakespeare, Milton, Pope, Wordsworth) has after all been written in the more artful syllable-stress meter—not in the older, simpler, more directly natural strong-stress meter.

It is no doubt possible to think of many kinds of interplay, with many resulting kinds of total poetic feel. Maybe some of the languor and soft drag of Tennyson's verse, for instance, comes sometimes from the interplay between the rising iambic motion of the line and the falling trochaic character of a series of important words.

> It little profits that an idle king . . .

> To follow knowledge, like a sinking star . . .

Again, and very frequently in English verse of the tradition, the special rhythmic effects arise from the fact that the stress pattern of the iambics either more or less coincides with or more or less fails to coincide with the pattern of the stronger logical stresses, thus producing a movement either slow or fast, heavy or light.

That, like a wounded snake, drágs its slów leńgth alóng . . .

Flies o'er th'unbending corn, and skíms alóng the máin.

The same kind of thing combines further with the number and length of the words involved in a line to produce contours of tension so special as perhaps better not translated into any other kind of meaning but simply regarded as shapes of energy. The 10,565 lines of Milton's *Paradise Lost*, all but two or three of them iambic pentameter lines, abound in illustrations of Milton's virtuosity. To show two extremes in one respect, recall a line we have already quoted and set beside it another.

Rocks, caves, lakes, fens, bogs, dens, and shades of death . . .

Immutable, immortal, infinite . . .

Eight strong stresses in one line; three in the other. But five *metric* stresses in either. And if that were not so, there would be nothing at all remarkable about the difference between eight and three.

It is, finally, possible, as we have already observed, that a given line in a given poet may invite scanning in either the older strong-stress way or in the Chaucer-Tennyson syllable-stress way—four beats by the old, five beats by the new. If a poem written on the whole in syllable-counting pentameters happens to show here and there lines which have one somewhat lighter stress and hence four stronger stresses, this is not very remarkable. For in the nature of things, as we have already observed, five stresses will always include one weakest. We have already sufficiently illustrated this phenomenon. But if a poem written on the whole in a meter of four strong stresses, with indeterminate number of syllables, at some point tightens up, counts syllables, and tilts minor accents into an iambic pentameter, this is something else. A wise and shifty modern poet, always in search of rhythmical invention, writes a stanza containing in the middle such a line as:

> Her hair over her arms and her arms full of flowers,

and at the end:

> Sometimes these cogitations still amaze
> The troubled midnight and the noon's repose.

This is playing in and out of the metrical inheritance. Part V of *The Waste Land* begins:

> After the torchlight red on sweaty faces
> After the frosty silence in the gardens
> After the agony in stony places . . .

Coming after four parts of a poem written largely in strong-stress meter, these lines, with their marked swinging parallel of construction, will most likely be read at a fast walk as strong-stress meter, four stresses to the first, three each to the second and the third. But each is also a perfectly accurate pentameter line, each complicated in the same two traditional ways, the inverted beginning and the hypermetric ending. ("Whether 'tis nobler in the mind to suffer . . .")

It is probably not until about the time of Mr. Eliot and his friends that the free and subtle moving in and out and coalescing of strong-stress and syllable-stress meters in the same poem, the same stanza, begins to appear with any frequency. This is something remarkable in the history of metrics. But the understanding of it depends precisely upon the recognition of the few homely and sound, traditional and objective, principles of prosody upon which we have been insisting throughout this essay. Without recognition of the two distinct principles of strong-stress and of syllable-stress meter, it seems doubtful if anything at all precise or technical can be said about Mr. Eliot's peculiar rhythms and tensions.

NORTHROP FRYE

The Rhythm Of Recurrence: Epos

[Frye "scans" his verse musically. He is careful, however, to select verse showing unmistakable musical influence. The distinction emerging from his discussion is an important one: the four-stress, or strong-stress, line has the closest affinity with musical structure. Love in the Valley moves to a two-beat musical bar; doubtless Meredith had a two-beat "tune in his head" when he composed his melodic lines.

[Frye perhaps underrates traditional syllable-stress metric; he does acknowledge that ". . . iambic pentameter provides a field of syncopation in which stress and metre can to some extent neutralize one another." Historically, English verse began in the four-stress line, moved away from it during the Renaissance; and has, with the meters of Hopkins and Eliot, returned to it in modern times.

[Melos, Frye tells us, is "musical poetry, that is, poetry which resembles in its structure the music contemporary with it." When Eliot wrote Sweeney Agonistes he had been listening to Stravinsky's Rite of Spring and the rhythms of jazz:

> Let Mr. Sweeney continue his story.
> I assure you, Sir, we are very interested.
>
> I knew a man once did a girl in. . .

A four-beat line (in common time) marked by heavy cross-rhythms reveals a clear modern instance of Frye's melos.]

The regular pulsating metre that traditionally distinguishes verse from prose tends to become the organizing rhythm in epos or extended oratorical forms. Metre is an aspect of recurrence, and the two words for recurrence, rhythm and pattern, show that recurrence is a structural principle of all art, whether temporal or spatial in its primary impact. Besides metre itself, quantity and accent (or stress) are elements in poetic recurrence, though quantity is not an element of regular recurrence in modern English, except in experiments in which the poet has to make up his own rules as he goes along. The relation of accent or stress to metre needs, perhaps, a different kind of explanation from what is usually given it.

A four-stress line seems to be inherent in the structure of the English language. It is the prevailing rhythm of the earlier poetry, though it changes its scheme from alliteration to rhyme in Middle English; it is the common rhythm of popular poetry in all periods, of ballads and of most nursery rhymes. In the ballad, the eight-six-eight-six quatrain is a continuous four beat line, with a "rest" at the end of every other line. This principle of the rest, or a beat coming at a point of actual silence, was already established in Old English. The iambic pentameter provides a field of syncopation in which stress and metre can to some extent neutralize one another. If we read many iambic pentameters "naturally," giving the important words the heavy accent that they do have in spoken English, the old four-stress line stands out in clear relief against its metrical background. Thus:

> To bé, or nót to be: thát is the quéstion.
> Whéther 'tis nóbler in the mínd to súffer
> The slíngs and árrows of outrágeous fórtune,
> Or táke up árms against a séa of tróubles . . .
>
> Of mán's fírst disobédience, and the frúit
> Of that forbídden trée, whose mórtal táste
> Brought déath into the wórld and áll our wóe,
> With lóss of Éden, till one gréater Mán
> Restóre us, and regáin the blíssful séat . . .

The stopped couplet of Dryden and Pope, as we should expect, has a higher percentage of five-stress lines, but any rhythmical license such as a feminine caesura is likely to bring back the old beat:

Forgét their hátred, and consént to féar.   (Waller)

Nor héll a fúry, like a wóman scórn'd.   (Congreve)

A líttle leárning is a dángerous thíng.   (Pope)

Any period of metrical uncertainty or transition will illustrate the native strength of the four-stress line. After the death of Chaucer and the change from middle to modern English, we find ourselves in the strange metrical world of Lydgate, in which we are strongly tempted to apply to Lydgate himself what the Minstrel says to Death in the *Danse Macabre*:

This newe daunce / is to me so straunge
Wonder dyverse / and passyngli contrarie
The dredful fotynge / doth so ofte chaunge
And the mesures / so ofte sithes varie.

But there is a dance there all the same: let us look at the preceding stanza, Death's speech to the Minstrel:

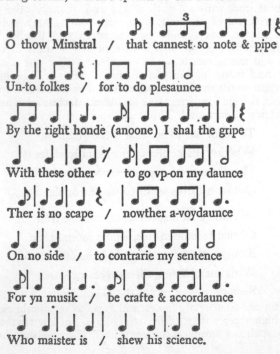

O thow Minstral / that cannest so note & pipe

Un-to folkes / for to do plesaunce

By the right honde (anoone) I shal the gripe

With these other / to go vp-on my daunce

Ther is no scape / nowther a-voydaunce

On no side / to contrarie my sentence

For yn musik / be crafte & accordaunce

Who maister is / shew his science.

This stanza will give us a bad time if we try to analyze it as a pentameter stanza of Chaucer's *ABC* type: the last line, for instance, is not a pentameter at all. Read as a continuous four-beat line, it is fairly simple; and such a reading will bring out what the prosodic analysis could never do, the grotesque, leaping-skeleton lilt of the voice of Death ending in the measured irony of the last line. I do not claim to know the details of Lydgate's prosody, what e's he might have preferred to pronounce or elide or what foreign words he might have accented differently. It is possible that neither Lydgate nor the fifteenth-century reader was entirely clear on all such points either; but a line with four main stresses and a variable number of syllables between the stresses is the obvious device for getting over such problems, as a good deal can be left to the individual reader's choice. In any case I am not indicating how the passage is to be read so much as how it may most easily be scanned: as with metrical scansion, every reader will make his own modification of the pattern.

The "Skeltonic" line is also usually a four-beat line: the spirited prelude to *Philip Sparowe* is a quick-march rhythm,

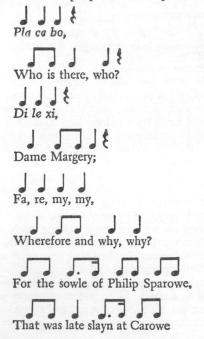

Pla ca bo,

Who is there, who?

Di le xi,

Dame Margery;

Fa, re, my, my,

Wherefore and why, why?

For the sowle of Philip Sparowe,

That was late slayn at Carowe

with more rests and more accented beats coming close together than we found in Lydgate.

In short, the "new principle" on which Coleridge constructed *Christabel* was about as new as principles usually are in literature. It is clear too that the Finnish inspiration of *Hiawatha* was no more fundamentally exotic than such inspirations usually are. *Hiawatha* fits the four-stress pattern of English very snugly, which explains perhaps why it is one of the easiest poems in the language to parody. Meredith's *Love in the Valley*, also, is most easily scanned as a four-stress line very similar in its rhythmical make-up to Lydgate's:

Under yonder beech-tree single on the green-sward

Couched with her arms behind her golden head,

Knees and tresses folded to slip and ripple idly,

Lies my young love sleeping in the shade.

These examples have, perhaps, begun to illustrate already something of what the word "musical," Aristotle's *melos*, really means as a term in modern literary criticism. In the music contemporary with English poetry since Lydgate's time, we have had almost uniformly a stress accent, the stresses marking rhythmical units (measures) within which a variable number of notes is permitted. When in poetry we have a predominating stress accent and a variable number of syllables between two stresses (usually four stresses to a line, corresponding to "common time" in music), we have musical poetry, that is, poetry which resembles in its structure the music contemporary with it. We are speaking now of *epos* or extended poetry in a continuous metre: the music most closely analogous to such poetry is music in its more extended instrumental forms, in which the organizing rhythm has descended more directly from dance than from song.

This technical use of the word musical is very different from the sentimental fashion of calling any poetry musical if it sounds nice. In practice the technical and the sentimental uses are often directly opposed, as the sentimental term would be applied to, for example, Tennyson, and withdrawn from, for example, Browning. Yet if we ask the external but relevant question: Which of these two poets knew more about music, and was a priori more likely to be influenced by it? the answer is certainly not Tennyson. Here is a passage from Tennyson's *Oenone*:

> O mother Ida, many-fountain'd Ida,
> Dear mother Ida, harken ere I die.
> I waited underneath the dawning hills,
> Aloft the mountain lawn was dewy-dark,
> And dewy dark aloft the mountain pine:
> Beautiful Paris, evil-hearted Paris,
> Leading a jet-black goat white-horn'd, white-hooved,
> Came up from reedy Simois all alone.

And here is a passage from Browning's *The Flight of the Duchess*:

> I could favour you with sundry touches
> Of the paint-smutches with which the Duchess
> Heightened the mellowness of her cheek's yellowness
> (To get on faster) until at last her
> Cheek grew to be one master-plaster
> Of mucus and fucus from mere use of ceruse:
> In short, she grew from scalp to udder
> Just the object to make you shudder.

In the Browning passage speed is a positive factor: one has the sense of a metronome beat. Tennyson has tried to minimize the sense of movement; his passage should be read slowly and with much dwelling on the vowels. Both passages repeat sounds obtrusively, but the repetitions in Tennyson are there to slow down the advance of ideas, to compel the rhythm to return on itself, and to elaborate what is essentially a pattern of sound. In Browning the rhymes sharpen the accentuation of the beat and help to build up a cumulative rhythm. The speed and the sharp accent in Browning's poetry are musical features in it, and it is difficult to see what the words in parentheses can be except a musical direction, an English translation of *più mosso*.

Such phrases as "smooth musical flow" or "harsh unmusical diction" belong to the sentimental use of the word musical, and are perhaps derived from the fact that the word "harmony" in ordinary English, apart from music, means a stable and permanent relationship. In this figurative sense of the word harmony, music is not a sequence of harmonies at all, but a sequence of discords ending in a harmony, the only stable and permanent "harmony" in music being the final resolving tonic chord. It is more likely to be the harsh, rugged, dissonant poem (assuming of course some technical competence in the poet) that will show in poetry the tension and the driving accented impetus of music. When we find a careful balancing of vowels and consonants and a dreamy sensuous flow of sound, we are probably dealing with an unmusical poet. Pope, Keats, and Tennyson are all unmusical. This term, I need hardly observe, is not pejorative: *The Rape of the Lock* is unmusical, just as it is a bad example of blank verse, because it is something else altogether. When we find sharp barking accents, crabbed and obscure language, mouthfuls of consonants, and long lumbering polysyllables, we are probably dealing with *melos*, or poetry which shows an analogy to music, if not an actual influence from it.

The musical diction is better fitted for the grotesque and horrible, or for invective and abuse. It is congenial to a gnarled intellectualism of the so-called "metaphysical" type. It is irregular in metre (because of the syncopation against stress), leans heavily on enjambement, and employs a long cumulative rhythm sweeping the lines up into larger rhythmical units such as the paragraph. The fact that Shakespeare shows an increasing use of *melos* as he goes on is the principle employed for dating his plays on internal evidence. When Milton says that rhymed heroic verse is "of no true musical delight," because musical poetry must have "the sense variously drawn out from one verse into another," he is using the word musical in its technical sense. When Samuel Johnson speaks of "the old manner of continuing the sense ungracefully from verse to verse," he is speaking from his own consistently anti-musical point of view. *The Heretic's Tragedy* is a musical poem; *Thyrsis* is not. *The Jolly Beggars* is; the *Ode on a Grecian Urn* is not. Pope's *Messiah* is not musical, but Smart's *Song to David*, with its pounding thematic words and the fortissimo explosion of its coda, is a musical *tour de force*. Crashaw's hymns and Cowley's Pindarics are musical, with their fluent, variable, prevailingly four-stress lines and their relentless pushing enjambement; Herbert's stanzaic poems and Gray's Pindarics are not. Skelton, Wyatt, and Dunbar are musical; Gavin Douglas and Surrey are not. Alliterative verse is usually accentual and musical; elaborate stanza forms usually are not. The use of *melos* in poetry does not, of course, necessarily imply any technical knowledge of music on the part of the poet, but it often goes with it. Such a technically musical poem as Crashaw's *Musicks Duell* (a Baroque aria with instrumental accompaniment) is an example.

And occasionally it is at least conceivable that some exposure to music would have guided a tendency to *melos* in verse. One feels that Southey, for instance, never quite clarified his remarkable experiments in *epos* rhythm: if so, it may be instructive to set beside Milton's incisive list of the musical qualities of poetry the stammer and mumble of the preface to *Thalaba*: "I do not wish the *improvisatorè* tune;—but something that denotes the sense of harmony, something like the accent of feeling,—like the tone which every poet necessarily gives to poetry." The conception of *melos*, too, may throw more light on what Wordsworth was trying to do in *Peter Bell* and *The Idiot Boy*. Wordsworth's remarks about metre as the source of excitement in verse apply more particularly to accent, in which the physical pulsation of the dance is present. What metre in itself gives is rather the pleasure of seeing a relatively predictable pattern filling up with the inevitably felicitous words. Pope's "What oft was thought, but ne'er so well expressed" is a metrical conception: as we listen to his couplets, we have a sense of fulfilled expectation which is the opposite of obviousness. The greater violence in the imagery of Donne's satires is appropriate to the greater energy of a more accentually-conceived rhythm.

If we turn to the contrasting group of what we have called the unmusical poets, Spenser, Pope, Keats, Tennyson, we find slower and more resonant rhythms. Four-stress lines are much rarer in *The Faerie Queene* than in *Paradise Lost*, and the opposite tendency is marked by the recurrent Alexandrine. The practice of this group of poets is finely expressed by Johnson in his anti-musical dictum: "The musick of the English heroic line strikes the ear so faintly that it is easily lost, unless all the syllables of every line co-operate together; this co-operation can be obtained only by the preservation of every verse unmingled with another, as a distinct system of sounds." The implication is that as the only musical elements in poetry that Johnson is considering have been lost for good with the loss of pitch accent and quantity, English poetry should think in terms of sound-pattern rather than cumulative rhythm.

The relations between poetry and the visual arts are perhaps more far-fetched than those between poetry and music. Unmusical poets are often "pictorial" in a general sense: they frequently use their more meditative rhythms to build up, detail by detail, a static picture, as in the careful description of the nude Venus in *Oenone* or in the elaborate tapestry-like pageants in *The Faerie Queene*. Where we do have something really analogous to *opsis*, however, is in the rhetorical device known as imitative harmony or onomatopoeia, as described and exemplified by Pope in the *Essay on Criticism*:

'Tis not enough no harshness gives offence,
The sound must seem an echo to the sense . . .
When Ajax strives some rock's vast weight to throw,
The line too labours, and the words move slow;
Not so, when swift Camilla scours the plain,
Flies o'er th' unbending corn, and skims along the main.

This device is easy to recognize, and has been remarked on ever since Aristotle, in his treatise on rhetoric, illustrated in Homer's line about the stone of Sisyphus the sound of a large stone rolling downhill:

αὖτις ἔπειτα πέδονδε κυλίνδετο λᾶας ἀναιδής

Pope's translation renders this line "Thunders impetuous down, and smoaks along the ground," and won for once the approval of Johnson, Johnson being in general very doubtful about imitative harmony. He ridicules it in one of the *Idler* papers in the figure of Dick Minim the critic, who points out that the words bubble and trouble cause "a momentary inflation of the cheeks by the retention of the breath, which is afterwards forcibly emitted, as in the practice of blowing bubbles." All that the ridicule really illustrates, however, is that onomatopoeia is a linguistic as well as a poetic tendency, and that the poet takes advantage of whatever his language offers as a matter of course. The English language has many excellent sound-effects, though it has lost a few: in Old English *The Wanderer* can express cold weather as a modern poem cannot:

Hreosan hrim ond snaw   hagle gemenged

But because such devices are linguistic as well as literary, they are continually being re-created in colloquial speech. Colloquial speech, when good, is frequently called "picturesque" or "colorful," both words being pictorial metaphors. The narrative passages of *Huckleberry Finn* have an imitative flexibility about them that the narrative passages of *Tom Sawyer*, for instance, hardly attain to:

. . . Then there was a racket of ripping and tearing and smashing, and down she goes, and the front wall of the crowd begins to roll in like a wave.

The most remarkably sustained mastery of verbal *opsis* in English, perhaps, is exhibited in *The Faerie Queene*, which we have to read with a special kind of attention, an ability to catch visualization through sound. Thus in

> The Eugh obedient to the bender's will,

the line has a number of weak syllables in the middle that makes it sag out in a bow shape. When Una goes astray the rhythm goes astray with her:

> And Una wandring farre in woods and forrests . . .

Part of the effect of this line is due to the weak rhyme of "forrests" against "guests." When the subject is wreckage, the rhythm is wrecked with the same kind of disappointment-rhyme:

> For else my feeble vessell crazd, and crackt
> Through thy strong buffets and outrageous blowes,
> Cannot endure, but needs it must be wrackt
> On the rough rocks, or on the sandy shallowes.

When Florimell finds her way difficult to scan, so does the reader:

> Through the tops of the high trees she did descry . . .

When the subject is harmony in music, we have an identical rhyme on one of the few appropriate words in the language:

> To th' instruments diuine respondence meet:
> The siluer sounding instruments did meet . . .

When the subject is a "perillous Bridge," we have:

> Streight was the passage like a ploughed ridge,
> That if two met, the one mote needes fall ouer the lidge.

Renaissance readers had been put on the alert for such effects by their school training in rhetoric: a harmless looking line from Spenser's *January*, for instance, is promptly sandbagged by E. K. as "a prety Epanorthosis . . . and withall a Paronomasia." The source of Pope's passage quoted above is Vida's *Art of Poetry*, which is earlier than Spenser. After Spenser the poet who showed the most consistent—or persistent—interest in imitative harmony was Cowley, who uses it so freely in *Davideis* as to draw a hoarse growl from Johnson that he saw no reason why a pine tree should be taller in Alexandrines than in pentameters. Some of Cowley's effects however are interesting enough, such as his use of the oracular hemistich. Here, for instance, three feet of a pentameter line are assigned to silent contemplation:

> O who shall tell, who shall describe thy Throne,
> Thou great Three-One?

The first line in the passage quoted from Pope (" 'Tis not enough no harshness gives offence") implies that a sharp discord or apparent bungle in the writing may often be interpreted as imitative decorum. Pope uses such intentional discords in the same poem when he gives horrible examples of practices he disapproves of, and Addison's discussion of the passage in *Spectator* 253 shows how lively an interest such devices still aroused. Here, for example, is the way that Pope describes constipated genius:

> And strains, from hard-bound brains, eight lines a year.

Spenser, naturally, employs the same device constantly. A tasteless misuse of alliteration marks a speaker (Braggadocchio) as a liar and hypocrite:

> But minds of mortall men are muchell mard,
> And mou'd amisse with massie mucks vnmeet regard.

and when the false Duessa tempts St. George, the grammar, rhythm, and assonance could hardly be worse: the worthy knight's ear should have warned him that all was not well:

> Yet thus perforce he bids me do, or die.
> Die is my dew; yet rew my wretched state
> You . . .

Certain imitative devices become standardized in every language, and most of them in English are too familiar to need recapitulation here: beheaded lines increase speed, trochaic rhythms suggest falling movement, and so on. The native stock of English words consists largely of monosyllables, and a monosyllable always demands a separate accent, however slight. Hence long Latin words, if skilfully used, have the rhythmical function of lightening the metre, in contrast to the sodden unrhythmical roar that results "When ten low words oft creep in one dull line." A by-product of this latter phenomenon in English is more useful: the so-called broken-backed line with a spondee in the middle has since Old English times (when it was Sievers' type C) been most effective for suggesting the ominous and foreboding:

Thy wishes then dare not be told.   (Wyatt)

Depending from on high, dreadful to sight.   (Spenser)

Which tasted works knowledge of good and evil.   (Milton)

Imitative harmony may of course be employed occasionally in any form of writing, but as a continuous effect it seems to adhere most naturally to epos in verse, where it takes the form of variants from a sustained normal pattern. Dramatists and prose writers use it very sparingly: in Shakespeare it occurs only for some definite reason, as when Lear calls to the storm on the heath in the accents of the storm itself. In lyrics its introduction has the effect of a *tour de force* which absorbs most of the interest and turns the poem into an epigram. An example is the brilliant little fourteenth-century poem *The Blacksmiths*, which uses the alliterative line to represent hammering:

> Swarte smekyd smethes smateryd wyth smoke
> Dryue me to deth wyth den of here dyntes . . .

Recurrently in the history of rhetoric some theory of a "natural" relation between sound and sense turns up. It is unlikely that there is any such natural relation, but that there is an onomatopoeic element in language which is developed and exploited by the poet is obvious enough. It is simpler to think rather of imitative harmony as a special application of a rhetorical feature which is analogous to Classical quantity, but would be better described as "quality": the patterns of assonance made by vowels and consonants. It is not difficult to distinguish epos with a continuous "quality" or sound-pattern, such as *Hyperion*, from the epos of, say, *Red Cotton Nightcap Country*, where the sound exists primarily for the sake of the sense, and is consequently felt to be closer to prose. We have an indication that there is no consistent sound-pattern when there are two equally satisfactory versions of the same poem differing in texture, as in the Prologue to Chaucer's *Legend of Good Women*.

The main reason for the confused use of the term musical in literary criticism is that when critics think of music in poetry, they seldom think of the actual music contemporary with the poetry they are discussing, with its stress accent and dance rhythm, but of the (very largely unknown) structure of Classical music, which was presumably closer to song and to pitch accent. We have stressed imitative harmony because it illustrates the principle that while in Classical poetry sound-pattern or quantity, being an element of recurrence, is part of the *melos* of the poetry, it is part of the *opsis* in ours.

RONALD SUTHERLAND

Structural Linguistics and English Prosody

[This essay makes modest claims for linguistic science and its ability to aid the prosodist. Certainly if we understand prosody to include more than the mechanical scansion of verse, then the terminology and the descriptive finesse Sutherland employs can be of value. Unfortunately, Sutherland's readings are offered as improvements or expansions on those of Brooks and Warren. Traditional graphic prosody can be handled with more sensitivity than Brooks and Warren show: thus Sutherland's readings lose some of their novelty and added attraction.

[The line from Yeats is the case in point. Brooks and Warren scan it:

$$\text{Spéech} \mid \text{ăf těr lóng} \mid \text{sĭ léncĕ;} \mid \text{ĭt} \mid \text{ĭs ríght} \ldots$$

They find in one line an anapest, a trochee, two monosyllabic feet, and one iamb. Such a mixture could only produce prose. But the line has a rhythm which is that of verse, not that of prose; its scansion, to my ears, reads more nearly:

$$\text{Spéech ăf} \mid \text{těr lóng} \mid \text{sĭ} \mid \text{léncĕ; ĭt} \mid \text{ĭs ríght} \ldots$$

"Springing," by the anomalous third foot, gives this line its particular rhythmic character. Tension builds up to the monosyllabic foot, then is resolved by the normally iambic fourth and fifth feet. The initial trochee hardly counts as a variation; it is so usual a feature of the iambic line as to count as a convention.

Reprinted from College English, XX, 1 (October 1958). Used by permission of the author.

[My quarrel with Brooks and Warren is more than a quibble or a "subjective" difference in hearing. Unless Yeats' line can be understood and read in its proper metrical context, its rhythmical form remains unrealized. The reading suggested by Brooks and Warren turns a line of sinuous rhythmical power into nerveless prose. Unless the line retains some usual features of iambic form, there can be no tension, no "springing." In music we have no syncopation unless there is an established pulse against which syncopation is possible. In verse we cannot have expressive variation unless a clear metrical pattern already exists.]

IT SEEMS likely that future generations will look upon the present age as one which witnessed not only the birth of the guided missile, but also the death of the misguided grammarian. The science of linguistics has completely revamped our notions of the English language. Former grammarians, who attempted to ram this language into the alien patterns of Latin and Greek, were in error; for it has been proven that English has a structure uniquely its own, requiring unique grammatical description. But what of the field of literary criticism? Can the findings of linguistic scientists affect that field in any way? To date, although many suggestions have been made, a conclusive answer has not been supplied.

Various theorists, including John C. McGalliard, have generalized on the matter, lamenting that structural linguists tend to be cultural philistines and calling for a liaison between them and the literary critics.[1] René Wellek and Austin Warren, however, attempted to pinpoint the situation and made the following prophetic statement: "Phonemics seems indispensable for comparative metrics and a proper analysis of sound patterns."[2] The purpose of this inquiry will be to ascertain exactly what the science of linguistics can contribute to English prosody.

In the Summer 1956 Kenyon Review, a series of papers dealt with this very subject. Harold Whitehall and Seymour Chatman, both structural linguists, argued for linguistic-based metrical analysis, while John Crowe Ransom and Arnold Stein

[1] Norman Foerster, et al., Literary Scholarship, Its Aims and Methods (1941), p. 35.
[2] René Wellek and Austin Warren, Theory of Literature (1949), p. 179.

supported conventional prosody. Although several important ideas were forwarded, after digesting all these papers one concluded that the linguists were taking a wrong approach. Of course their system permits highly accurate representation of any particular recitation, but the purpose of metrical analysis, most critics will agree, is not to discover the idiosyncrasies of particular readings of a poem, but to examine in broad terms how the meaning and effect of a poem are reinforced. In other words, the ideal is to get as far away as possible from the relative and as near as possible to the standard; structural linguistics, it would seem, can only reverse this process. Moreover, in the eyes of many literary men, that science encourages the cardinal sin of separating words from meaning.

Accordingly, if the science of linguistics is going to bestow anything on English prosody, a new approach is needed. In Brooks and Warren's *Understanding Poetry*, which has become a sort of bible in many of our schools, one finds:

> This is not to say that any system of indicating scansion, certainly not the rather rudimentary system suggested in this book, will render the enormous subtlety, the complication and shading, of rhythm and texture in language when it is well used. We must depend upon the tact and discrimination of our ear to do that. But the use of a system will help us. It will give us a sort of standard, however crude, to which we can refer the actual language. And it is to the actual language that we always want to come back. That is where poetry exists.[3]

Now the "rather rudimentary" system employed by Brooks and Warren probably represents the peak of development in conventional metrics. Although it is unlikely and unnecessary that any system "render the enormous subtlety, the complication and shading, of rhythm and texture in language"— and we have already observed that such a system could never be universally meaningful—there is every probability that the present system can be relieved of some of its crudity to become a more polished "sort of standard." If this can be done, then the most salient key to its accomplishment is Whitehall's suggestion in the *Kenyon Review* that linguistics information about pitch and juncture should be part of the prosodist's equipment. To substantiate this point, I shall examine closely one of the most complete and rewarding analyses in *Under-*

---

[3] Cleanth Brooks and Robert Penn Warren, *Understanding Poetry* (1950), pp. 124-125.

standing Poetry. But first, a brief statement of the pertinent linguistics information must be made.[4]

There are four degrees of stress: primary ($/$), secondary ($\wedge$), tertiary ($\setminus$), and weak ($\smile$). Corresponding to these are four pitches: low (1), mid (2), high (3), and extra high (4). Since hardly anything, and especially not poetry, is spoken in a level monotone, the voice goes higher and lower in the course of an utterance, and this is known as change in pitch. When a person speaks more loudly than normally, the greater amount of air employed causes an increase in the vibrations of the vocal apparatus, often resulting in a rise of pitch; although loudness can also be combined with low pitch, as in the case of bass drums and bassoons. Also, when a person puts emphasis on a certain word, it is usually by means of a correlative increase in stress and pitch; for assisted by junctures these two factors condition every word, producing, as Whitehall so aptly puts it, chords rather than notes—the essence of what has been known to many men as "verbal music." Closely connected with the idea of pitch are the differing junctures between words and syllables. In the normal flow of a phrase, the various sounds run into one another; yet there is something between most words which allows us to distinguish them as separate. This slight pause, as it were, is called the "transitional juncture" ($+$). But there are three other junctures indicating greater divisions. The end of a statement is usually accompanied by a lowering of pitch and a fading of the voice into silence, and the resulting hiatus is described as a "fading juncture" ($\searrow$). To the conventional prosodists, this type of juncture is known as the "caesura"; without being able to explain why, the conventional prosodists also know that such a juncture causes unusual emphasis to be placed on the initial following syllable, and their knowledge is happily corroborated by linguistics' research. Since the voice fades into silence, the next sound to be heard is a fresh mark on a clean slate, like the first note of a solo violinist after the orchestra has hushed. When, as in the case of a good many questions, a group of words ends with a rise in pitch, we have a "rising juncture" ($\nearrow$). This type of pause ordinarily creates an expectancy of more to come; its precise explanation in

---

[4] With certain modifications, this information is based upon H. A. Gleason's *An Introduction to Descriptive Linguistics* (1955). Mr. Gleason lists three clause terminals ($\rightarrow \nearrow \rightarrow$) and one open transition ($+$); these are all called junctures above.

terms of linguistics' data clarifies the prosodist's general notion of "secondary pauses." Sometimes the gap between two units of language is characterized by a sustention of pitch, like a taut clothesline between two poles, causing the syllable before the gap to be "prolongated." Most noticeable when the pitch is high, this type of pause is known as the "sustentional juncture" ($\rightarrow$).

With the above information in mind, we shall now turn to the analysis of William Butler Yeats's "After Long Silence" in *Understanding Poetry* (pp. 116-121). The poem:

> Speech after long silence; it is right,
> All other lovers being estranged or dead,
> Unfriendly lamplight hid under its shade,
> The curtains drawn upon unfriendly night,
> That we descant and yet again descant
> Upon the supreme theme or Art and Song:
> Bodily decrepitude is wisdom; young
> We loved each other and were ignorant.

Now the first line of this poem is scanned by Brooks and Warren as follows:

$$\wedge \text{Speech} \mid \text{after long} \mid \text{silence;} \mid \text{it} \mid \text{is right,}$$

With the information we have acquired above, we might modify this scansion to:[5]

$$\wedge {}^2\text{Speech} + \text{after} + \text{long} {}^2 \nearrow {}^3\text{silence;}^1 \searrow {}^2\text{it} + \text{is} + \text{right,}^3 \nearrow$$

Brooks and Warren go on to say that "the fact that the reader must hurry over the two unaccented syllables of *after* before he can rest on the accent of *long* makes the emphasis on *long* greater than it would otherwise be; and this heavy emphasis on *long* fortifies the meaning of the word." To this we can add that the rising juncture after *long*, causing the sound volume of that word to be sustained as the pitch rises, is another reason for the emphasis. The study continues: "This emphasis is further increased by the fact that the accented syllable *si*—of the trochaic foot *silence* follows the accented *long* without an intervening unaccented syllable. But when two accented syllables are thrust together in this way, the reader is

[5] Only changes in pitch and the pitches before and after a juncture need be marked. Tertiary and secondary stresses are indicated here as a means of suggesting slightly less than a primary stress and slightly more than a weak. Since this is a more or less subjective distinction, there is no interference with the conventional notions of feet and meter.

forced to take a slight pause between them. The effect of such a condition is to increase the emphasis on the accented syllables, because the reader has lingered at that point in the verse." The "slight pause," of course, is a rising juncture; and since the stressed initial syllable *si* has a pitch of (3), we can explain further that the increased emphasis upon it is due to a harmonic of stress and pitch.

Brooks and Warren go on to say that "The heavy pause after *silence* (a pause dictated by rhetorical construction) gives the effect of the speaker's meditating a moment . . . . The word *it* receives, by reason of the weak syllable (the second syllable of *silence*) and the pause which precede it, more than its ordinary emphasis. This emphasis, again, is dramatically right . . . ." In other words, *silence* is followed by silence; the "heavy pause" is a fading juncture, giving the word *it* all the emphatic quality of an initial note which breaks a silence.

". . . For the word *it*, usually a fairly unimportant word and lightly stressed, in this context is important. When the word occurs we do not yet know what the *it* refers to; and what it does refer to—what the speaker says is 'right'—constitutes the basic statement of the poem. Explaining the *it* gives us the body of the poem." Furthermore, the word-group *it is right* ends with a rising juncture, instilling, as is usually the case with such junctures, a sense of expectancy concordant with the dramatic pattern of the poem.[6]

Of the second line in the poem, not much needs to be said. Brooks and Warren point out the emphasis on *estranged*; we might add that the line ends with a fading juncture, which observation will be of some use later.

The conventional and modified scansions of the third line are as follows:

$$\text{Un}\overset{\smile}{\text{friend}}|\overset{\smile}{\text{ly}}\ \text{lamp}|\text{light}\ \text{hid}|\overset{\smile}{\text{under}}|\overset{\smile}{\text{its}}\ \text{shade},$$

$$^2\text{Unfriendly}+\text{lamp}+\text{light}^3{\rightarrow}^3\text{hid}+\text{under}+\text{its}+\text{shade},^1\searrow$$

"The third line," reads the analysis, "offers two slight variations from the norm. There is a strong *secondary accent* on the syllable *-light*, for in the compound word *lamplight*, as is

[6] It is interesting to note that in Paul Robert's *Understanding Grammar* (1954), p. 251, the word *it* as used in this poem is classified as "Situation It." Mr. Roberts, who based much of his work on linguistics research, points out that "When we use this *it*, we withhold for a moment the name and nature of the substantive we want to mention; consequently we introduce a bit of suspense and make the substantive more emphatic when it comes."

true of most such compounds (*midnight, bookcase*), there is a marked secondary accent . . . . The result is to give the accent in the foot *-light hid* a hovering effect rather than that of a decisive fixing on one of the two syllables." Here we have a most interesting phenomenon. Brooks and Warren describe the foot *-light hid* as having a "hovering effect"; one look at our modified scansion tells us exactly what they mean and how the situation is brought about. Between *-light* and *hid* is a sustentional juncture, which, it will be recalled, causes the prolongation of the first syllable as the pitch is sustained. It should also be observed that this line, like the second, ends with a fading juncture.

Now the analysis has nothing to say about the metrical patterns of lines four and five, they being regular iambic pentameter; however, I believe they contain a point of some interest. Unlike lines two and three, ending with low-pitched words and fading junctures, line four ends with a high pitch on the word *night* followed by a rising juncture. If the fourth line be interchanged with lines two or three, the meaning of the poem will remain perfectly intact; yet, an attempt to read the work with these three lines arranged other than they are will swiftly convince one that something is thereby lost. The fact of the matter is that the rising juncture at the end of line four at once recalls the similar ending of line one (*it is right* ↗) and waves the reader on to the beginning of line five, consummating the construction (*It is right that we descant*). Neither line two nor line three, since each ends with the kind of juncture that does not create a sense of expectancy, could do this so well. We might also note incidentally that line five ends with a transitional juncture, carrying, as grammatical structure would lead one to expect, that line into the next.

Brooks and Warren next center the attention on the sixth line:

Upon|the supreme|theme|of Art|and Song:

It is interesting that they add in a note: "Some students may prefer to scan the line as follows:

Upon|the su|preme theme|of Art|and Song:

though this alternate scansion is somewhat arbitrary in that it gives a primary accent to *su-* and thus suggests that it is on something of the same stress level as *-preme*, a syllable actually much more heavily accented." Here we have these two gentlemen admitting a troublesome kind of inadequacy in their system, to a certain extent illustrating what they meant by "rather rudimentary." They know that -*preme* has a heavier accent than *su*-, yet they are not completely happy about giving *su*- either a weak or a strong stress. The whole problem might be solved by the following scansion:

²Upon + the + supreme³→³theme + of + Art + and + Song:²→

Although, as was intimated earlier, the meticulous marking of four stresses will likely only cause a system of metrics to become less a significant norm and more a subjective evaluation, there are bound to be situations like the above when the prosodist will welcome four defined stresses at his disposal, when, ironically, their use will enable him to establish a more significant norm. It will be noticed that our modified scansion labels the accent on *su*- as midway between the weak stress and the less-than-primary stress indicated by Brooks and Warren's alternate scansions.

The analysis has more to say about line six: "The second foot, *the supreme*, is anapaestic; this means that the syllable -*preme* receives a more than normally emphatic pronunciation. The next foot is imperfect, containing only the syllable *theme*; a lingering on the syllable -*preme* and a pause compensate for the missing syllable in the next foot. This situation, as we have already seen from line 1, gives unusual emphasis." Here again, we are in a position to explain what has been observed. A sustentional juncture constitutes the "pause" between -*preme* and *theme*, and this combined with two high pitches accounts for the "lingering on the syllable -*preme*." Harmonics of high pitch and primary stress on both *theme* and -*preme* magnify their accents so that the emphasis upon them is indeed unusual. Unlike any of the others, this line ends with a sustentional juncture, and this observation should be kept in mind as we move on to the seventh line, the conventional and modified scansions for which are:

Bodily|decre|pitude|is wis|dom; young

²Bodily + decrepitude + is + ³wisdom;

¹↘²young²↗

Brooks and Warren mention that because of the three unaccented syllables, "The reader is forced, as it were, to accelerate the pace to reach the second accent." Another factor contributing to this acceleration is the sustentional juncture at the end of line six. Since the pitch is sustained, the reader does not have to start at the bottom of the hill again; he simply coasts on.

They go on to say that "After the pause, therefore, the reader is forced to stress, and linger on, the syllable *young*, for only by this accent does the line achieve any metrical system . . . . *Young*, is, obviously, a very important word here . . . . The unusual emphasis forced on it by the metrical arrangement of the line fortifies the whole meaning of the word in the poem." Our scansion shows the word *young* to be strategically situated between two junctures: it is the initial word after a fading juncture, and although the body of the word is not high-pitched, there is no drop-off in volume and a sharp rise in pitch before its sound has disappeared. All this adds up to a unique kind of accentuation, and the rising juncture acts as an invitation to the concluding line of the poem. There does not seem to be anything we can add to the description of the regular, iambic pentameter last line.

Before I go on to seek conclusions from the examination just conducted, one more thing must be said. I have no doubt that a linguistic scientist could manipulate his descriptive devices with much more precision than I have demonstrated. Moreover, he could apply much more complicated notions, such as voice qualifiers, differentiators and all the recent discoveries of metalinguistics and microlinguistics, provided—and this is the important point—provided he were dealing with a particular reading of a poem. But as I have mentioned, the purpose of prosody is to seek a norm, a standard from which individual interpretations can move. Now that years of detailed research lie behind the science of linguistics, only a fool would question the ability of a qualified structural linguist to analyze particular speech performances, but he is equally foolish who thinks that the exact description of such a performance would constitute what literary scholars call "a metrical analysis." It follows, then, that much of the information accumulated by this new science is inconsequential to English prosody.

Prior to examining "After Long Silence," we made a selection from available linguistics information. Armed with a general understanding of pitch, junctures, and two extra stresses, we proceeded to experiment with a long-standing metrical analysis made by two reputable conventional prosodists. We were not able, except in one minor case, to arrive at a greater understanding of how the language pattern of the poem reinforced its effect and meaning; however, I venture to say that we did achieve a *clearer* understanding. In many instances, when Brooks and Warren seemed to be groping for appropriate words ("hovering effect," "slight pause," "heavy pause," "unusual emphasis"), we had precise descriptions ready. We did not transcend the norm established by Messrs. Brooks and Warren, but within the limits they defined, we were operating more efficiently. In effect, we illustrated how the application of linguistics principles does not have to interfere with the purposes, general methodology, or conclusions of the prosodist, but can help fulfill his purposes, clarify his methodology and fortify his conclusions.

Our conclusion, therefore, seems obvious. The science of linguistics does have something to offer to English prosody, and thus to English literary criticism. The adoption of certain selected descriptive devices will hardly revolutionize the old system of metrics, nor even provide for greater insight into poetry. The analysis found in *Understanding Poetry* is striking evidence that the old system works; there is no necessity for an overhaul, yet the addition of a few linguistics-manufactured accessories will expedite the achievement of its end. The prosodist who realizes this can still travel on the same road, enjoy the same scenery, reach the same destination—only in a slightly more efficient machine.

Part Three

THREE ESSAYS IN CRITICISM

ARNOLD STEIN

Meter and Meaning

[Too many prosodists have expanded their efforts in tax-
onomy: in counting, arranging, and classifying metrical phenomena. The structural linguists and the acousticians, as well
as the traditional prosodists, all have accumulated reams of
data that tell us so many lines of verse contain so many pauses
and stresses, so many dactyls and so many spondees. It is the
rare metrist who attempts the critical task of showing how the
pattern of sound controls and modifies the pattern of propositional sense.

[Stein's essay will require more than one careful reading;
however, the effort will be well repaid. Not only does Stein
offer a subtle and brilliant examination of Donne's poetry, he
also suggests a general approach to poetic structure that takes
into full account the interplay of meter and meaning.]

The point was made earlier that we should need to qualify
the working hypothesis that Donne was interested more in the
immediacies of meaning than in the immediacies of grace.
The various discussions of sense, of rhetoric and lyric, of simplicity, of the poet's voice—all have indicated that Donne
could not properly be said to use the affective resources of
metrical language merely to drive home rhetorical points. We
come now to a place in the exposition where we must look
more closely at the relations between sound and meaning.

We may begin with the simplest kind of example, the familiar use of sound to imitate directly the sense of what is being said. At one extreme the resources of style can be used to
convey the effect of a physical state. Pope writes the classic
examples of the doctrine that "The sound must seem an echo
to the sense"—soft strains for zephyr, or rough, heavy, swift,
whichever "echo" is appropriate. The doctrine is based on the

power of music, which "all our hearts allow"; but the examples are those of a rather literal, and limited, kind of program music. A less mechanical use of the doctrine may be dramatic on a restricted plane—in giving an external sense of the immediate situation.

Donne delights in the immediate, in the actually moving scene and in the natural, or rehearsed, inflections of the voice speaking the part that is required. As for the more obvious use of sound to imitate the sense, Donne hardly ever plays this game seriously. Even in his two virtuoso pieces describing the storm and the calm, where the opportunities for program music were most inviting, he preferred to create situations almost entirely by other means. He is quite willing to make the sound emphasize the sense, but not imitate it. The one big exception is the comic or satiric context. For example, in Elegy IV, he writes:

> Thy little brethren, which like Faiery Sprights
> Oft skipt into our chamber, those sweet nights.

But the charm of the children and the spontaneous joy of their skipping movement, which we are made to feel and respond to with a natural innocence that matches their own, turn out to be a trap. The next morning the children are bribed, on the father's knee, to tell what they saw. This same elegy has two other examples of imitative sound: "The grim eight-foot-high iron-bound serving-man," and "I taught my silkes, their whistling to forbeare." These lines have no ironic turn, or counterpoint; they are straight, like Pope's examples. They illustrate something rare in Donne, presumably evoked by the general comic tone of the elegy.

If Donne does not write this way more often, it is not from want of ability. He can exhibit his own mastery of delicate sensuousness:

> As the sweet sweat of roses in a Still,
> As that which from chaf'd muskats pores doth trill,
>
> And like that slender stalke, at whose endstands
> The wood-bine quivering, are her armes and hands.[1]

But the delicacy is cultivated only for the occasion, that of an enormous joke that Donne is contriving. And in the following example it is for the sake of the ironic turn that the sound imitates the sense:

[1] Elegy VIII

> So carelesse flowers strow'd on the waters face,
> The curled whirlepooles suck, smack, and embrace,
> Yet drowne them; so, the tapers beamie eye
> Amorously twinkling, beckens the giddie flie,
> Yet burnes his wings.[2]

It is in his satires that Donne makes freest use of imitative sound, though seldom in any literal way. And this qualification is no doubt a commentary on his attitude toward the device. It is not to be taken very seriously, but it can do charming things, particularly if the imitation works through exaggerated emphasis in the manner of the caricaturist.

> He, like to a high stretcht lute string squeakt, O Sir,
> 'Tis sweet to talke of Kings.[3]

When the imitation works in this way, qualities that are presented as external are made to suggest something of the internal as well. So it is not only a mocking version of the fop's voice that we hear; the lines also require us to imagine facial expressions and perhaps bodily movements. This is another way of saying that the sound is less imitative than suggestive and interpretative. In the following lines, which create a whole scene, we sense much of the fop's personality from the way he speaks; and we fill out a picture of his actions partly from the erratic impetuousness with which the verse moves, and then droops:

> Now leaps he upright. Joggs me, & cryes, Do you see
> Yonder well favoured youth? Which? Oh, 'tis hee
> That dances so divinely; Oh, said I,
> Stand still, must you dance here for company?
> Hee droopt.

But the verse that creates a physical situation and suggests a personality requires more than imitative sound if it is to present more than external drama:

> Yet though he cannot skip forth now to greet
> Every fine silken painted foole we meet,
> He them to him with amorous smiles allures,
> And grins, smacks, shrugs, and such an itch endures,
> As prentises, or schoole-boyes which doe know
> Of some gay sport abroad, yet dare not goe.[4]

[2] Elegy VI
[3] Satire IV
[4] Satire I

The third line is delightful physical caricature; one cannot read it aloud without putting the mouth through motions of alluring smiles that feel like grimaces. But only "dare" of the last line really penetrates far below the surface of the fop's personality. The rhythmic arrangement helps, of course, and performs an important role in the psychological drama. But this takes us to our next series of examples, in which the structure of sound does more than echo the sense or convey the immediacy of an external situation.

At one simple extreme we need only remind ourselves of Donne's favorite device of making his sound go along with his meaning for the rhetorical emphasis. The device, even when it is mostly rhythmical, can manage very fine shades of meaning. But we need not pause for simple illustrations of this kind of rhetoric in Donne. Almost any line quoted would serve as example, and we shall soon consider some complex uses which include the simple. Let us instead note another kind of example. A pattern of sound may be used as a kind of musical symbol to evoke a meaning that does not coincide with the formal emphasis. For instance, in the following lines where certain conventional satiric objects are presented for illustration, the verse takes on a roughness that refers less to the immediate objects than to a personal kind of satiric attitude that has been awakened.

> Th'hydroptique drunkard, and night-scouting thiefe,
> The itchy Lecher, and selfe tickling proud
> Have the remembrance of past joyes, for reliefe
> Of comming ills. To (poore) me . . .[5]

Once he has called up the satiric attitude (which is excessive and not strictly relevant to the limited situation), Donne can shift the ready-made contempt where he wants it, to himself.

A pattern of sound can also act as a musical symbol to suggest conflict within the structure of a poem. The line "Tell me, where all past yeares are" is, as I read it, quite different in tone from the lines dealing with the flippant impossibilities of catching a falling star and the like. The incantation evokes a sense of serious magic that is contrary to the dominant tone. The imaginative range of the line is also greater, and not merely because of the potential seriousness. But if one looks at the

[5] Holy Sonnet III

whole poem from this point of view, the single line may seem
to represent a significant disproportion. The lavish imaginative
detail, the intense exaggeration that gives the poem its special
quality—these too produce a sense of disproportion in a poem
that is, formally at least, an epigrammatic joke.

Or consider the more substantial example of these lines
from "Loves Growth":

> Gentle love deeds, as blossomes on a bough,
> From loves awakened root do bud out now.

The delicacy of spring's miracle is in the words, along with a
rationalistic perception of the source of its power; but the special lyrical qualities of the second line also suggest something
of the illusion possible in a sight that is being looked at too
closely. The delicate beauty is there, so delicate that it cannot
possibly last long, so irrepressible ("do bud out now") that it
cannot help returning, every spring.

Our next examples will attempt to demonstrate a more
deeply involved relationship between meter and rhetorical emphasis. These examples, though they are intended to exhibit
Donne as a consummate rhetorician in verse, do not conclude
this part of the argument but are instead transitional. For
whenever we try to trace with full detail the exact emergence
of metaphorical meaning, we go beyond the useful rhetorical
categories. The full case, and the conclusions to be drawn,
must wait until the end of the chapter, until we have been
able to study the means by which the meaning of a whole
poem takes shape.

How shall we read the last three words of this line from
Elegy X?[6]

> So, if I dreame I have you, I have you.

The first "have," reinforced by the meter, is very emphatic,
and so creates a pressure that is felt by the second "have." But
the second "have" must resist at least part of that pressure; it
cannot coincide with the meter, any more than it can avoid
the influence of the rhetorical emphasis. One may imagine
that the ear, with a swiftness and sureness which outstrip
thought and have been acquired as by second nature, experimentally listens ahead. The trained ear senses in advance that

[6] The following two passages and my analysis of them have been
discussed by Seymour Chatman and John Crowe Ransom, in *Kenyon
Review*, XVIII (1956).

the "I" and the "you" are the regular but unlikely places for stress to fall. The mind informed by such an ear may recognize that a stressed "I" and "you" will mean that out of the dream a real *I* will possess a real *you*, but with far less emphasis on the reality of the possession than on the reality of the identity. However, the deliberate suppression of the "have" would be extreme and unlikely. Yet let us assume that the ingenious ear swiftly tries out the possibility and records it.

Or let us consider that the ear could solve its problem boldly with a stress shift in the fifth foot—like a swift stream encountering an obstacle temporarily too big to flow around. This would throw the weight on the final "I" and especially on the "have." The emphasis would then suggest an egoistic reality of possession, and would suit an assertive, supercilious tone. Or the ear might, at last, attempt its final and most complicated possibility, a spondee in the last foot. It cannot be an exact spondee, with both of the last syllables receiving absolutely equal stress. Of course, we know that this is always true in the transformation of meter into rhythm, but in this particular case we have the privilege of seeing some of the complicating elements openly in action. The "have," because of its rhetorical position, demands a striking emphasis. But then the "you" may be left without enough stress either to make a decent spondee or to satisfy the established expectation of the complex meaning. The result, inevitably influenced also by the obstacle of that egoistic, dominating "I," which resists being suppressed, would then tend toward the assertive tone of the stress shift. The ear, I think, will be sensitive to the imbalance and will compensate in behalf of the "you"—but not too much, lest the reality of the you dominate the reality of the possession, or even cancel its effect.

And so, finally, I think one may say that all of the possibilities are contained in the reading the ear at last prefers. The result is a kind of ambiguous hovering that includes (in the pyrrhic-spondee of the last four syllables) both the reality of possession and the reality of identity, and includes them in their dynamic relationship to each other. Needless to say, the voice attempting to register these fine things will require some special effects. It would be naive, however, to assume that all of the potential of a rich line must be heard at each performance. The analogy of musical performance can be instructive here.

The opening lines of the same elegy present us with a similar situation, where the play between meter and rhetorical emphasis holds the key to the metaphorical meaning:

> Image of her whom I love, more then she,
>   Whose faire impression in my faithfull heart,
> Makes mee her *Medall*, and makes her love mee,
>   As Kings do coynes, to which their stamps impart
> The value; goe, and take my heart from hence.

It is the first three lines I am concerned with, and particularly the problem of how we shall read the third. Let us be elementary and inductive. "Makes mee" may be taken as a spondee, and the first syllable of "*Medall*" is plainly stressed. "Makes her," because of the parallel with "Makes mee" and because it follows two unstressed syllables, requires two stresses. So that leaves us with only the last two words seriously in question. (Perhaps I should add that my spondees are relative and are based on a built-up sense of Donne's metrical style. In another style, say Milton's, there is nothing in the line, except the last two words, that could not work within the ample flexibility of the iambic. The "and" would require a little artificial stiffening, but that can always be made available out of the accumulated credit, as it were, of a style.[7] My spondees, I repeat, are not equal in stress, though they would sound nearly equivalent in emphasis by means of other resources of vocal intensification. The tension to be expressed is not only within each spondee but in the interrelationship between the two "makes" and between "mee" and "her.")

The metrical possibilities for reading the last two words are again, I think, three. If "love mee" is heard as an iamb, the emphasis will make "mee" more important, as if to assert that the effect is more significant than the cause. One might then say that the coin grants the stamp the favor of reality and makes what was an abstract form into a reality of value. The second possibility is a stress shift that will make "love" clearly dominate "mee," with the resulting changes to the emphasis and the complex of meaning. The third possibility involves a compromise, I think necessary, between the other two. That is, treat "love mee" as another spondee. Hesitating among alternatives, as he must, the reader becomes aware that the metrical uncertainty is a part of the larger ambiguity carefully balanced in the whole complex metaphor of the coining. Unable to decide whether "love" or "mee" is dominant, one hesitates and

[7] See, for instance, my "A Note on Meter," *Kenyon Review*, XVIII (1956).

is forced into the compromise of stressing both. In the hesitation one discovers a buried syntactical ambiguity: "love" may be not a verb but a noun parallel to "Medall." Then we should have something like this: the image that creates her medal (me) also creates her love (me); her love is me and I am her love, brought into being, as a medal, by her image.

Let us try another paraphrase from our present vantage. I love her image more than she does for this reason—that, through her image and its stamp on me, she must love me. Her love of her image gives me (stamped with it) my being in love, so her love is me. And so I love her image more than she does. I also love her image more than I love her (the female She who *has no image* or idea, but is only She—"forget the Hee and Shee"). For it is her image and its effect on me that causes her to love me, that transforms me into her love, that transforms me into an image of her image. But her image is a kind of Platonic idea that (anti-Platonically) depends for its expression, perhaps for its existence, upon me. It may be my idea of her image that makes her love it and so me. If I love her image, then she depends for her existence as a loved object upon my idea of her image, and so *I* am her love as her love is *me*. The identification is established by reciprocal actions, and a philosophical problem is solved by a metaphor to which the metrical structure is an indispensable key.

Our two final examples are brief. They will indicate something of Donne's power to extend imaginative meaning sensuously. First, this familiar line from "The Relique":

A bracelet of bright haire about the bone.

The first effect of "A bracelet of bright haire" is to excite the imagination in a way that always increases the willing expectation of new experience, and therefore seems to open up and extend the potential range of meaning. But "about the bone" imposes a countering sense of limit. "Bone" is absolute and needs no further descriptive designation than "the."

If we narrow our view to the structure of sound we may see a similar pattern of development. The dominating vowels of "A bracelet of bright haire"—at least in reference to the sense of the words, and to the sense and sound of the rest of the line —help convey an effect of warmth and animation. "Haire" is the metrical high point of the line, and it builds upon a vowel and consonant more briefly articulated earlier. At this point, where stress and sound coincide in climax, the imaginative

sensuousness of the line is at its furthest extent. But the
limit which the second half of the line brings into effect also
builds on an earlier sound. The neutral b of "bracelet" and
"bright" is shaped by the positive b of "about" and "bone."

Our final example is the famous last line of this stanza from
"A Valediction: Forbidding Mourning":

> Our two soules therefore, which are one,
>   Though I must goe, endure not yet
> A breach, but an expansion,
>   Like gold to ayery thinnesse beate.

It is possible to remark a certain conflict in the line, though
the dominant impression is that of marvelous order and precision. "Ayery," for instance, threatens both rationally and
sensuously to break through the limits of the controlling idea,
that by which the parting is to avoid material rupture and is to
remain instead an admirable connection however extended.
"Ayery" is followed by "thinnesse," which is the metrical
climax of the line. "Thinnesse" as a word in the mouth suggests a delicacy that carries the magic of airiness a step closer
to immateriality. But it is a definite word too, at least more
definite than "ayery," and its full ambivalence is defined by
the word which follows. The emphatically physical "beate"
makes the thinness more definite, even as the thinness becomes
beaten materially thinner. And so one may say that gold, the
concrete substance, and gold, the symbol of infinite association, together move toward airiness while, with a counter motion, the imaginative limits are fixed and the balance holds
firm.

T. S. Eliot And The Music Of Poetry

[*This section, abridged from my book* Sound and Form in
Modern Poetry, *examines the metrics of Eliot's* Four Quartets.
*My position as a prosodist can be summarized by a statement
from an earlier section of the book:* "We need the basic approaches and techniques of literary criticism to place prosodic
analysis in the larger context of humanistic scholarship."]

Eliot has given us unforgettable rhythms—rhythms which
echo and re-echo in the mind's ear. We need only go to our
memories for prosodical touchstones: lines grasped long ago
by the "auditory imagination" and never lost. They recover
an emotion from personal or racial origins, recall some shud-
dering gesture of the spirit, or catch the flat intonation of a
bored voice. It is the heard rhythms which animate these lines:

> Where worried bodies of drowned men drift down in the
> green silence . . .

> Whispers and small laughter between leaves and
> hurrying feet
> Under sleep, where all waters meet.

> The awful daring of a moment's surrender
> Which an age of prudence can never retract

> Let Mr. Sweeney continue his story.
> I assure you, Sir, we are very interested.

Eliot's rhythms, capable of such variety in movement and
sonority, return us to the musical function of prosody. No
modern poet has so effectively used rhythm to evoke a "knowl-

Abridged from Chapter VII of Sound and Form in Modern Poetry.
Copyright 1964 by The University of Michigan Press. Used by permission of The University of Michigan Press.

edge of how feelings go"; no rhythms have shown such power to summon emotion to the forefront of consciousness.

Eliot has been aware of prosody-as-music. Whether he speaks, dry-mouthed and stammering,

> And no rock
> If there were rock
> And also water
> And water
> A spring . . .
>
> (The Waste Land)

or smoothly sings of a frozen moment, "suspended in time":

> In windless cold that is the heart's heat,
> Reflecting in a watery mirror
> A glare that is blindness in the early afternoon . . .
>
> (Little Gidding)

the patterns of stress and pause, quantity, dynamics, and syntax reach down and "make conceivable" the richness of the inner life of feeling. Eliot has quarreled with Pater's ethical notions, but Eliot's prosody—the function of the "auditory imagination"—aspires toward the condition of music.

Eliot does not approach the condition of music in order to submerge his ideas in his form or merely to create pleasing sounds. To Eliot "the music of poetry" means a great deal more than melodious verse, achieved through smooth textures and verbal tone color. The music of poetry is not "the elemental sound of brasses, strings, or wood-winds, but the intellectual and written word in all its glory—music of perfect fullness and clarity, the totality of universal relationships."[1] Alliteration and assonance, or such onomatopoeia as "Forlorn! the very word is like a bell" are not the essential music of poetry: it lies in "the totality of universal relationships."

Eliot's verse first establishes these relationships through the articulating structures of syntax. Syntax, the order of words as they arrange themselves into patterns of meaning, is the analogue to harmony in music. Like harmony, syntax generates tension and relaxation, the feelings of expectation and fulfillment which make up the dynamics of poetic life. Susanne Langer remarks:

> The tension which music achieves through dissonance, and the reorientation in each new resolution to harmony,

[1] Stéphane Mallarmé, Selected Prose Poems, Essays, and Letters, tr. Bradford Cook (Baltimore, 1956), p. 42.

find their equivalents in the suspensions and periodic decisions of propositional sense in poetry. Literal sense, not euphony, is the "harmonic structure" of poetry; word melody in literature is more akin to tone color in music.[2]

Syntax gives us the arc of "literal sense," the articulations of meaning. Like harmony in music, syntax makes connections, strengthens ideas, and relates thematic material. Eliot himself emphasizes that music in poetry does not inhere in word melody and tone color, but in the harmony of meanings and connections:

> It would be a mistake, however, to assume that all poetry ought to be melodious, or that melody is more than one of the components of the music of words. . . . The music of a word is, so to speak, at a point of inter-section: it arises from its relation first to the words immediately preceding and following it, and indefinitely to the rest of its context; and from another relation, that of its immediate meaning in that context to all the other meanings which it had in other contexts, to its greater or less wealth of association.[3]

The reverberation of words, their semantic resonances, are the shifting tones in the harmony of intersections and associations.

Eliot's syntax carries the bass line of his prosody. Through a deliberate and idiosyncratic use of repeated grammar and repeated words, Eliot achieves qualities common to both music and poetry—the feelings of arrest and motion, of beginnings and endings, of striving and stillness. "Musical syntax" forms a basic element in the Eliotic style and method. Although Eliot had experimented with musical forms and techniques in his earlier verse, we can hear the richest and most moving syntactical music in *Four Quartets*. I offer first the opening lines of *Burnt Norton*:

> Time present and time past
> Are both perhaps present in time future,
> And time future contained in time past.
> If all time is eternally present
> All time is unredeemable.

These lines present neither images nor metaphors, the sup-posed quintessential materials of poetry. Everything is handled

[2] Susanne K. Langer, *Philosophy in a New Key* (Cambridge, Mass., 1942), p. 261.
[3] T. S. Eliot, *On Poetry and Poets* (New York, 1957), pp. 24-25.

through the silent rhythms of syntax and the audible rhythms
of isochronism and strong-stress meter. We hear the echoing
repetitions of individual words and phrases; we hear the more
subtle repetitions of syntactical structure, the persistently un-
varying grammatical forms. The syntax is static: the noun
Time, the modifiers past, present, future, the copulatives is or
are, all follow in strict order. We hear the literal sense modified
by each repetition of word and phrase; we hear how each
repetition fits into an overall pattern of incantation.

Note the grammatical marking time in these lines:

> If all time is eternally present
> All time is unredeemable . . .

Eliot tells how time can be immovable, without direction. But
there comes a point where Eliot must resolve his meaning,
where a composer would introduce a cadence to tell us where
his music is going, harmonically speaking. Then Eliot changes
his syntax; he drops the copulatives and allows the movement
of the preceding lines to pivot on the transitive verb point:

> What might have been and what has been
> Point to one end, which is always present . . .

Eliot has suspended syntactical movement by using only the
verbs is and are for nine lines running. The verb point releases
us into a new idea, and we modulate into a new syntactical
unit:

> Footfalls echo in the memory
> Down the passage which we did not take
> Towards the door we never opened
> Into the rose-garden. My words echo
> Thus, in your mind . . .

Now the verbs are active; the repeated echo develops a special
burden of sound and meaning. And we hear again a haunting
syntactical melody: "Down the passage . . . Towards the
door . . . Into the rose-garden. . . ."

Another kind of music is heard in the lyrical fourth section
of Burnt Norton:

> Will the sunflower turn to us, will the clematis
> Stray down, bend to us: tendril and spray
> Clutch and cling?
> Chill
> Fingers of yew be curled
> Down on us? After the kingfisher's wing

> Has answered light to light, and is silent,
>   the light is still
> At the still point of the turning world.

We have the insistent repetitions as in the first section: "turn to us . . . bend to us . . . Down on us." These are the melodies. We have, however, an effect which, to quote Mrs. Langer again, involves "the suspense of literal meaning by a sustained ambiguity resolved in a long-awaited key word."[4] Reading the penultimate line, we briefly poise on the word *still*. Meter and rhyme (with *chill*) enforce our usual tendency to pause slightly at the end of the line, and we understand *still* as an adjective modifying *light*. Moving down to the next line, we see that *still* is more exactly an adverb whose effect is strong enough to modify the sense of both lines. The light is *even yet* at the still point of the turning world.

We realize the ambiguity here, and how the word functions as a grammatical pivot on which the movement and meaning of the lines turn. The effect is analogous to an ambiguous harmonic structure which hovers between tonalities, a structure which might take any of a number of possible directions, but which is suddenly resolved by an unexpected cadence.

In *East Coker* we note another "effect of harmony"; we might call it "the illusion of tonality." The poem opens in this key:

> In my beginning is my end. In succession
> Houses rise and fall, crumble, are extended,
> Are removed, destroyed, restored, or in their place
> Is an open field, or a factory, or a by-pass . . .

At the end of the first section, we have:

> Dawn points, and another day
> Prepares for heat and silence. Out at sea
>   the dawn wind
> Wrinkles and slides. I am here
> Or there, or elsewhere. In my beginning.

Again Eliot builds tension through repeated syntax: ". . . or in their place . . . or a factory . . . or a by-pass." This pattern is repeated, in diminution, just before Eliot restates his theme: "I am here / Or there, or elsewhere. In my beginning." The familiar, almost expected, syntax acts as a return section, preparing us for the new entrance of the theme in its initial

[4] Susanne K. Langer, *op. cit.*, p. 261.

"tonality." We stress this musical preparation through syntax. Many have recognized Eliot's use of repeated thematic material without realizing how complex Eliot's musical procedures actually are. At the end of *East Coker*, we hear the same hesitant syntax announcing the theme, in inversion:

> The wave cry, the wind cry, the vast waters
> Of the petrel and the porpoise. In my end is
>   my beginning.

The striking effect created by each return of the theme is not gained through simple verbal repetition or modification. It is gained through the manipulation of syntax which gives this "illusion of tonality." Eliot's procedure parallels sonata form where the principal tonality is reestablished at the end of the movement, and the main theme makes its final appearance.

We "hear" Eliot's music in the meanings of words and the structures of grammar. I qualify *hear* with quotes because the rhythms of meaning and syntax are silent; they achieve tension and resolution not in phonological but in intellectual realms. The explicit, heard music of Eliot's verse sounds in Eliot's meters and the rhythmic effects occurring within the context of formally ordered metrical patterns. I shall treat later the more technical aspects of Eliot's meters: his varied handling of syllable-stress and strong-stress meter; his uses of open rhythm and nonmetrical techniques. However, we return to *Burnt Norton* for a moment to examine the musical aspects of Eliot's explicit sound patterns and the rhythms they inspire.

The falling strong-stress lines of *Burnt Norton*'s opening develop a single rhythmic idea, a motif which slowly accumulates emotional force. Individual word groups form themselves into apparent isochronic units; the four-beat strong-stress line resembles common measure (4/4) in music. If we assign note values to Eliot's word groups, we get something like this.[5]

Eliot's accelerating rhythm persists in our memories, modifying meaning and feeling: as the units of the phrase expand, we feel the arc of propositional sense tighten. The rhythm quickens with the thought. The statements about the nature of time in the first three lines are followed by the taut proposition of lines four and five: "If all time is eternally present, / All time is unredeemable." This is awesome; the notion challenges the imagination. We accept the opening statements as curious, teasing, the speculations of a poet with a taste for conundrums. But lines four and five have accumulated the tension (through repeated syntax as well as rhythmic expan-

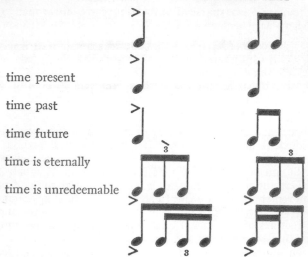

time present

time past

time future

time is eternally

time is unredeemable

sion) appropriate to the idea: that everything we have done is still *doing*, that everything we *shall do* is already taking place. Metaphysics is implicit in the paradigms of verbs; the possibilities of human action (what might have been; what has been) are conjugated in Eliot's syntax. The whole grows to thought in slow rhythmic expansion, moving along the metric closest to musical structure. The ear hears a gently insistent four-beat line; the imagination responds to the infinitely subtle music of feeling. . . .

The syntactical music of *Four Quartets* represents Eliot's highest technical achievement; hearing Eliot read the *Quartets* is as genuine a musical experience as hearing the Budapest Quartet play Beethoven's Opus 132. This is not analogical nonsense; Eliot's hint about Beethoven's later works provides an important clue to the form and substance of *Four Quartets*. J. W. N. Sullivan, whose influence on Eliot has been convincingly demonstrated by Herbert Howarth, describes below Beethoven's Quartets in B Flat, Opus 130, C# Minor, Opus 131, and A Minor, Opus 132; he is also describing, with uncanny precision, Eliot's *Four Quartets*:

In these quartets the movements radiate, as it were, from a central experience. They do not represent stages in a journey, each stage being independent and existing in its own right. They represent separate experiences, but the meaning they take on in the quartet is derived from their relation to a dominating, central experience. This is characteristic of the mystic vision, to which everything in the world appears unified in the light of one fundamental experience. In these quartets, then, Beethoven is not describing to us a spiritual history; he is presenting to us a vision of life. In each quartet many elements are surveyed, but from one central point of view. They are presented as apprehended by a special kind of awareness, they are seen in the light of one fundamental experience. It is not any kinship between the experiences described in the separate movements themselves, but the light in which they are seen, that gives to these works their profound homogeneity.[5]

The formal prosody of Four Quartets grows out of this "dominating central experience" and "profound homogeneity." Each movement, in Eliot's five-movement scheme, has its characteristic metric; yet, throughout the Quartets, Eliot sustains an overall consistency in metrical tone. This consistency is first established by the close musical structure, derived in all probability from Beethoven's Quartet in A Minor, Opus 132.[6] Eliot had been using musical structures and techniques long before he composed Four Quartets; The Waste Land was an experiment in the use of repeated thematic material as well as being orchestral in its elaborate handling of contrasting sonorities. Eliot's methods in the Quartets are more strictly musical; we find the pervasive repetitions of themes, images, and rhythms. We find, in addition, devices Eliot may have absorbed in his listening to Beethoven: variation of theme, inversion, diminution, rhythmic contraction and expansion.

The metrical modes complement the musical form. The first movements of Burnt Norton, East Coker, and Little Gidding are set in Eliot's flexible strong-stress lines. Line lengths vary but the number of stresses remains close to the normative four:

Drý the poól, || drý concréte, || brówn édged,

And the poól was fílled with wáter || out of súnlíght,

And the lótos róse, || quíetly, quíetly,

The súrface glíttered || out of heárt of líght . . .

                          [Burnt Norton]

The measure is the same in Little Gidding, but the alliteration gives an archaic flavor—a suggestion of Piers Plowman:

[5] J. W. N. Sullivan, Beethoven, His Spiritual Development (New York: Mentor Books, 1949), pp. 127-128.

[6] Stephen Spender and Herbert Howarth both suggest the A Minor Quartet as a possible musical model. Harvey Gross sees closer analogues in the C♯ Minor Quartet, Opus 131: see his "Music and the Analogue of Feeling," Centennial Review, Summer 1959.

Midwinter spring is its own season
Sempiternal though sodden towards sundown,
Suspended in time, between pole and tropic,
When the short day is brightest, with frost and fire,
The brief sun flames the ice, on pond and ditches,
In windless cold that is the heart's heat,
Reflecting in a watery mirror
A glare that is blindness in the early afternoon . . .

The complex positioning and counterpointing of vowel length
against the meter add a luster not present in the sparse lines
opening *Burnt Norton*.[7] The long vowel will sometimes coincide with metrical stress, as in this line:

A gláre that is blíndness || in the éarly afternóon . . .

The vowel may be duplicated at the analogous metrical position:

When the shórt day is bríghtest,   with fróst and fíre . . .

Long and short vowels may be inverted and balanced, short,
long followed by long, short:

Suspénded in tíme, between pole ánd tropic . . .

Or the long vowels may occur on the off-beats, cross-rhythmi-
cally:

Sempitérnal though sódden towards súndown . . .

A rhythmic crescendo marks the fifth line of our passage
from *Little Gidding*,

The bríef | sun flámes | the íce, | on·pónd | and
    dít | ches . . .

and we see the line falls into blank verse. The next line moves
back into the four-stress mode,.

In wíndless cóld || that is the héart's héat . . .

with a crowding together of the two final stresses. Again we
discover that the principle of Eliot's metric resides in ". . . the
contrast between fixity and flux, this unperceived evasion of
monotony, which is the very life of verse."[8] The opening of
The Dry Salvages skillfully avoids the monotony usually occasioned by triple meter in English; although the lines move

[7] "I suspect that the element which prosodists will concentrate on in
the future is the use Eliot makes of quantity to counterpoint his
stress . . ." Helen Gardner, *The Art of T. S. Eliot* (London, 1940).
[8] T. S. Eliot, "Reflections on Vers Libre," *The New Statesman*, March
3, 1917.

METRICAL MODES IN FOUR QUARTETS

	I Landscape	II Lyric	III Didactic	IV Lyric	V Didactic
BURNT NORTON	Four-stress line	1. Irregularly rhymed tetrameter 2. Hexameters and septenaries 3. Loose blank verse and four-stress line	1. Four-stress 2. Three-stress	1. Irregular iambic, rhymed	1. Four-stress 2. Three-stress
EAST COKER	Four-stress line	1. Irregularly rhymed tetrameter 2. Four-stress	1. Hexameter 2. Irregular five- and four-stress	1. Regular tetrameter stanzas	1. "Hexameters" 2. Four-stress
THE DRY SALVAGES	1. Five-stress anapestic/dactylic 2. Four-stress	1. Adapted sestina 2. Probably nonmetrical, merging into four-stress	1. "Hexameters" 2. Four-stress	1. Five-line stanza unrhymed; falling rhythm	1. Four-stress 2. Three-stress
LITTLE GIDDING	1. Four-stress 2. Irregular blank verse; four-stress	1. Regular trimeter and tetrameter stanzas 2. Blank verse in "terza rima"	1. "Hexameters" 2. Three-stress	1. Regular tetrameter and trimeter stanzas	1. Four-stress with irregular blank verse 2. Three-stress

in almost regular trisyllabic feet, anapests and dactyls, there is neither the solemn torpor of *Evangeline* nor the galloping frenzy of *The Destruction of Sennacherib*:

> I do not know much about gods; but I think that the river
> Is a strong brown god—sullen, untamed and intractable,
> Patient to some degree, at first recognized as a frontier,
> Useful, untrustworthy, as a conveyor of commerce;
> Then only a problem confronting the builder of bridges . . .

Each line has five principal stresses and a strongly felt caesura; the meter is anapestic pentameter with dactylic and spondaic substitutions. But the ear is not assaulted by anapests and dactyls; it hears the slow and primitive music of the Mississippi as it flows through past and present, recalling Eliot to childhood memories. The ear hears the infinitely subtle inflections of human feeling.

The second movement of each quartet opens with a rhyming lyric. The precision of the natural order is "figured" in regular tetrameter,

> We move above the moving tree
> In light upon the figured leaf
> And hear upon the sodden floor
> Below, the boarhound and the boar
> Pursue their pattern as before
> But reconciled among the stars . . .
>
> [*Burnt Norton*]

as are the disturbances of the spring, "not in time's covenant":

> Comets weep and Leonids fly
> Hunt the heavens and the plains
> Whirled in a vortex that shall bring
> The world to that destructive fire
> Which burns before the ice-cap reigns . . .

The second movement of *The Dry Salvages* introduces a variation on sestina form. The pattern is complicated, and as it unfortunately turns out, clumsy and self-defeating. The endrhymes of the first stanza

> Where is there an end of it, the soundless *wailing*,
> The silent withering of autumn *flowers*
> Dropping their petals and remaining *motionless*;
> Where is there an end to the drifting *wreckage*,
> The prayer of the bone on the beach, the *unprayable*
> Prayer at the calamitous *annunciation*?

undergo an increasingly desperate metamorphosis until we get *sailing* and *bailing*, and *devotionless*, *oceanless*, and *erosionless*. The ineffable *weariness* here brings to mind Eliot's own parody of this mood:

> O when will the creaking heart cease?
> When will the broken chair give ease?
> Why will the summer day delay?
> When will Time flow away?
> [Lines to a Persian Cat]

A longer section, of greater philosophic density, follows the lyrical interludes. In *Burnt Norton* Eliot penetrates to the unity of all experience; these lines, among all that Eliot has written, certainly approach the *poetry beyond poetry*:

> At the still point of the turning world. Neither flesh nor
>   fleshness;
> Neither from nor towards; at the still point, there the
>   dance is,
> But neither arrest nor movement. And do not call it fixity,
> Where past and future are gathered. Neither movement
>   from nor towards,
> Neither ascent nor decline. Except for the point,
>   the still point,
> There would be no dance, and there is only the dance . . .

Though the lines contain six and seven principal stresses, they move with all the ease and grace of the celestial dance they describe. Equally remarkable is the parallel section of *Little Gidding*, the "Inferno" episode. Eliot's adaptation of Dante's stanza avoids rhyme but alternates masculine and feminine endings to achieve the interlocking effect of *terza rima*:

> In the uncertain hour before the morning
>   Near the ending of interminable night
>   At the recurrent end of the unending
> After the dark dove with the flickering tongue
>   Had passed below th' horizon of his homing
>   While the dead leaves still rattled on like tin . . .

The first five lines follow Dante's *endecasillabo*, even to observing the ellision of a final vowel before *h*:

> Had passed below th' horizon of his homing

We are not dealing, however, with syllabic meter but blank verse. Eliot's "familiar compound ghost" speaks in grave, measured pentameter:

> Let me disclose the gifts reserved for age
>> To set a crown upon your lifetime's effort.
>> First, the cold friction of expiring sense
> Without enchantment, offering no promise
>> But bitter tastelessness of shadow fruit
>> As body and soul begin to fall asunder . . .

The final allusion to *Hamlet* reminds us that Eliot's versification owes as much to Shakespeare as to Dante; it may also be
Old Possum's little joke that the "compound ghost," ingeni-
ously fashioned from a dozen literary sources,[9] is only that sad
spook, the ghost of Hamlet's father:

> The day was breaking. In the disfigured street
>> He left me, with a kind of valediction,
>> And faded on the blowing of the horn . . .

Some readers have been dismayed by Eliot's weariness, his
repetitive circling of ideas, and his flaccid rhythms in the
Quartets. Karl Shapiro complains

> Eliot
> Himself in the *Quartets* (in my opinion
> His most depressing prosody) makes shift
> Of rhythms one thought he had exhausted ten
> Or fifteen years before. Symptoms of doubt
> Lie in reiteration; we sense confusion,
> The anxiety of the sensitive to mistakes.

> [*Essay on Rime*]

Donald Davie, in a devastating analysis of *The Dry Salvages*,
speaks of its ". . . stumbling, trundling rhythms . . . inarticu-
late ejaculations of reach-me-down phrases . . . debased cur-
rency of the study circle. . . ."[10] Exhaustion and even clumsi-
ness certainly mar passages in *East Coker* and *The Dry Salvages*; the two inner *Quartets* suffer the most from Eliot's
bemused prosiness and the grinding futility of disillusion
chasing its tail. We are often dulled by purposeless rhythms
or bored by

> The loud lament of the disconsolate chimera.

[9] See Grover Smith, Jr. *T. S. Eliot's Poetry and Plays* (Chicago,
1956), p. 286.
[10] Donald Davie, "T. S. Eliot: The End of an Era," in *T. S. Eliot:
A Collection of Critical Essays*, ed. Hugh Kenner (New Jersey,
1962), p. 195.

I agree with Mr. Davie that these lines are dismal in every respect:

> It seems, as one becomes older,
> That the past has another pattern, and ceases to be
> a mere sequence—
> Or even development: the latter a partial fallacy
> Encouraged by superficial notions of evolution . . .

Eliot allows too many weak syllables to intervene between strong stresses:

En cour aged by super fi cial no tions of e vo lu tion . . .

Since it is nearly impossible to tell which syllables are dynamically strong, the metrical checkpoints are obscured. The obsessive parenthetical qualification disrupts syntactical movement,

> Which becomes, in the popular mind . . .
>
> The moments of happiness—not the sense of well-being . . .

> I sometimes wonder if that is what Krishna meant—
> Among other things—or one way of putting the same
> thing . . .

and there are sections of The Dry Salvages when Eliot, usually so precise, loses control of his grammar.

But we need not judge the Quartets by their arid or tired moments. The vigorous opening of The Dry Salvages (quoted above), the section beginning,

> The river is within us, the sea is all about us;

continuing with the magnificent,

> The sea has many voices,
> Many gods and many voices.
> The salt is on the briar rose,
> The fog is in the fir trees . . .

and concluding with the sonorous and mysterious,

> And the ground swell, that is and was from the beginning,
> Clangs
> The bell . . .

redeem the weak sestina and the unilluminated metaphysics of "what Krishna meant."

Far from containing Eliot's "most depressing prosody,"

Little Gidding concludes the *Quartets* with a consistently strong and unbroken rhythmic impulse. While the other *Quartets* struggle with definition and direction, *Little Gidding* reaches a resolution of both technique and idea. The large formal rhythm (the five-movement divisions of landscape, lyric, didactic, lyric, didactic) is firmly settled as a pattern; the *Gestalt* of the other three *Quartets* is impressed on our minds. The expected sequence of metrical modes (see the chart on p. 211) now seems inevitable; we react with a sense of prepared surprise to the changes from four-stress verse to regular iambics, and from irregular pentameter to regular three-stress verse. Within each movement Eliot achieves his surest rhythms against an always discernible controlling meter.

The opening, with its balance between strong-stress and pentameter verse, offers these superb lines:

> And glow more intense than blaze of branch, or brazier,
> Stirs the dumb spirit: no wind, but pentecostal fire
> In the dark time of the year. Between melting and freezing
> The soul's sap quivers. There is no earth smell
> Or smell of living thing. This is the spring time
> But not in time's covenant.

The lines at first expand toward five stresses and blank verse; as the overall rhythm turns downward, reaching toward conclusion, the line turns back to four stresses:

> But this is the nearest, in place and time,
> Now and in England.
>
>   If you came this way . . .
>
>   Is England and nowhere. Never and always.

The lyrics of Sections II and IV have the simple regularity of songs; their mixture of iambic with trochaic and anapestic feet derives largely from the examples of Blake and Tennyson—and their great example, the Shakespearean song:

Ásh on | an óld | man's sléeve

Is áll | the ásh | the burnt ró | ses léave.

Dúst in | the áir | sus pén | ded

Márks | the pláce | where a stó | ry én | ded . . .

As in many of Shakespeare's songs, the iambic line begins on the strong syllable (trochaic or monosyllabic substitution): where the musical beat would naturally fall.

A hiatus, indicated by a visual pause, intervenes between the two strophes of Section V:

> So while the light fails
> On a winter's afternoon, in a secluded chapel
> History is now and England.
>
> With the drawing of this Love and the voice
>   of this Calling
>
> We shall not cease from exploration
> And the end of all our exploring
> Will be to arrive where we started
> And know the place for the first time.

The break is charged with silent energy; the poet stops, catches his breath for his final statement. The concluding movement (in three-stress lines) draws together motifs from all the *Quartets*; the falling rhythm of

> Quick now, here, now, always—

is transformed upward:

> When the tongues of flame are in-folded
> Into the crowned knot of fire
> And the fire and the rose are one.

As God's testing fire merges with the Rose of His Love, the rhythm slowly rises and ends the sequence of the *Quartets* in quiet triumph.

THEODORE ROETHKE

What Do I Like?

[Theodore Roethke's elegant jeu d'esprit concludes this volume. He draws on his own verse for examples of metrical procedure; he also shows how certain poetic rhythms originate in popular verse and early Tudor lyrics. Roethke's immense skill and zest are evidence of a rare spirit. The same imagination that shaped his poetry energizes the sharp analyses here.

[Especially valuable are Roethke's observations on what Eliot calls "the contrast between fixity and flux. . . ." Indeed, Roethke (doubtless subconsciously) closely approximates a formulation from Eliot's early and immensely important essay, "Reflections on Vers Libre" (New Statesman, March 3, 1917): ". . . the ghost of some simple metre should lurk behind the arras in even the 'freest' verse; to advance menacingly as we doze, and withdraw as we rouse. Or freedom is only truly freedom when it appears against the background of an artificial limitation."

[Robert Graves ("Harp, Anvil, Oar") quarrels with (and, in my opinion, misunderstands) this basic aesthetic fact: that a formal structure, such as meter, exists to be evaded, varied, or departed from. Mere regularity is monotony; unconsidered or unconscious freedom is anarchy. And to quote Eliot again: "There is no escape from metre; there is only mastery."]

What do I like? Listen.

> Hinx, minx, the old witch winks,
> The fat begins to fry,
> There's nobody home but Jumping Joan,
> And Father, and Mother, and I.

Reprinted from Conversations on the Craft of Poetry. Edited by Cleanth Brooks and Robert Penn Warren (A transcript of the tape recording made to accompany UNDERSTANDING POETRY, Third Edition.) Copyright © 1961 by Holt, Rinehart and Winston, Inc. Used by permission.

Now what makes that catchy, to use Mr. Frost's phrase? For one thing, the rhythm. Five stresses out of a possible six in the first line. Though maybe "old" doesn't take quite as strong a stress as the others. And three—keep noticing that magic number—internal rhymes, hinx, minx, winks. And notice too the apparent mysteriousness of the action. Something happens right away—the old witch winks and she sets events into motion. The fat begins to fry, literally and symbolically. She commands—no old fool witch this one. Notice that the second line, "The fat begins to fry," is absolutely regular metrically. It's all iambs, a thing that often occurs when previous lines are sprung or heavily counterpointed. The author doesn't want to get too far from his base, from his ground beat. The third line varies again with an anapaest and variations in the "O" and "U" sound. "There's nobody home but Jumping Joan." Then the last line—anapaest lengthening the line out to satisfy the ear, "And Father, and Mother, and I." Sometimes we are inclined to feel that Mother Goose, or the traditional kind of thing, is almost infallible as memorable speech. The phrase is Auden's but this is by no means so. There is another version that goes,

> Hink, mink, the old witch stinks,
> The fat begins to fry
> Nobody's home but Jumping Joan,
> Jumping Joan and I.

Well, the whole situation has obviously altered, for the better perhaps from the standpoint of the speaker at least. But in his excitement he has produced a much inferior poem. First, deleting the "S's" takes some of the force away from the three rhyming words—"Hinx, minx, the old witch winks,"—the triad. What's more, he has become tiresomely naturalistic. The old witch stinks—hardly a fresh piece of observation. Stink's a splendid old word, but here it is a bore. It is a prerogative of old witches to stink. Part of their stock in trade as it were, and nobody mentions it. Take the change from minx, which means of course a pert little vixen of a girl, and carries with it overtones of tenderness or, further back, a wanton, a roaring girl. And the mink, a wonderful little predatory animal with a characteristic odor. But if we keep that in mind the line becomes an olfactory horror. It's some fusty little cave these two have in the absence of father and mother. And their absence takes away the real drama from the situation. It's a roll in the hay, and nothing more.

Allow me another I love.

> IN spells in.
> I was in my kitchin,
> Doin' a bit of stitchin'
> Old Father Nimble,
> Came 'n took my thimble.
> I got a great big stone.
> Hit him on the belly bone.
> O U T spells out.

Here we see how light "i" and short "i" and feminine endings can make for speed and rhythmical quickness, velocity and then, with the words following the action, that truly awesome and portentous line with its spondees, "I got a great big stone," and then the sudden speedup in the action, the triumphant release from a frustration, I suppose the Freudians would say, "Hit him on the belly bone. O U T spells out." Take another, a single line, which is always a test. "Great A, little a, bouncing B." There are three shifts of pace—it's a triad again, lovely alliterations, the long full vowels combined. Names themselves can be a love in half the poem.

> Julius Caesar Pompey Green
> Wore a jacket of velveteen.

Here we're cranked up by four trochees in the first line. The second line would be dull by itself, but that first line, the impetus of it is still bearing us along.

What's my real point by these little examples? It's this. That while our genius in the language may be essentially iambic, particularly in the formal lyric, much of memorable or passionate speech is strongly stressed, irregular, even sprung, if you will. Now we see that the name itself, the direct address, makes for the memorable, for rhythmical interest; often it means an implied dialogue. Take the ridiculous

> Oh Father dear, do ships at sea
> Have legs way down below?
> Of course they do, you goosey you,
> Or how else could they go?

Or, if you can stand my Scots,

> Says Tweed to Till—
> "What gars ye rin sae still?"
> Says Till to Tweed—"Though we rin with speed

> And I rin slaw,
> For ae man that ye droon
> I droon twa!"

But, you may protest, these are the rhythms of children, of folk material, strongly stressed—memorable perhaps, but do they appear in poetry today. The answer is yes, certainly in some poets. For instance Auden's

> The silly fool, the silly fool
> Was sillier in school
> But beat the bully as a rule.
>
> The youngest son, the youngest son
> Was certainly no wise one
> Yet could surprise one.
>
> Or rather, or rather
> To be posh, we gather,
> One should have no father.

Then the cryptic and elliptical end,

> Simple to prove
> That deeds indeed
> In life succeed
> But love in love
> And tales in tales
> Where no one fails.

Not all Mother Goosie to be sure. And the "rather-father" rhyme maybe comes from Sam Johnson's

> If a man who turnips cries,
> Cries not when his father dies
> It must prove that he would rather
> Have a turnip than a father.

Or take an example from myself, a piece, "I Need, I Need." In the first section the protagonist, a little boy, is very sad. Then there is a jump-rope section in which two children chant in alternate aggressive dialogue. Then their aggression trails off into something else. This goes,

> Even steven all is less:
> I haven't time for sugar,
> Put your finger in your face,
> And there will be a booger.

A one is a two is
I know what you is:
You're not very nice,—
So touch my toes twice.

I know you are my nemesis
So bibble where the pebble is.
The Trouble is with No and Yes
As you can see I guess I guess.

I wish I was a pifflebob
I wish I was a funny
I wish I had ten thousand hats,
And made a lot of money.

Open a hole and see the sky:
A duck knows something
You and I don't.
Tomorrow is Friday.

Not you I need.
Go play with your nose.
Stay in the sun,
Snake-eyes.

Some of the poems I cherish from the dramatists have heavily
pronounced, strongly stressed spot rhythms. They are written
to be sung, or maybe danced to. Here from *Ralph Roister
Doister*,

I mun be married a Sunday;
I mun be married a Sunday;
Whosoever shall come that way,
I mun be married a Sunday.

Roister Roister is my name;
Roister Doister is my name;
A lusty brute I am the same;
I mun be married a Sunday.

Christian Custance have I found;
Christian Custance have I found;
A widow worth a thousand pound;
I mun be married a Sunday.

and so on. Notice that shift in the second stanza, in tone, and
feeling—how it goes into another speed rhythmically, George
Peele, that wonderful poet, abounds in incantatory effects in
the same propulsion. Here is the opening of a dialogue.

Fair and fair, and twice so fair,
As fair as any may be,
The fairest shepherd on our green, A love for any lady.

And later,

> And of my love my roundelay,
> My merry, merry, merry roundelay,
> Concludes with Cupid's curse:
> They that do change old love for new,
> Pray gods they change for worse!

Repetition in word and phrase and in idea is the very essence
of poetry and particularly of *this* kind of poetry. Notice how
these poets can and do change the pace, and the change is
right psychologically. We say the command, the hortatory,
often makes for the memorable. We're caught up, involved.
It is implied we do something, at least vicariously. But it can
also be very tricky—it can seem to have a factitious strength.
The emotion must be strong and legitimate and not fabri-
cated. Thus when Eleanor Wylie writes,

> Go study to disdain
> The frail, the overfine

I can't get past the first line. There is no conviction, no natural rhythm of speech. I suppose there must be an element of
the startling, or the strange, or the absurd. Yeats is magnificent, often, at getting the right tone, seizing the attention:

> "Call down the hawk from the air;
> Let him be hooded or caged wild"

or

> Come swish around, my pretty punk,
> And keep me dancing still
> That I may stay a sober man
> Although I drink my fill.

Or Donne's "So, so, breake off this last lamenting kisse, . . ." I
think of Bogan's "Come, Break with Time" as a supreme
example of this kind of thing.

> Come, break with time,
> You who were lorded
> By a clock's chime
> So ill afforded.
> If time is allayed.
> Be not afraid.
>
> *I shall break, if I will.* Break, since you must.
> Time has its fill,
> Sated with dust. Long the clock's hand

Burned like a brand.

> Take the rock's speed
> And the earth's heavy measure.
> Let buried see
> Drain out time's pleasure,
> Take time's decrees.
> Come, cruel ease.

Here is a strong stress again, and the emotion powerful. We are into the theme immediately, a great theme always but one that few can handle. Say anything new about today. Notice a cunning shift of rhythm in the last stanza, the pick-up in energy. The change reminding me always (and perhaps this is deliberate) of the Wordsworthian

> No motion has she now, no force;
> She neither hears nor sees;
> Rolled round in earth's diurnal course
> With rocks, and stones, and trees.

In some more serious poetry we see again how the direct address can pull us up sharply. We are used to this in spoken language. Maybe we hark back to the condition of the child when we are being told. Almost invariably a dramatic situation, some kind of opposition, is indicated. Thus in Charlotte Mew's

> Sweetheart, for such a day
> One mustn't grudge the score; . . .

Or Donne's

> When by thy scorne, O murderess, I am dead, . . .

Or the action itself can be dramatic, as in Herbert's "I struck the board, and cry'd 'No more; . . .'" Or the situation can be given dramatically, as in Kunitz'

> Within the city of the burning cloud,
> Dragging my life behind me in a sack
> Naked I prowl, . . .

Nor must we forget the rhetorical question, as in W. H. Davies' lovely and little known poem, "V is for Venus":

> Is that star dumb, or am I deaf?
> Hour after hour I listen here

To catch the lovely music played
By Venus down the evening air.

Before the other stars come out,
Before the Moon is in her place—
I sit and watch those fingers move,
And mark the twitching of her face.

Hour after hour I strain my ears
For the lovely notes that will not come:
Is it my mortal flesh that's deaf,
Or that long-fingered star that's dumb?

And he ends with a question, you see. To question and to affirm, I suppose, are among the supreme duties of a poet.

But what about the rhythm and the motion of the poem as
a whole? Are there any ways of sustaining it, you may ask? We
must keep in mind that rhythm is the entire movement, the
flow, the recurrence of stress and unstress that is related to the
rhythms of the blood, the rhythms of nature. It involves certainly stress, time, pitch, the texture of the words, the total
meaning of the poem. We've been told that a rhythm is invariably produced by playing against an established pattern. Blake
does this admirably in "The Poison Tree":

I was angry with my friend:
I told my wrath, my wrath did end.
I was angry with my foe:
I told it not, my wrath did grow,

And I watered it in fears
Night and morning with my tears,
And I sunned it with smiles
And with soft deceitful wiles.

And it grew both day and night,
Till it bore an apple bright,
And my foe beheld it shine,
And he knew that it was mine,—

And into my garden stole
When the night had veiled the pole;
In the morning, glad I see
My foe outstretched beneath the tree.

The first and third lines in the first stanza have really only two
stresses. The lines said in an absolute rush, "I was angry with
my friend," "I was angry with my foe." But each is followed
by a perfectly regular iambic four-beat line, "I told my wrath,

my wrath did end." "I told it not, my wrath did grow." The whole poem is a masterly example of variation in rhythm, of playing against meter. It's what Blake has called "the bounding line," the nervousness, the tension, the energy in the whole poem. And this is a clue to everything. Rhythm gives us the very psychic energy of the speaker, in one emotional situation at least.

But there are slow rhythms too, for we're not always emotionally high. And these, as any practitioner will find, are very difficult to sustain in poetry without boring the reader. Listen to Janet Lewis' "Girl Help":

> Mild and slow and young,
> She moves about the room,
> And stirs the summer dust
> With her wide broom.
>
> In the warm, lofted air,
> Soft lips together pressed,
> Soft wispy hair,
> She stops to rest,
>
> And stops to breathe,
> Amid the summer hum,
> The great white lilac bloom
> Scented with days to come.

Here we see particularly the effect of texture, especially the vowel sounds as well as the effect of the dentates, the "D's" and "T's." The first line sets the pace. It can't be said fast. "Mild and slow and young." It's a little vignette, very feminine, absolutely true emotionally. The drowsy adolescent. But the poem is not static. The girl moves, she stirs, she stops to rest, and stops to breathe. At last, a real pick-up in motion. And the girl, virtually embraced by the season, is part of herself. It's nonsense, of course, to think that memorableness in poetry comes solely from rhetorical devices, or the following of certain sound patterns, or contrapuntal rhythmical effects. We all know that poetry is shot through with appeals to the unconscious, to the fears and desires that go far back into our childhood, into the imagination of the race. And we know that some words, like hill, plow, mother, window, bird, fish, are so drenched with human association, they sometimes can make even bad poems evocative. I remember the first time I heard Robert Frost read, in 1930. Suddenly a line, I think it was from Shakespeare, came into his head. He recited it. "Listen to that," he said. "Just like a *hiss*, just like a *hiss*." It is what Eliot has called "the auditory imagination." The sinuousness. A rhythm like the tail of a fish, a cadence like the sound of the sea or the arbor bees, a droning, a hissing, a sighing. I find it in early Auden:

> Shall memory restore
> The steps and the shore,
> The face and the meeting place;
> Shall the bird live,
> Shall the fish dive,
> And sheep obey
> In a sheep's way;
> Can love remember
> The question and the answer,
> Or love recover
> What has been dark and rich and warm all over?

Or to quote from my own "The Lost Son," the protagonist, we are told, is hunting, hunting along the river down among the rubbish, the bug-riddled foliage, by the muddy pond edge, by the bog holes, by the shrunken lake, hunting, in the heat of summer.

> The shape of a rat?
> It's bigger than that.
> It's less than a leg.
> And more than a nose,
> Just under the water
> It usually goes.

> Is it soft like a mouse?
> Can it wrinkle its nose?
> Could it come in the house
> On the tips of its toes?

> Take the skin of a cat
> And the back of an eel,
> Then roll them in grease,—
> That's the way it would feel.

> It's sleek as an otter
> With wide webby toes
> Just under the water
> It usually goes.

Curiously, we find this primitiveness of the imagination cropping up in the most sophisticated poetry. In Eliot; in Stevens' "She sang beyond the genius of the sea," and he keeps play-

ing with that wavelike repetitive motion until the whole poem
reverberates, and resounds to the pitch and swell of the sea
itself. Stevens can also intone and doodle platonically. But it's
the wildly nutty ones of his that I cherish thus:

> The garden flew round with the angel,
> The angel flew round with the clouds,
> And the clouds flew round and the clouds flew round
> And the clouds flew round with the clouds.
>
> Is there any secret in skulls,
> The cattle skulls in the woods?
> Do the drummers in black hoods
> Rumble anything out of their drums?
>
> Mrs. Anderson's Swedish baby
> Might well have been German or Spanish,
> Yet that things go round and again go round
> Has rather a classical sound.

A real piece of sophisticated looniness. We haven't lost, we
have recovered, in Stevens at least, the secret of being lyri-
cally funny. We are closer, rhythmically I think, to the nursery
rhyme, the poem of the common speech. If we concern ourselves with more primitive effects in poetry, we come inevitably to consideration, I think, of verse that is closer to prose.
And here we jump rhythmically to a kind of opposite extreme.
For many *strong* stresses, or a playing against an iambic pattern to a loosening up, a longer, more irregular foot. I agree
that free verse is a denial in terms. There is, invariably, the
ghost of some other form, often blank verse, behind what is
written, or the more elaborate rise and fall of the rhythmical
prose sentence. Let me point up, to use Mr. Warren's phrase,
in a more specific way the difference between the formal poem
and the more proselike piece. Mr. Ransom has read his beautiful elegy, "Bells for John Whiteside's Daughter"; I'd like to
read "Elegy for Jane" on the same theme, a poem, I'm proud
to say, Mr. Ransom first printed.

> I remember the neckcurls, limp and damp as tendrils;
> And her quick look, a sidelong pickerel smile;
> And how, once startled into talk, the light syllables leaped
>   for her,
> And she balanced in the delight of her thought,
> A wren, happy, tail into the wind,
> Her song trembling the twigs and small branches.
> The shade sang with her;

The leaves, their whispers turned to kissing;
And the mold sang in the bleached valleys under the rose.

Oh, when she was sad, she cast herself down into such a
    pure depth,
Even a father could not find her:
Scraping her cheek against straw;
Stirring the clearest water.

My sparrow, you are not here,
Waiting like a fern, making a spiny shadow.
The sides of wet stones cannot console me,
Nor the moss, wound with the last light.

If only I could nudge you from this sleep,
My maimed darling, my skittery pigeon.
Over this damp grave I speak the words of my love:
I, with no rights in this matter,
Neither father nor lover.

I think any reader would agree that Mr. Ransom's is a superior
piece; the emotion subtler, more complex and kept in control,
the psychological distance maintained with great skill. The un-
derstatement of "brown study," for instance, and the rhythms,
the light "i's," the off-rhymes, the feminine endings—"the
body," "study." The whole thing in beautiful balance, a truly
classical restraint. Behind this piece, as in a Hardy lyric, lies
a whole world. There is an immense tenderness, that rare
quality in modern poetry, in Mr. Ransom's elegy. It makes
me want to love all of the South, and that's an undertaking!
But let me indicate one or two technical effects in my little
piece. For one thing, the enumeration, the favorite device of
the more irregular poem. We see it again and again in Whitman and Lawrence. "I remember," then the listing, the ap-
positions, and the absolute construction. "Her song trem-
bling," etc. Then the last three lines in the stanza lengthen
out:

The shade sang with her;
The leaves, their whispers turned to kissing;
And the mold sang in the bleached valleys under the rose.

A kind of continuing triad. In the last two stanzas exactly the
opposite occurs, the final lines being,

Over this damp grave I speak the words of my love:
I, with no rights in this matter,
Neither father nor lover.

There is a successive shortening of the line length, an effect I have become inordinately fond of, I'm afraid. This little piece indicates in a way some of the strategies for the poet writing without the support of a formal pattern—he can vary his line length, modulate, he can stretch out the line, he can shorten. If he is a real master, he can, like Christopher Smart, make virtually every line an entity in itself, a poem, as he does in his magnificent ode to his cat, Jeoffrey. Here are a few excerpts:

For I will consider my Cat Jeoffrey.
For he is the servant of the Living God, duly and daily serving him.
For at the First glance of the glory of God in the East he worships in his way.
For is this done by wreathing his body seven times round with elegant quickness.
. . . For he is of the Lord's poor and so indeed is he called by benevolence perpetually—Poor Jeoffrey! poor Jeoffrey! the rat has bit thy throat.
For I bless the name of the Lord Jesus that Jeoffrey is better.
For the divine spirit comes about his body to sustain it in complete cat.
For he can jump over a stick which is patience upon proof positive . . .
For he can catch the cork and toss it again . . .
For he is good to think on, if a man would express himself neatly . . .
For by stroking of him I have found out electricity . . .
For God has blessed him in the variety of his movements.
For, tho he cannot fly, he is an excellent clamberer.
For his motions on the face of the earth are more than any other quadrupede.
For he can tread to all the measures upon the music.
For he can swim for life.
For he can creep.

It was Lawrence, a master of this sort of poem (I think I quote him more or less exactly) who said, "It all depends on the pause, the natural pause." In other words the breath unit, the language that is natural to the immediate thing, the particular emotion. Think of what we'd have missed in Lawrence, in Whitman, in Charlotte Mew or more lately, in Robert Lowell, if we denied this kind of poem. There are areas of experience in modern life that simply cannot be rendered by either the formal lyric or straight prose. We need the catalogue in our time. We need the eye close on the object, and the poem about the single incident—the animal, the child. We must permit poetry to extend consciousness as far, as deeply, as particularly as it can, to recapture, in Stanley Kunitz' phrase, "what it has lost to some extent to prose." We must realize, I think, that the writer in freer forms must have an even greater fidelity to his subject matter than the poet who has the support of form. He must keep his eye on the object, and his rhythm must move as a mind moves, must be imaginatively right, or he is lost. On the simplest level, something must happen in this kind of poem. The Smart sort of piece, or the biblical catalogue, is really easier to do than the free poem in the shorter line length. Let me end with a simple and somewhat clumsy example of my own, in which we see a formal device giving energy to the piece, that device being, simply, participial or verbal forms that keep the action going.

Big Wind

Where were the greenhouses going,
Lunging into the lashing
Wind driving water
So far down the river
All the faucets stopped?—
So we drained the manure-machine
For the steam plant,
Pumping the stale mixture
Into the rusty boilers,
Watching the pressure gauge
Waver over to red,
As the seams hissed
And the live steam
Drove to the far
End of the rose-house,
Where the worst wind was,
Creaking the cypress window-frames,
Cracking so much thin glass
We stayed all night,
Stuffing the holes with burlap;
But she rode it out,
That old rose-house,
She hove into the teeth of it,
The core and pith of that ugly storm,
Ploughing with her stiff prow,
Bucking into the wind-waves
That broke over the whole of her,
Flailing her sides with spray,

Flinging long strings of wet across the roof-top,
Finally veering, wearing themselves out, merely
Whistling thinly under the wind vents;
She sailed until the calm morning,
Carrying her full cargo of roses.

So we'll leave Roethke and his manure machine.

APPENDIXES

APPENDIXES

RAYMOND MACDONALD ALDEN

The Foot and The Verse

English verse is commonly measured by feet, a determinate number of which go to form a verse or line. The foot is determined by the distance from one accented syllable to another in the regular scheme of the metre. The usual metrical feet are either dissyllabic or trisyllabic. The dissyllabic foot is commonly called an *iambus* (or *iamb*) if the unaccented syllable precedes the accented, and a *trochee* if the accented precedes the unaccented. The trisyllabic foot is commonly called an *anapest* if the two unaccented syllables precede the accented syllable, and a *dactyl* if they follow the accented syllable.[1] It will be observed that the fundamental rhythm of both iambic and trochaic verse is the same, as is also that of both anapestic and dactylic verse; the distinction belonging only to the metre as measured into regular lines. Iambic and anapestic verse (in which the light syllables commonly open the verse) are sometimes called "ascending rhythm"; trochaic and dactylic verse (in which the accented syllables commonly open the verse) "descending rhythm." Ascending rhythm is very greatly in predominance in English poetry.

Reprinted and edited from English Verse: Specimens Illustrating its Principles and History. *First published by Henry Holt and Company, 1902. Copyright renewed 1930, expired 1958.*

[1] The names of the several kinds of feet are of course borrowed from classical prosody, where they are used to mark feet made up not of accented and unaccented, but of long and short syllables. The different significance of the terms as applied to the verse of different languages has given rise to some confusion, and it is proposed by some to abandon the classical terms; their use, however, seems to be too well established in English to permit of change. Some would even abandon the attempt to measure English verse by feet, contending that its rhythm is too free to admit of any such measuring process; thus, see Mr. J. M. Robertson, in the Appendix to *New Essays toward a Critical Method,* and Mr. J. A. Symonds in his *Blank Verse.* See also in Mr. Robert Bridges's *Milton's Prosody,* Appendix G "On the Use of Greek Terminology in English Prosody." (1901 ed. p. 77.)

The normal verse of any poem is therefore described by indicating the name of the foot and the number of feet in the verse. The number of feet is always indicated by the number of stresses or principal accents in the normal verse. As the light or unaccented syllables may vary from the typical number, it may also be necessary to indicate that the line is longer than its name would imply, by reason of Feminine Ending (a light syllable added at the end) or Anacrusis (a light syllable prefixed); or that it is shorter than its name would indicate by reason of Catalexis or Truncation (the light syllable at the end—or less frequently at the beginning—being omitted).

In like manner, any particular verse or line is fully described by indicating: (1) the typical foot; (2) the number of feet; (3) the place of the cesura; (4) the presence or absence of a final pause ("end-stopped" or "run-on"); (5) the presence of such irregularities as

(a) Anacrusis or feminine ending,
(b) Catalexis (or truncation),
(c) Substitution of exceptional feet for the tyical foot,
(d) Pauses other than the cesural.

One-stress iambic.

> Thus I
> Pass by
>   And die
> Unknown
>   And gone.

(HERRICK: *Upon his Departure Hence.* 1648.)

Two-stress iambic.

> Most good, most fair,
> Or things as rare
> To call you 's lost;
> For all the cost
> Words can bestow
> So poorly show, . . .

(DRAYTON: *Amouret Anacrontic.* ab. 1600.)

Two-stress trochaic.

> Could I catch that
> Nimble traitor,
> Scornful Laura,
> Swift-foot Laura,
> Soon then would I
> Seek avengement.

(CAMPION: Anacreontics, in *Observations in the Art of English Poesie.* 1602.)

(Catalectic, and in combination with three-stress:)
>   Summer's crest
>   Red-gold tressed,
>   Corn-flowers peeping under;—
>   Idle noons,
>   Lingering moons,
>   Sudden cloud,
>   Lightning's shroud,
>   Sudden rain,
>   Quick again
>   Smiles where late was thunder.

(GEORGE ELIOT: Song from *The Spanish Gypsy*, Bk. i. 1868.)

The trochaic measures in *The Spanish Gypsy* are in imitation of the similar forms in Spanish poetry.

Two-stress anapestic.
(In combination with three-stress:)
>   Like a gloomy stain
>   On the emerald main
>   Alpheus rushed behind,—
>   As an eagle pursuing
>   A dove to its ruin
>   Down the streams of the cloudy wind.
>   (SHELLEY: *Arethusa*. 1820.)

(With feminine ending:)
>   He is gone on the mountain,
>   He is lost to the forest,
>   Like a summer-dried fountain,
>   When our need was the sorest.
>   The font, reappearing,
>   From the raindrops shall borrow,
>   But to us comes no cheering,
>   To Duncan no morrow!

(SCOTT: Coronach, from *The Lady of the Lake*, Canto 3. 1810.)

These specimens, as is usual in anapestic verse, show considerable freedom in the treatment of the part of the foot containing the light syllables, substituted iambi being very common. Note the iambi in the Shelley stanza, line 1, second foot, and line 5, first foot. In the latter case, however, the first light syllable of line 5 is really supplied by the syllable added to make the feminine ending of line 4. In like manner, in the

Scott stanza, the first syllable of line 8 is really supplied by the
-ing of line 7; and where we have both feminine ending (in
line 1) and a full anapest following, the effect is that of a
hypermetrical syllable which must be hurried over in the reading. In the specimen from Browning we find an iambus in the
opening foot in lines 2 and 6 (also, of course, in lines 1 and
5).

Two-stress dactylic.

> One more Unfortunate,
> Weary of breath,
> Rashly importunate,
> Gone to her death!
>
> Take her up tenderly,
> Lift her with care;
> Fashioned so slenderly,
> Young, and so fair!

(THOMAS HOOD: *The Bridge of Sighs*. ab. 1830.)

Here the alternate lines are catalectic, both light syllables
being wanting.

> Pale beech and pine so blue
>   Set in one clay,
> Bough to bough cannot you
>   Live out your day?
> When the rains skim and skip,
> Why mar sweet comradeship,
> Blighting with poison drip
>   Neighbourly spray?

(HARDY: *In a Wood*. 1887.)

The final foot of the indented lines is catalectic, lacking the
two unstressed syllables.

Two-stress irregular.

> On the ground
> Sleep sound:
> I'll apply
> To your eye,
> Gentle lover, remedy.
> When thou wak'st,
> Thou tak'st
> True delight
> In the sight
> Of thy former lady's eye.

(SHAKESPEARE: Puck's Song in *Midsummer Night's Dream*,
   III. ii. ab. 1595.)

> Live thy Life,
>   Young and old,
> Like yon oak,
> Bright in spring,
>   Living gold;
>
> Summer-rich
>   Then; and then
> Autumn-changed,
> Soberer-hued
>   Gold again.
>
> All his leaves
>   Fallen at length,
> Look, he stands,
> Trunk and bough,
>   Naked strength.
>   (TENNYSON: *The Oak.* 1889.)

We can scan these lines either as iambic with initial
catalexis, or as trochaic with final catalexis. Our ears prefer
falling rhythm, influenced doubtless by the subject and elegiac
tone. The possibility of one-stress dactylic also suggests itself:

Live thy life, | Young and old |, ctc.

Three-stress iambic.
> O let the solid ground
>   Not fail beneath my feet
> Before my life has found
>   What some have found so sweet;
> Then let come what may,
> What matter if I go mad,
> I shall have had my day.
>   (TENNYSON: Song in *Maud,* xi. 1855.)

(In combination with verse of four, five, and six stresses:)
>   The Oracles are dumb;
>   No voice or hideous hum
> Runs through the arched roof in words deceiving.
>   Apollo from his shrine
>   Can no more divine,
> With hollow shriek the steep of Delphos leaving:
>   No nightly trance or breathed spell
> Inspires the pale-eyed priest from the prophetic cell.
(MILTON: *Ode on the Morning of Christ's Nativity.* 1629.)

Here, in line 5, we have an instance of a verse truncated at
the beginning,—rare in modern English poetry.

Three-stress trochaic.

> All the night in woe
> Lyca's parents go
> Over vallies deep,
> While the desarts weep.
>
> Tired and woe-begone,
> Hoarse with making moan,
> Arm in arm seven days
> They trac'd the desart ways.
> (BLAKE: *The Little Girl Found.* 1794.)

Here the lines are catalectic, omitting the final unstressed syllable. The last line above is actually iambic.

(In combination with four-stress trochaic:)

> Little Lamb, who made thee?
> Dost thou know who made thee?
> Gave the life, & bid thee feed
> By the stream & o'er the mead;
> Gave thee clothing of delight,
> Softest clothing, wooly bright;
> Gave thee such a tender voice,
> Making all the vales rejoice?
> Little Lamb, who made thee?
> Dost thou know who made thee?
> (BLAKE: *The Lamb.* 1789.)

(In combination with six-stress verses:)

> Hail to thee, blithe Spirit!
> Bird thou never wert,
> That from heaven, or near it,
> Pourest thy full heart
> In profuse strains of unpremeditated art.
>
> Higher still and higher
> From the earth thou springest,
> Like a cloud of fire
> The blue deep thou wingest,
> And singing still dost soar, and soaring ever singest.
> (SHELLEY: *To a Skylark.* 1820.)

Here lines 2 and 4 are catalectic.

Three-stress anapestic.

> I am monarch of all I survey;
> My right there is none to dispute;
> From the centre all round to the sea
> I am lord of the fowl and the brute.
> (COWPER: *Verses supposed to be written by Alexander Selkirk.* 1782.)

In this specimen lines 2, 5, 6, and 8 show initial truncation, the first light syllable being missing.

(With two-stress verse:)

> His desire is a dureless content,
>   And a trustless joy;
> He is won with a world of despair
>   And is lost with a toy. . . .
>
> But true love is a durable fire,
>   In the mind ever burning,
> Never sick, never old, never dead,
>   From itself never turning.

(SIR WALTER RALEIGH (?): *Pilgrim to Pilgrim*. In Ms. Rawl. 85; in Schelling's *Elizabethan Lyrics*, p. 3.)

Three-stress dactylic.
(Catalectic:)

> This is a spray the Bird clung to,
>   Making it blossom with pleasure,
> Ere the high tree-top she sprung to,
>   Fit for her nest and her treasure.

(BROWNING: *Misconceptions.* 1855.)

Four-stress iambic: octosyllabic couplets.

> O god of science and of light,
> Apollo, through thy grete might,
> This litel laste bok thou gye!
> Nat that I wilne, for maistrye,
> Here art poetical be shewed;
> But, for the rym is light and lewed,
> Yit make hit sumwhat agreable,
> Though som vers faile in a sillable;
> And that I do no diligence
> To shewe craft, but o sentence.
> And if, divyne vertu, thou
> Wilt helpe me to shewe now
> That in myn hede y-marked is—
> Lo, that is for to menen this,
> The Hous of Fame to descryve—
> Thou shalt see me go, as blyve,
> Unto the nexte laure I see,
> And kisse hit, for hit is thy tree.

(CHAUCER: *House of Fame*, II. 1091-1108. ab. 1385.)

It was Gower and Chaucer, in the fourteenth century, who brought the use of the eight-syllable couplet to the point of accuracy and perfection. Gower made it the vehicle of the interminable narrative of the *Confessio Amantis*, using it with regularity but with great monotony. Chaucer transformed it into a much more flexible form (with freedom of cesura, *enjambement*, and inversions), using it in about 3500 lines of his poetry (excluding the translation of the *Roman de la Rose*), but early leaving it for the decasyllabic verse. In modern English poetry this short couplet has rarely been used for continuous narrative of a serious character, except by Byron and Wordsworth.

> But let my due feet never fail
> To walk the studious cloister's pale,
> And love the high embowed roof,
> With antique pillars massy proof,
> And storied windows richly dight,
> Casting a dim religious light.
> There let the pealing organ blow,
> To the full-voiced choir below,
> In service high, and anthems clear,
> As may with sweetness, through mine ear,
> Dissolve me into ecstasies,
> And bring all heaven before my eyes.
> (MILTON: *Il Penseroso*, 11. 155-166. 1634.)

A sect whose chief devotion lies
In odd, perverse antipathies,
In falling out with that or this
And finding something still amiss;
More peevish, cross, and splenetic
Than dog distract or monkey sick:
That with more care keep holyday
The wrong, than others the right way;
Compound for sins they are inclined to
By damning those they have no mind to. . . .
Rather than fail they will defy
That which they love most tenderly;
Quarrel with mince-pies, and disparage
Their best and dearest friend plum-porridge,
Fat pig and goose itself oppose,
And blaspheme custard through the nose.
(SAMUEL BUTLER: *Hudibras*, Part I. 1663.)

Butler made the octosyllabic couplet so entirely his own, for the purposes of this jogging satiric verse, that ever since it has frequently been called "Hudibrastic."

> Stella this Day is Thirty-four,
> (We shan't dispute a Year or more:)
> However, Stella, be not troubled,
> Although thy Size and Years are doubled,
> Since first I saw thee at Sixteen,
> The brightest Virgin on the Green.

So little is thy Form declin'd;
Made up so largely in thy Mind.
  (SWIFT: *Stella's Birthday.* 1718.)

See, whilst Thou weep'st, fair Cloe, see
The World in Sympathy with Thee.
The chearful Birds no longer sing,
Each drops his Head, and hangs his Wing.
The Clouds have bent their Bosom lower,
And shed their Sorrows in a Show'r.
  (PRIOR: *To Cloe Weeping,* 1718.)

When chapman billies leave the street,
And drouthy neibors, neibors meet;
As market days are wearing late,
And folk begin to tak the gate,
While we sit bousing at the nappy,
An' getting fou and unco happy,
We think na on the lang Scots miles,
The mosses, waters, slaps and stiles,
That lie between us and our hame,
Where sits our sulky, sullen dame,
Gathering her brows like gathering storm,
Nursing her wrath to keep it warm.
(BURNS: *Tam O'Shanter,* ll. 1-12. 1790.)

  Three Virgins at the break of day:
  "Whither young man, whither away?
  "Alas for woe! alas for woe!"
  They cry, & tears for ever flow.
  The one was Cloth'd in flames of fire,
  The other Cloth'd in iron wire,
  The other Cloth'd in tears & sighs
  Dazzling bright before my Eyes.
  (BLAKE: *The Golden Net.* c. 1803.)

Four-stress trochaic.
  Honour, riches, marriage-blessing,
  Long continuance, and increasing,
  Hourly joys be still upon you!
  Juno sings her blessings on you.
(SHAKESPEARE: Juno's Song in *The Tempest,* IV. i. ab. 1610.)

(Catalectic:)
  When the stars threw down their spears,
  And water'd heaven with their tears,
  Did he smile his work to see?
  Did he who made the Lamb make thee?

Tyger! Tyger! burning bright
In the forests of the night,
What immortal hand or eye,
Dare frame thy fearful symmetry?
(BLAKE: *The Tyger*. 1794.)

Souls of Poets dead and gone,
What Elysium have ye known,
Happy field or mossy cavern,
Choicer than the Mermaid Tavern?
Have ye tippled drink more fine
Than mine host's Canary wine?
Or are fruits of Paradise
Sweeter than those dainty pies
Of venison? O generous food!
Drest as though bold Robin Hood
Would, with his maid Marian,
Sup and bowse from horn and can.
(KEATS: *Lines on the Mermaid Tavern*. 1820.)

Four-stress anapestic.
What I speak, my fair Chloe, and what I write, shows
    The difference there is betwixt nature and art:
I court others in verse; but I love thee in prose:
    And they have my whimsies; but thou hast my heart.
(PRIOR: *A Better Answer*. ab. 1710.)

Prior's anapests well illustrate the appropriateness of the measure for light tripping effects, such as are sought in *vers de société*. See also the measure of Goldsmith's *Retaliation*, especially the passage beginning—

"Here lies David Garrick, describe me who can;
An abridgment of all that was pleasant in man."

The Assyrian came down like the wolf on the fold,
And his cohorts were gleaming in purple and gold;
And the sheen of their spears was like stars on the sea,
When the blue wave rolls nightly on deep Galilee.
(BYRON: *The Destruction of Sennacherib*. 1815.)

Four-stress dactylic.
After the pangs of a desperate Lover,
When day and night I have sigh'd all in vain,
Ah what a pleasure it is to discover
In her eyes pity, who causes my pain!

When with unkindness our love at stand is,
And both have punish'd our selves with the pain,
Ah what a pleasure the touch of her hand is,
Ah what a pleasure to press it again!

> When the denyal comes fainter and fainter,
> And her eyes give what her tongue does deny,
> Ah what a trembling I feel when I venture,
> Ah what a trembling does usher my joy!
>
> When, with a Sigh, she accords me the blessing,
> And her eyes twinkle 'twixt pleasure and pain;
> Ah what a joy 'tis beyond all expressing,
> Ah what a joy to hear, shall we again?
> (DRYDEN: Song in *An Evening's Love*. 1671.)

Of this song Mr. Saintsbury says that it is "one of the rare examples of a real dactylic metre in English, where the dactyls are not, as usual, equally to be scanned as anapests." (*Life of Dryden*, Men of Letters Series, p. 62.) Here, as almost always in English, the measure is catalectic, a final dactyl being instinctively avoided, except in short two-stress lines.

Five-stress iambic: rhymed.

> A good man was ther of religioun,
> And was a povre Persoun of a toun;
> But riche he was of holy thoght and werk.
> He was also a lerned man, a clerk,
> That Cristes gospel trewely wolde preche;
> His parisshens devoutly wolde he teche.
> Benigne he was, and wonder diligent,
> And in adversitee ful pacient; . . .
> He wayted after no pompe and reverence,
> Ne maked him a spyced conscience,
> But Cristes lore, and his apostles twelve,
> He taughte, and first he folwed it himselve.

(CHAUCER: Prologue to *Canterbury Tales*, ll. 477-484, 525-528. ab. 1385.)

With Chaucer we have the first deliberate use of the five-stress couplet, in continuous verse, known to English poetry. His earliest use of the pentameter line was in the *Compleynt to Pitee* (perhaps written about 1371), in the "rime royal" stanza; his earliest use of the pentameter couplet was in the *Legend of Good Women*, usually dated 1385. From that time the measure became almost his only instrument, and we find altogether in his poetry some 16,000 lines in the couplet, besides some 14,000 more in rime royal. Too much praise cannot be given Chaucer's use of the couplet. Although it was an experiment in English verse, it has perhaps hardly been used since his time with greater skill. He used a variety of cesuras (see ten Brink's monograph for the enumeration of them), a very large number of feminine endings (such as the still pro-

nounced final -e and similar syllables easily provided), free
inversions in the first foot and elsewhere, and many run-on
lines (in a typical 100 lines some 16 run-on lines and 7 run-on
couplets appearing). The total effect is one of combined freedom and mastery, of fluent conversational style yet within the
limits of guarded artistic form.

> But the false Fox most kindly played his part;
> For whatsoever mother-wit or art
> Could work, he put in proof: no practice sly,
> No counterpoint of cunning policy,
> No reach, no breach, that might him profit bring,
> But he the same did to his purpose wring. . . .
> He fed his cubs with fat of all the soil,
> And with the sweet of others' sweating toil;
> He crammed them with crumbs of benefices,
> And fill'd their mouths with meeds of malefices.
> . . . No statute so established might be,
> Nor ordinance so needful, but that he
> Would violate, though not with violence,
> Yet under color of the confidence
> The which the Ape repos'd in him alone,
> And reckon'd him the kingdom's corner-stone.
> (SPENSER: *Mother Hubbard's Tale* ll. 1137-1166. 1591.)

Spenser's use of the heroic couplet for the *Mother Hub-
bard's Tale* is the earliest instance of its adoption in English
for satirical verse,—a purpose for which its later history showed
it to be peculiarly well fitted.

> Upon her head she wore a myrtle wreath,
> From whence her veil reach'd to the ground beneath:
> Her veil was artificial flowers and leaves,
> Whose workmanship both man and beast deceives:
> Many would praise the sweet smell as she past,
> When 'twas the odor which her breath forth cast;
> And there for honey bees have sought in vain,
> And, beat from thence, have lighted there again.
> About her neck hung chains of pebble-stone,
> Which, lighten'd by her neck, like diamonds shone.
> (MARLOWE: *Hero and Leander*, ll. 17-26.
> ab. 1590, pub. 1598.)

> Too popular is tragic poesy,
> Straining his tip-toes for a farthing fee,
> And doth beside on rimeless numbers tread;
> Unbid iambics flow from careless head.
> Some braver brain in high heroic rhymes
> Compileth worm-eat stories of old times:

And he, like some imperious Maronist,
Conjures the Muses that they him assist.
Then strives he to bombast his feeble lines
With far-fetch'd phrase. — ...
Painters and poets, hold your ancient right:
Write what you will, and write not what you might:
Their limits be their list, their reason will.
But if some painter in presuming skill
Should paint the stars in centre of the earth,
Could ye forbear some smiles, and taunting mirth?
(JOSEPH HALL: Virgidemiarum Libri VI.,
bk. i. satire 4. 1597.)

Joseph Hall was the most vigorous satirist of the group of
Elizabethans who, in the last decade of the sixteenth century,
were imitating the satires of Horace, Juvenal, and Persius.
Hall's satires have a curiously eighteenth-century flavor, and
his couplets are frequently very similar to those of the age of
Pope.

On the other hand, the verse of the satires of John Donne,
from which the following specimen is taken, is the roughest
and most difficult of all the satires of the group. The reputa-
tion of Donne's satires for metrical ruggedness has affected
unjustly that of his other poetry and that of the Elizabethan
satires in general. Dryden said: "Would not Donne's Satires,
which abound with so much wit, appear more charming if he
had taken care of his words and of his numbers?" (Essay on
Satire.) And Pope "versified" two of them, so as to bring them
into a form pleasing to the ear of his age.

Therefore I suffered this: towards me did run
A thing more strange than on Nile's slime the sun
E'er bred, or all which into Noah's ark came:
A thing which would have posed Adam to name;
Stranger than seven antiquaries' studies,
Than Afric's monsters, Guiana's rarities; ...
Sleeveless his jerkin was, and it had been
Velvet, but 'twas now (so much ground was seen)
Become tufftaffaty; and our children shall
See it plain rash awhile, then nought at all.
This thing hath travelled, and faith, speaks all tongues,
And only knoweth what to all states belongs.
(JOHN DONNE: Satire iv. ll. 17 ff. ab. 1593.)

This gallant pins the wenches on his sleeve.
Had he been Adam, he had tempted Eve.
He can carve too, and lisp: why, this is he
That kiss'd his hand away in courtesy;

This is the ape of form, monsieur the nice,
That, when he plays at tables, chides the dice
In honorable terms: nay, he can sing
A mean most meanly, and, in ushering,
Mend him who can: the ladies call him sweet;
The stairs, as he treads on them, kiss his feet.
> (SHAKESPEARE: *Love's Labor's Lost*,
> V. ii. 315-330. ab. 1590.)

The use of rimed couplets in Shakespeare's dramas is especially characteristic of his earlier work. In this play, *Love's Labor's Lost*, Dowden says, "there are about two rhymed lines to every one of blank verse" (*Shakespeare Primer*, p. 44). In the late plays, on the other hand, rime disappears almost altogether. It will be observed that while Shakespeare's heroic verse is usually fairly regular, with not very many run-on lines, it yet differs in quality from that of satires. The dramatic use moulds it into different cadences, and the single couplet is, perhaps, less noticeably the unit of the verse.

Shepherd, I pray thee stay. Where hast thou been?
Or whither goest thou? Here be woods as green
As any; air likewise as fresh and sweet
As where smooth Zephyrus plays on the fleet
Face of the curled streams; with flowers as many
As the young spring gives, and as choice as any;
Here be all new delights, cool streams and wells,
Arbors o'ergrown with woodbines, caves, and dells;
Choose where thou wilt, whilst I sit by and sing,
Or gather rushes, to make many a ring
For thy long fingers; tell thee tales of love,—
How the pale Phoebe, hunting in a grove,
First saw the boy Endymion, from whose eyes
She took eternal fire that never dies;
How she conveyed him softly in a sleep,
His temples bound with poppy, to the steep
Head of old Latmus, where she stoops each night,
Gilding the mountain with her brother's light,
To kiss her sweetest.
> (FLETCHER: *The Faithful Shepherdess*,
> I. iii. ab. 1610.)

Fletcher uses the couplet in this drama with a freedom hardly found elsewhere until the time of Keats.

If Rome so great, and in her wisest age,
Fear'd not to boast the glories of her stage,
As skilful Roscius, and grave Æsop, men,

Yet crown'd with honors, as with riches, then;
Who had no less a trumpet of their name
Than Cicero, whose every breath was fame:
How can so great example die in me,
That, Allen, I should pause to publish thee?
Who both their graces in thyself hast more
Outstript, than they did all that went before:
And present worth in all dost so contract,
As others speak, but only thou dost act.
Wear this renown. 'Tis just, that who did give
So many poets life, by one should live.
(BEN JONSON: *Epigram LXXXIX, to Edward Allen*. 1616.)

Jonson is thought by some to have been the founder of the classical school of the seventeenth and eighteenth centuries, which made the heroic couplet peculiarly its own. See on this subject an article by Prof. F. E. Schelling, "Ben Jonson and the Classical School," in the *Publications of the Modern Language Association*, n. s. vol. vi. p. 221. Professor Schelling finds in Jonson's verse all the characteristics of the later couplet of Waller and Dryden: end-stopped lines and couplets, a preference for medial cesura, and an antithetical structure of the verse. "No better specimen of Jonson's antithetical manner could be found," he says further, than the Epigram here quoted. So far as this antithetical quality of Jonson's verse is concerned, Professor Schelling's view cannot be questioned; but that Jonson shows any singular preference for end-stopped lines and couplets may be seriously questioned.

These mighty peers placed in the gilded barge,
Proud with the burden of so brave a charge,
With painted oars the youths begin to sweep
Neptune's smooth face, and cleave the yielding deep;
Which soon becomes the seat of sudden war
Between the wind and tide that fiercely jar.
As when a sort of lusty shepherds try
Their force at football, care of victory
Makes them salute so rudely breast to breast,
That their encounters seem too rough for jest;
They ply their feet, and still the restless ball,
Tossed to and fro, is urged by them all:
So fares the doubtful barge 'twixt tide and winds,
And like effect of their contention finds.
(WALLER: *Of the Danger his Majesty [being Prince]
escaped in the Road at St. Andrews*. 1623?)

Edmund Waller is the chief representative of the early classical poetry of the seventeenth century, and of the polish-

ing and regulating of the couplet which prepared the way for
the verse of Dryden and Pope. The dominant characteristic
of this verse is its avoidance of *enjambement*, or run-on lines,
still more of run-on couplets. The growing precision of French
verse at the same time was perhaps influential in England.
Malherbe, who was at the French court after 1605, set rules
for more regular verse, and forbade, among other things, the
use of run-on lines—a precept which held good in French
poetry until the nineteenth century. The influence of Waller
in England was, for a considerable period, hardly less than that
of Malherbe in France.

> My eye, descending from the hill, surveys
> Where Thames amongst the wanton valleys strays;
> Thames, the most loved of all the Ocean's sons
> By his old sire, to his embraces runs . . .
>
> O could I flow like thee, and make thy stream
> My great example, as it is my theme!
> Though deep, yet clear, though gentle, yet not dull,
> Strong without rage, without o'erflowing full.
>   (SIR JOHN DENHAM: *Cooper's Hill*. 1642.)

"Denham," says Mr. Gosse, "was the first writer to adopt
the precise manner of versification introduced by Waller."
(Ward's *English Poets*, vol. ii. p. 279.) The last four lines of
the specimen here given have been universally admired.

> Of these the false Achitophel was first,
> A name to all succeeding ages curst:
> For close designs and crooked counsels fit,
> Sagacious, bold, and turbulent of wit,
> Restless, unfixed in principles and place,
> In power unpleased, impatient of disgrace;
> A fiery soul, which, working out its way,
> Fretted the pigmy body to decay,
> And o'er-informed the tenement of clay.
> A daring pilot in extremity.
> Pleased with the danger, when the waves went high,
> He sought the storms; but, for a calm unfit,
> Would steer too nigh the sands, to boast his wit.
> Great wits are sure to madness near allied,
> And thin partitions do their bounds divide;
> Else, why should he, with wealth and honor blest,
> Refuse his age the needful hours of rest?
>   (DRYDEN: *Absalom and Achitophel*,
>   part I. ll. 150-179. 1681.)

Dryden was the first great English poet after Chaucer to

make the heroic couplet his chief vehicle of expression, and he
put far more variety and vigor into it than had been achieved
by his nearer predecessors. As Pope said:

> "Waller was smooth, but Dryden taught to join
> The varying verse, the full resounding line,
> The long majestic march, the energy divine."
> *(Epistle ii., 267.)*

And Gray, some years later, symbolized Dryden's couplet in
these fine lines of the *Progress of Poesy*:

> "Behold, where Dryden's less presumptuous car,
> Wide o'er the fields of glory bear
> Two coursers of ethereal race,
> With necks in thunder clothed, and long-resounding pace."

> Why boast we, Glaucus, our extended reign
> Where Xanthus' streams enrich the Lycian plain,
> Our numerous herds that range the fruitful field,
> And hills where vines their purple harvest yield,
> Our foaming bowls with purer nectar crowned,
> Our feasts enhanced with music's sprightly sound?
> Why on those shores are we with joy surveyed,
> Admired as heroes, and as gods obeyed;
> Unless great acts superior merit prove,
> And vindicate the bounteous powers above?
> 'Tis ours, the dignity they give to grace;
> The first in valor, as the first in place:
> That when with wondering eyes our martial bands
> Behold our deeds transcending our commands,
> Such, they may cry, deserve the sovereign state,
> Whom those that envy dare not imitate!
> Could all our care elude the gloomy grave,
> Which claims no less the fearful than the brave,
> For lust of fame I should not vainly dare
> In fighting fields, nor urge the soul to war.
> But since, alas! ignoble age must come,
> Disease, and death's inexorable doom;
> The life which others pay let us bestow,
> And give to fame what we to nature owe;
> Brave though we fall, and honored if we live,
> Or let us glory gain, or glory give!
> *(POPE: Iliad, bk. xii.)*

Pope's couplet, while less vigorous and varied than Dryden's, has been generally considered the most perfect development of the typical measure of the classical school. Mr.

Courthope thinks that in this speech from the *Iliad*, Pope "perhaps attains the highest level of which the heroic couplet is capable."

(*Works of Pope*, vol. v. p. 167.)

> Darkness begins to reign; the louder wind
> Appals the weak and awes the firmer mind;
> But frights not him whom evening and the spray
> In part conceal—yon prowler on his way.
> Lo, he has something seen; he runs apace,
> As if he feared companion in the chase;
> He sees his prize, and now he turns again,
> Slowly and sorrowing—"Was your search in vain?"
> Gruffly he answers, " 'Tis a sorry sight!
> A seaman's body: there'll be more to-night!"
> (CRABBE: *The Borough*, letter i. 1810.)

Crabbe's poems are the latest to use the strict Popean couplet for narrative and descriptive purposes, and his couplets have a certain characteristic reticence and vigor.

> Behold! in various throngs the scribbling crew,
> For notice eager, pass in long review:
> Each spurs his jaded Pegasus apace,
> And rhyme and blank maintain an equal race;
> Sonnets on sonnets crowd, and ode on ode;
> And tales of terror jostle on the road;
> Immeasurable measures move along;
> For simpering folly loves a varied song,
> To strange mysterious dulness still the friend,
> Admires the strain she cannot comprehend.
> Thus Lays of Minstrels—may they be the last!—
> On half-strung harps whine mournful to the blast;
> While mountain spirits prate to river sprites,
> That dames may listen to the sound at nights;
> And goblin brats, of Gilpin Horner's brood,
> Decoy young border-nobles through the wood,
> And skip at every step, Lord knows how high,
> And frighten foolish babes, the Lord knows why.
> (BYRON: *English Bards and Scotch Reviewers*. 1809.)

> Hanging thick clusters from light boughs; in short,
> All the sweet cups to which the bees resort;
> With plots of grass, and leafier walks between
> Of red geraniums, and of jessamine,
> And orange, whose warm leaves so finely suit,
> And look as if they shade a golden fruit;

And midst the flowers, turfed round beneath a shade
Of darksome pines, a babbling fountain played,
And 'twixt their shafts you saw the water bright,
Which through the tops glimmered with showering light.

(LEIGH HUNT: *The Story of Rimini*. 1816.)

Of this poem Mr. C. H. Herford says: "*The Story of Rimini* is the starting-point of that free or Chaucerian treatment of the heroic couplet, and of the colloquial style, eschewing epigram and full of familiar turns, which Shelley in *Julian and Maddalo* and Keats in *Lamia* made classical." (*Age of Wordsworth*, p. 83.) The treatment of the couplet is still characterized by but slight use of run-on lines, and a preference for the medial cesura; but on the other hand there is a large degree of freedom in the inversion of accents and other alterations of the regular stress.

A thing of beauty is a joy forever:
Its loveliness increases; it will never
Pass into nothingness; but still will keep
A bower quiet for us, and a sleep
Full of sweet dreams, and health, and quiet breathing.
Therefore, on every morrow are we wreathing
A flowery band to bind us to the earth,
Spite of despondence, of the inhuman dearth
Of noble natures, of the gloomy days,
Of all the unhealthy and o'er-darkened ways
Made for our searching: yes, in spite of all,
Some shape of beauty moves away the pall
From our dark spirits. Such the sun, the moon,
Trees old and young, sprouting a shady boon
For simple sheep; and such are daffodils
With the green world they live in; and clear rills
That for themselves a cooling covert make
'Gainst the hot season; the mid-forest brake,
Rich with a sprinkling of fair musk-rose blooms;
And such too is the grandeur of the dooms
We have imagined for the mighty dead;
All lovely tales that we have heard or read:
An endless fountain of immortal drink,
Pouring unto us from the heaven's brink.

(KEATS: *Endymion*, ll. 1-24. 1818.)

In the couplet of Keats and of a number of his successors, we have a really different measure from the "heroic couplet" proper. The individual line and the couplet alike cease to be prominent units of the verse. The effect is therefore closely allied to that of blank verse; the rimes, not being emphasized

by marked pauses, serving rather as means of tone color than
as organizers of the verse.

> Past thought and speech her maiden motions were,
> And a more golden sunrise was her hair.
> The very veil of her bright flesh was made
> As of light woven and moonbeam-colored shade
> More fine than moonbeams; white her eyelids shone
> As snow sun-stricken that endures the sun,
> And through their curled and colored clouds of deep
> Luminous lashes, thick as dreams in sleep,
> Shone as the sea's depth swallowing up the sky's
> The springs of unimaginable eyes.
>> (SWINBURNE: *Tristram of Lyonesse;*
>> *the Sailing of the Swallow.*)

It will be noticed that in Swinburne's use of the couplet the
single line is even less the unit of measure than in Keats and
Shelley; the periods correspond closely to those in the blank
verse of Milton and Tennyson.

Five-stress iambic: blank verse.

Unrimed five-stress verse early became the accepted form
for English dramatic poetry, and in the modern English period
has become the favorite form for long continuous poems, narrative and reflective as well. In general, as will appear from
the specimens, it is marked not only by the absence of rime
but by a prevalent freedom of structure rarely found in the
couplet.

> By night she flies amid the cloudy sky,
> Shrieking, by the dark shadow of the earth,
> Ne doth decline to the sweet sleep her eyes:
> By day she sits to mark on the house top,
> Or turrets high, and the great towns affrays;
> As mindful of ill and lies as blazing truth.
>> (EARL OF SURREY: *Æneid*, book IV. 223-242.
>>> ab. 1540. pub. 1557.)

Surrey's translation of two books of the *Æneid* may have
been suggested by the translation (1541) made by Francesco
Maria Molza, attributed at the time to Cardinal Ippolito de
Medici. This was in Italian unrimed verse. (See Henry Mor-
ley's *First Sketch of English Literature*, p. 294, and his *English
Writers*, vol. viii. p. 61.) The verse of Surrey, like Wyatt's,

shows a somewhat mechanical adherence to the syllable-count-ing principle, in contrast to regard for accents. Thus we find such lines as:

> "Each palace, and sacred porch of the gods."
> "By the divine science of Minerva."

> O Jove, how are these people's hearts abused!
> What blind fury thus headlong carries them,
> That, though so many books, so many rolls
> Of ancient time record what grievous plagues
> Light on these rebels aye, and though so oft
> Their ears have heard their aged fathers tell
> What just reward these traitors still receive,—
> Yea, though themselves have seen deep death and blood
> By strangling cord and slaughter of the sword
> To such assigned, yet can they not beware,
> Yet cannot stay their lewd rebellious hands,
> But, suff'ring too foul reason to distain
> Their wretched minds, forget their loyal heart,
> Reject all truth, and rise against their prince?
> (SACKVILLE and NORTON: Gorboduc, or Ferrex and Porrex,
>   V. ii. 1-14. 1565.)

This tragedy, although Dryden curiously instanced it in defence of the use of rime on the stage, was the earliest English drama in blank verse. The metre is decidedly more monoto-nous than Surrey's, and gives little hint of the possibilities of the measure for dramatic expression. In general, the early experiments in blank verse suggest—what they must often have seemed to their writers the mere use of the decasyllabic couplet deprived of its rime. Nevertheless, as Mr. Symonds remarks of a passage in Gorboduc, "we yet may trace variety and emphasis in the pauses of these lines beyond what would at that epoch have been possible in sequences of rhymed couplets." (Blank Verse, p. 20.)

>   Ah, Faustus,
> Now hast thou but one bare hour to live,
> And then thou must be damned perpetually!
> Stand still, you ever-moving spheres of Heaven,
> That time may cease, and midnight never come:
> Fair Nature's eye, rise, rise again, and make
> Perpetual day; or let this hour be but
> A year, a month, a week, a natural day,
> That Faustus may repent and save his soul!

O lente, lente, currite noctis equi!
The stars move still, time runs, the clock will strike,
The Devil will come, and Faustus must be damned.
O, I'll leap up to my God! Who pulls me down?
See, see where Christ's blood streams in the firmament!
One drop would save my soul—half a drop: ah, my Christ!
Ah, rend not my heart for naming of my Christ!
Yet will I call on him: O spare me, Lucifer!
(MARLOWE: *Doctor Faustus*, sc. xvi. ll. 65-81. Printed 1604;
    written before 1593.)

Marlowe is universally and rightly regarded as the first English poet who used blank verse with the hand of a master, and
showed its possibilities. With him it became practically a new
measure. Mr. Symonds says: "He found the ten-syllabled
heroic line monotonous, monosyllabic, and divided into five
feet of tolerably regular alternate short and long. He left it
various in form and structure, sometimes redundant by a syllable, sometimes deficient, enriched with unexpected emphases
and changes in the beat. He found no sequence or attempt at
periods; one line succeeded another with inspired regularity,
and all were made after the same model. He grouped his verse
according to the sense, obeying an internal law of melody, and
allowing the thought contained in his words to dominate their
form. . . . Used in this fashion, blank verse became a Proteus.
It resembled music, which requires regular time and rhythm;
but, by the employment of phrase, induces a higher kind of
melody to rise above the common and despotic beat of time.
. . . It is true that, like all great poets, he left his own peculiar
imprint on it, and that his metre is marked by an almost
extravagant exuberance, impetuosity, and height of coloring."
(*Blank Verse*, pp. 22-27.) In the earlier verse of *Tamburlaine*,
while showing these new qualities of a metrical master, Marlowe yet kept pretty closely to the individual, end-stopped line;
in his later verse, as illustrated in the fragmentary text of
Faustus, he seems to have attained much more freedom, resem-
bling that of the later plays of Shakespeare.

Is it mine eye, or Valentinus' praise,
Her true perfection, or my false transgression,
That makes me, reasonless, to reason thus?
She's fair, and so is Julia that I love,—
That I did love, for now my love is thawed,
Which, like a waxen image 'gainst a fire,
Bears no impression of the thing it was.
Methinks my zeal to Valentine is cold,

And that I love him not, as I was wont:
O! but I love his lady too too much;
And that's the reason I love him so little.
How shall I dote on her with more advice,
That thus without advice begin to love her? . . .
If I can check my erring love, I will;
If not, to compass her I'll use my skill.

(SHAKESPEARE: *Two Gentlemen of Verona*, II. iv. 196-208;
213, 214. ab. 1590.)

Ay, but to die, and go we know not where;
To lie in cold obstruction and to rot;
This sensible warm motion to become
A kneaded clod; and the delighted spirit
To bathe in fiery floods, or to reside
In thrilling regions of thick-ribbed ice;
To be imprisoned in the viewless winds,
And blown with restless violence about
The pendant world; or to be worse than worst
Of those that lawless and incertain thoughts
Imagine howling,—'tis too horrible!
The weariest and most loathed worldly life,
That age, ache, penury, and imprisonment
Can lay on nature, is a paradise
To what we fear of death.

(SHAKESPEARE: *Measure for Measure*, III. i. 118-132. ab.
1603.)

This Mr. Symonds cites as "a single instance of the elasticity,
self-restraint, and freshness of the Shakespearean blank verse;
of its freedom from Marlowe's turgidity, or Fletcher's languor,
or Milton's involution; of its ringing sound and lucid vigor.
. . . It illustrates the freedom from adventitious ornament and
the organic continuity of Shakespeare's versification, while it
also exhibits his power of varying his cadences and suiting
them to dramatic utterance of his characters." (*Blank Verse*,
p. 31.)

Ye elves of hills, brooks, standing lakes, and groves;
And ye that on the sands with printless foot
Do chase the ebbing Neptune, and do fly him
When he comes back; you demi-puppets, that
By moonshine do the green-sour ringlets make,
Whereof the ewe not bites; and you, whose pastime
Is to make midnight mushrooms; that rejoice
To hear the solemn curfew; by whose aid
(Weak masters though ye be) I have bedimm'd
The noontide sun, called forth the mutinous winds,

And 'twixt the green sea and the azur'd vault
Set roaring war: to the dread rattling thunder
Have I given fire, and rifted Jove's stout oak
With his own bolt: the strong-bas'd promontory
Have I made shake; and by the spurs pluck'd up
The pine and cedar: graves, at my command,
Have wak'd their sleepers, op'd, and let them forth
Be my so potent art.
(SHAKESPEARE: *The Tempest*, V. i. 33-50. ab. 1610.)

No attempt can be made to represent adequately the blank verse of Shakespeare. The specimens, chosen respectively from his earlier, middle, and later periods, illustrate the trend of development of his verse. In the earlier period it was characterized by the slight use of feminine endings, and *enjambement*; in the later by marked preference for both, and by general freedom and flexibility. In other words, Shakespeare's own development represents, in a sort of miniature, that of the history of dramatic blank verse.

A sullen woman fear, that talks not to you;
She has a sad and darkened soul, loves dully;
A merry and a free wench, give her liberty,
Believe her, in the lightest form she appears to you,
Believe her excellent, though she despise you;
Let but these fits and flashes pass, she will show to you
As jewels rubbed from dust, or gold new burnished.
(FLETCHER: *The Wild-Goose Chase*, IV. i. 1621.)

The verse of Fletcher is highly individual among the Jacobean dramatists, though in a sense typical of the breaking down of blank verse, in the direction of prose, which was going on at this period. The distinguishing feature of Fletcher's verse is the constant use of feminine endings, and the extension of these to triple and even quadruple endings, by the addition of one or more syllables. Twelve-syllable lines (not alexandrines, but ordinary lines with triple endings) are not at all uncommon; and the additional syllable or syllables may even be emphatic. In general the tendency was in the direction of the freedom of conversational prose. Such a line as

"Methinks you are infinitely bound to her for her journey"

would not be recognized, standing by itself, as a five-stress iambic verse; properly read, however, it takes its place without difficulty in the scheme of the metre.

Middleton carried on the work of fitting blank verse for
plausibly conversational, as distinguished from poetic, effects.
Often his lines are more difficult to scan than Fletcher's, and
still less seek melodiousness for its own sake. Characteristic
specimens are verses like these:

"I doubt I'm too quick of apprehension now."
"With which one gentleman, far in debt, has courted her."
"To call for, 'fore me, and thou look'st half ill indeed."

What would it pleasure me to have my throat cut
With diamonds? or to be smothered
With cassia? or to be shot to death with pearls?
I know death hath ten thousand several doors
For men to take their exits; and 'tis found
They go on such strange geometrical hinges,
You may open them both ways; any way, for Heaven sake,
So I were out of your whispering. Tell my brothers
That I perceive death, now I am well awake,
Best gift is they can give or I can take. . . ,
— Pull, and pull strongly, for your able strength
Must pull down Heaven upon me:—
Yet stay; Heaven-gates are not so highly arched
As princes' palaces; they that enter there
Must go upon their knees.— Come, violent death,
Serve for mandragora to make me sleep!—
Go tell my brothers, when I am laid out,
They then may feed in quiet.
    (JOHN WEBSTER: *The Duchess of Malfi*, IV. ii. 1623.)

"Webster," says Mr. Symonds, "used his metre as the most
delicate and responsive instrument for all varieties of dramatic
expression. . . . Scansion in the verse of Webster is subor-
dinate to the purpose of the speaker." (*Blank Verse*, pp. 45-
47.) He also calls attention to such remarkable lines as—

"Cover her face; mine eyes dazzle; she died young."
"Other sins only speak; murder shrieks out."

                        . . . And now his heart
Distends with pride, and hardening in his strength
Glories: for never since created man
Met such embodied force; as nam'd with these
Could merit more than that small infantry
Warr'd on by cranes: though all the giant brood
Of Phlegra with th' heroic race were joined
That fought at Thebes and Ilium, on each side

Mixed with auxiliar gods; and what resounds
In fable or romance of Uther's son
Begirt with British and Armoric knights;
And all who since, baptiz'd or infidel,
Jousted in Aspramont or Montalban,
Damasco, or Morocco, or Trebizond,
Or whom Biserta sent from Afric shore
When Charlemagne with all his peerage fell
By Fontarabbia.

(MILTON: *Paradise Lost*, Book I. ll. 544-559; 571-587. 1667.)

In Milton's own prefatory note to *Paradise Lost*, he called
his blank verse "English heroic verse without rime." Rime he
spoke of as "the invention of a barbarous age, . . . graced
indeed since by the use of some famous modern poets,"—not
least among them, he might have said, being John Milton himself. He described also the special character of his verse in saying that "true musical delight . . . consists only in apt numbers, fit quantity of syllables, and the sense variously drawn out
from one verse to another,"—that is, by *enjambement*. "This
neglect then of rime so little is to be taken for a defect, . . .
that it rather is to be esteemed an example set, the first in
English, of ancient liberty recovered to heroic poem from the
troublesome and modern bondage of riming."

Through the hushed air the whitening shower descends,
At first thin wavering; till at last the flakes
Fall broad, and wide, and fast, dimming the day
With a continual flow. The cherished fields
Put on their winter-robe of purest white.
'Tis brightness all; save where the new snow melts
Along the mazy current. Low the woods
Bow their hoar head; and, ere the languid sun
Faint from the west emits his evening ray,
Earth's universal face, deep-hid and chill,
Is one wild dazzling waste, that buries wide
The works of man.

(THOMSON: *The Seasons; Winter.* 1726.)

Thomson's *Seasons* was undoubtedly the most influential of
the poems of the blank-verse revival of this period. Saintsbury
says: "His blank verse in especial cannot receive too much com-
mendation. With that of Milton, and that of the present Poet
Laureate [Tennyson], it must rank as one of the chief original
models of the metre to be found in English poetry." (Ward's
English Poets, vol. iii. p. 169.)

Instead of thrones, hard flint they sat upon,
Couches of rugged stone, and slaty ridge
Stubborn'd with iron. All were not assembled:
Some chain'd in torture, and some wandering.
Cœus, and Gyges, and Briareus,
Typhon, and Dolor, and Porphyrion,
With many more, the brawniest in assault,
Were pent in regions of laborious breath;
Dungeon'd in opaque element, to keep
Their clenched teeth still clench'd, and all their limbs
Lock'd up like veins of metal, crampt and screw'd;
Without a motion, save of their big hearts
Heaving in pain, and horribly convuls'd
With sanguine feverous boiling gurge of pulse.
                    (KEATS: *Hyperion*, book II. 1820.)

"In Keats at last," says Mr. Symonds, "we find again that
inner music which is the soul of true blank verse. . . . His
Hyperion is sung, not written. . . . Its music is fluid, bound
by no external measurement of feet, but determined by the
sense and intonation of the poet's thought, while like the cro-
talos of the Athenian flute-player, the decasyllabic beat main-
tains an uninterrupted undercurrent of regular pulsations."
(*Blank Verse*, p. 64.)

        There in a secret olive-glade I saw
    Pallas Athene climbing from the bath
    In anger; yet one glittering foot disturb'd
    The lucid well; one snowy knee was prest
    Against the margin flowers; a dreadful light
    Came from her golden hair, her golden helm
    And all her golden armor on the grass,
    And from her virgin breast, and virgin eyes
    Remaining fixt on mine, till mine grew dark
    For ever, and I heard a voice that said,
    "Henceforth be blind, for thou hast seen too much.
    And speak the truth that no man may believe."
                    (TENNYSON: *Tiresias*. 1883.)

Ah, sad and strange as in dark summer dawns
The earliest pipe of half-awaken'd birds
To dying ears, when unto dying eyes
The casement slowly grows a glimmering square;
So sad, so strange, the days that are no more.
                    (TENNYSON: *The Princess*, iv.;
                        "Tears, Idle Tears." 1847.)

The blank verse of Tennyson is probably to be regarded as the most masterly found among modern poets. Its flexibility is almost infinite, yet never unmelodious. The last of the specimens just quoted illustrates his use of blank verse for short lyrical poems—an unusual and notable achievement.

> —Oh, though first comer, though as strange at the work
> As fribble must be, coxcomb, fool that's near
> To knave as, say, a priest who fears the world—
> Was he bound brave the peril, save the doomed,
> Or go on, sing his snatch and pluck his flower,
> Keep the straight path and let the victim die?
> I held so; you decided otherwise,
> Saw no such peril, theerfore no such need
> To stop song, loosen flower, and leave path. Law,
> Law was aware and watching, would suffice,
> Wanted no priest's intrusion, palpably
> Pretence, too manifest a subterfuge!
> (BROWNING: Caponsacchi, The Ring and the Book. 1868.)

The Ring and the Book Professor Corson calls "the greatest achievement of the century . . . in the effective use of blank verse in the treatment of a great subject. . . . Its blank verse, while having a most complex variety of character, is the most dramatic blank verse since the Elizabethan era. . . . One reads it without a sense almost of there being anything artificial in the construction of the language; . . . one gets the impression that the poet thought and felt spontaneously in blank verse." (Primer of English Verse, pp. 224, 225.)

> I that was near your heart was removed therefrom
> To lose beauty in terror, terror in inquisition.
> I have lost my passion: why should I need to keep it
> Since what is kept must be adulterated?
> I have lost my sight, smell, hearing, taste and touch:
> How should I use them for your closer contact?
> (T. S. ELIOT: Gerontion. 1920.)

Eliot's blank verse is modeled, according to his own testimony, on the verse of the Jacobean dramatists. The principle behind Eliot's practice may be expressed in his formula: "the ghost of some simple metre should lurk behind the arras in even the 'freest' verse . . . freedom is . . . truly freedom when it appears against the background of an artificial limitation." ("Reflections on Vers Libre." 1917.)

Six, seven, and eight stress lines.

The attempts by English poets to write in lines of more than five stresses have been only occasionally and moderately successful. We find the six-stress line in numerous forms; the iambic hexameter (Alexandrine) can be illustrated by these lines from Sidney's famous sonnet:

Loving in truth, and fain in verse my love to show,
That she, dear she, might take some pleasure of my pain—
Pleasure might cause her read, reading might make her know,
Knowledge might pity win, and pity grace obtain. . . .
(SIDNEY: *Astrophel and Stella.* i. c. 1580.)

and the dactylic hexameter, based on Greek and Latin models, by the sleep-inducing sonorities of Longfellow's *Evangeline:*

This is the forest primeval. The murmuring pines and the
    hemlocks,
Bearded with moss, and in garments green, indistinct in the
    twilight,
Stand like Druids of eld, with voices sad and prophetic,
Stand like harpers hoar, with beards that rest on their bosoms.

Lines of seven and eight stresses are rarely encountered as such; the septenary or seven-stress line usually breaks down, in extended passages, into sharply divided sections of trimeter and tetrameter. Swinburne, the past master of all galloping meters, calls the lines below "anapestic heptameter"; most ears will hear the lines as successive four's and three's:

Come on then, ye dwellers by nature in darkness, and like
    to the leaves' generations,
That are little of might, that are moulded of mire, unendur-
    ing and shadowlike nations,
Poor plumeless ephemerals, comfortless mortals, as visions
    of creatures fast fleeing,
Lift up your mind unto us that are deathless, and dateless
    the date of our being.
(SWINBURNE: *The Birds*, from Aristophanes.)

Similarly, the eight-stress line will divide into equal hemistiches. Perhaps the most celebrated poem in eight-stress lines is Tennyson's *Locksley Hall* (eight-stress trochaics):

Far along the world-wide whisper of the south-wind rushing
    warm,
With the standards of the peoples plunging thro' the thunder-
    storm;

Till the war-drum throbb'd no longer, and the battle-flags
    were furl'd
In the Parliament of man, the Federation of the World.
            (TENNYSON: *Locksley Hall.* 1842.)

Certainly the most notorious poem in eight-stress trochaics is
Poe's *The Raven*:

Open then I flung the shutter, when, with many a flirt and
    flutter,
In there stepped a stately raven of the saintly days of yore.
Not the least obeisance made he; not an instant stopped or
    stayed he;
But, with mien of lord or lady, perched above my chamber
    door,—
Perched upon a bust of Pallas, just above my chamber door.
            (POE: *The Raven.* 1845.)

Poe's use of internal rhyme decisively cuts the line in two,
and reveals the basically four-stress structure of the verse.

Glossary of Terms

This is not a complete glossary of prosodical terminology but rather a list of hard words that have turned up in the previous essays. The student interested in more complete glossing should consult Karl Shapiro and Robert Beum's excellent *A Prosody Handbook* (New York: Harper & Row, 1965). For much useful information, especially on Greek and Latin metrics, the student will also want to look at the *Encyclopedia of Poetry and Poetics*, edited by Alex Preminger *et al* (Princeton, 1965).

● Accentual verse   Verse measured by count of stresses alone. In accentual verse the number of stressed syllables is usually constant; the number of unstressed syllables can vary considerably. A favorite nursery rhyme, "Oranges and Lemons" is a fine example of accentual verse, four stresses to the line:

Bull's eyes and targets ‖ say the bells of St. Marg'ret's.

Brickbats and tiles ‖ say the bells of St. Giles'.

Oranges and lemons ‖ say the bells of St. Clement's.

See remarks under strong-stress verse.

● Accidence   Grammatical inflection as it occurs in gender, number, case, person, voice, etc.

● Adonic   A metrical scheme in Latin and Greek poetry. It consisted of a dactyl and a spondee: $-\,\cup\cup\ \mid\ -\,-$

The adonic forms the last line in the Sapphic (q.v.) stanza.

● Alexandrine   Originally the French verse line of twelve syllables. As the carry-all metric of French poetry, it stands analogous to the iambic pentameter in English. Its appearance in English verse has been contemptuously remarked by Pope; the second line below is meant as a horrible example:

A needless Alexandrine ends the song,

That, like a wound ed snake drags its slow length a long,

The English Alexandrine contains six feet and six metrical stresses.

● Anacrusis   An extra syllable, or syllables, occurring in a metrical pattern. It is like the up-beat preceding the main accent in a musical bar. The last line of the stanza below is preceded by an extra unstressed syllable: an anapest for the expected iamb:

> O what can ail thee, knight-at-arms,
> So haggard, and so woe-begone?

The squirrel's granary is full,

And the har | vest's done.

(Keats, *La Belle Dame Sans Merci*)

⦿ Anaphora   Strictly speaking, a rhetorical rather than a prosodical device. However, anaphora, the repetition of a syntactical figure at the head of a line, can have rhythmical significance. Whitman uses anaphora with great freedom and effect:

Passing the visions, passing the night,

Passing, unloosing the hold of my comrades'
                                                    hands,

Passing the song of the hermit bird and the
                                tallying song of my soul . . .

(*When Lilacs Last in the Door-Yard Bloom'd*)

⦿ Arsis   A much confused term. Greek prosodists regarded the thesis as the long syllable of the foot, the arsis the remaining short syllables. However, the Latin theorists reversed the meaning of the two terms; arsis became the long syllable, and thesis the short syllables of a foot.

⦿ Brachycatalectic ·   A line lacking two syllables of its normal metrical scheme is called brachycatalectic. In the stanza below, the indented lines lack the two unstressed syllables of the normal dactylic foot; the omitted syllables are marked by a carat (∧):

Pale beech and | pine so blue

Set in one | clay, ∧∧

Bough to bough | can not you ·

Live out your | day? ∧∧   (Thomas Hardy)

⦿ Caesura (cesura)   A pause in the line of verse occasioned by normal syntactical phrasing or grammatical sense. Though of great prosodical importance, the caesura does not form part of the regular metrical scheme. Shakespeare often splits the metrical foot with a pronounced caesura (marked here with the double bar):

Whose ac | tion is | no strong | er ‖ than | a flower . . .

(Sonnet 65)

⦿ Catalexis, catalectic   Literally truncation. The omission of an expected final syllable in a line of verse. Trochaic lines are frequently catalectic, lacking the final unstressed syllable:

Pí ping | down the | val leys | wild, ∧

Pí ping | songs of | pleas ant | glee, ∧

On a | cloud I | saw a | child, ∧

And he | laugh ing | said to | me . . . ∧ (William Blake)

Lines lacking two omitted syllables are brachycatalectic (q.v.).

● Counterpoint, counterpoint rhythm   Gerard Manley Hopkins coined this term to designate the simultaneous appearance of two rhythms in a line of verse, ". . . two rhythms . . . in some manner running at once and we have something answerable to counterpoint in music . . ." A line of iambic pentameter verse may be counterpointed by the reversal of certain sensitive feet, usually the second and the fourth:

Cap tain | Car pen | ter rose | up in | his prime. . .

(John Crowe Ransom)

Successive spondees will also counterpoint a line of iambic verse:

Good strong | thick stu | pe fy | ing in | cense smoke. . .

(Browning)

● Decasyllabic   Containing ten syllables. A 'regular' line of English iambic pentameter is normally decasyllabic; however, dramatic blank verse may show great irregularity in syllable count:

Do anything but this thou doest. Empty
Old receptacles, or common shores, of filth;
Serve by indenture to the common hangman.
Any of these ways are yet better than this.
For what thou professest, a baboon, could he speak,
Would own a name too dear. Oh, that the gods
Would safely deliver me from this place!
Here, here's gold for thee.

(Shakespeare, Pericles, IV, vi.)

● Dipodic verse   Verse structured so that the metrical unit encompasses two feet. Good examples of dipodic verse may be found in the patter songs from the Gilbert and Sullivan operettas:

As some | day it | may hap | pen that | a vic | tim must | be found,

Of so ci e ty's of fend ers || who might well be un der ground . . .   (The Mikado)

The first line is scanned as conventional iambic heptameter; however, it is clear that the syllables marked with the double accent (//) receive the stronger stress. The scansion in the second line recognizes the double foot or dipody of two strong stresses separated by the strong medial pause or caesura. Such verse is sometimes termed double-iambic. Its descent from Old English strong-stress meter (q.v.) should be noted.

● Endecasillabo   See hendecasyllabic

● Elision   The practice of running together a final un-stressed, or short, vowel with the initial vowel or mute consonant of the following syllable. Elision allows greater freedom in building the line in conformity with the metrical scheme. Elision is a regular feature of Latin versification:

Pol li o et | in ci pi | ent mag | ni pro | ce de re | men ses. . .
                                           (Virgil, *Ecloga IV*)

The final o of *Pollio* and the initial e of *et* count, in the metrical scheme, as one syllable. Milton introduced elision in the blank verse of *Paradise Lost*, adapting the rules of quantitative verse for English syllable-stress verse:

Hurl'd head | long flam | ing from | the E the | real Sky. . .
                                         (I, 45)

● End Stopping   The practice of adjusting the syntax of the verse-line to the length of the line itself, as in these lines from James Thomson's *The Seasons*:

See, Winter comes, to rule the vary'd Year,
Sullen, and sad with all his rising Train;
Vapours, and Clouds, and Storms. Be these my Theme,
These, that exalt the Soul to solemn Thought,
And heavenly Musing. Welcome, kindred Glooms!
                                     (*Winter*, 1-5)

See enjambment below.

● Enjambment   The practice of 'running a line over,' so that "the sense be variously drawn out from one Verse into another," as in these lines from Keats:

A thing of beauty is a joy forever:
Its loveliness increases; it will never
Pass into nothingness; but still will keep
A bower quiet for us, and a sleep
Full of sweet dreams, and health, and quiet breathing.
                                     (*Endymion*, I, 1-5)

●Feminine ending   A hypermetrical (q.v.) line with a final unstressed syllable. The first four lines of Hamlet's famous soliloquy have feminine endings:

> To be, or not to be: that is the question:
> Whether 'tis nobler in the mind to suffer
> The slings and arrows of outrageous fortune,
> Or to take arms against a sea of troubles. . .
> (Shakespeare, Hamlet, III, i, 56-59)

●Hendecasyllabic .   A line of eleven syllables. Chaucer's lines may be thought of as hendecasyllabic if we pronounce the final e. The first two lines of The Canterbury Tales may be hendecasyllabic; the second two are decasyllabic:

> Whan that Aprille with his shoures soote
> And droghte of March hath perced to the roote
> And bathed every veyne in swich licour
> Of which vertu engendred is the flour.

See decasyllabic.

●Hexameter   In classical prosody the meter of both Homer's Iliad and Virgil's Aeneid. It was originally a quantitative line of six feet, conforming to this paradigm:

$$\underbrace{- \cup \cup}_{1} \quad \underbrace{- \cup \cup}_{2} \quad \underbrace{- \cup \cup}_{3} \quad \underbrace{- \cup \cup}_{4} \quad \underbrace{- \cup \cup}_{5} \quad \underbrace{- -}_{6}$$

The pattern, as may be seen, was five dactyls with a spondee in the sixth position. However, a spondee may substitute for a dactyl in any position except the last; a spondee rarely occurs in the fifth position: when it does, the entire line is named 'spondaic.' The opening line of the Aeneid scans:

> Ar ma vir| um que ca |no Troi |ae qui |pri mis ab| or is. . .

Longfellow adapted the quantitative hexameter to syllable-stress meter for his Evangeline.

●Hypermetrical   A line of verse containing more syllables than the paradigm allows. The loose blank verse of the Jacobean dramatists is characteristically hypermetrical; the lines often run to eleven, twelve, or more syllables:

> Why, no 'tis most apparent: this precise fellow
> Is the duchess' bawd:—I have it to my wish!
> This is a parcel of intelligency
> Our courtiers were cased up for: it needs must follow
> That I must be committed on pretence
> Of poisoning her; which I'll endure and laugh at.
> (Webster, The Duchess of Malfi, II, iii.)

● Iambic trimeter   In classical verse a line of three iambic dipodies (double feet):

ad sum | pro fun ‖ do Tar | ta ri̯e ‖ miss us | spe cu (Seneca)

This line was used with great freedom in dramatic dialogue, especially in later Roman comedy.

● Ictus   The heavy stress in classical verse, usually falling on the long syllable of the foot. However, metrical ictus and normal word accent do not necessarily coincide; Robert Bridges quotes this line from Virgil where normal word accent contradicts (or 'combats') the metrical expectation:

Flu mi na | que an ti | quos sub | ter la | ben ti a | mu ros. . .

● Internal rhyme   Rhyme occurring within the line of verse, as

    The fair breeze blew, the white foam flew,
    The furrow followed free;
    We were the first that ever burst
    Into that silent sea.
(Coleridge, *The Rime of the Ancient Mariner*, 103-106)

● Isochronic, isochronism   Some prosodists ('timers' and musical scanners) maintain that English meter is composed of units of equal time. Musical scanners believe that the foot is equivalent to the musical bar and that each foot occupies the same time interval. Others feel that isochronism is illusory, created by "the total effect of metrical organization which seemingly eliminates temporal discrepancies."

● Paradigm   In grammar all the inflected forms of a part of speech, arranged in systematic order. A *metrical paradigm* abstracts the ideal form of a particular metrical arrangement; thus the paradigm of the iambic pentameter line consists of five iambic feet in consecutive arrangement:

The pro | per stu | dy of | man kind | is man. . .

The paradigm is often departed from; in the following line a trochee substitutes (q.v.) for an iamb in the first foot:

Cha os | of Thought | and Pas | sion, all | con fus'd. . .

● Sapphic, Sapphics   A Greek stanzaic form named after the poetess Sappho—who may or may not have invented it. Its paradigm consists of three lines of Lesser Sapphics

— ◡ | — — | — ◡ ◡ | — ◡ | — —

followed by a fourth line, an Adonic (q.v.): — ◡ ◡ | — —

Swinburne, among others, has adapted the Sapphic stanza to English:

> All the night sleep came not upon my eyelids,
> Shed not dew, nor shook nor unclosed a feather,
> Yet with lips shut close and with eyes of iron
>   Stood and beheld me.
>
> (Sapphics)

● Septenary   A line consisting of seven metrical feet, as in T. S. Eliot's

> The yellow fog that rubs its back upon the window-panes. . .

● Sestina   A complicated Provençal verse form, invented, supposedly, by Arnaut Daniel. A sestina is a poem of thirty-nine lines divided into six stanzas of six lines each, and an envoy of three lines. Each stanza repeats the end-words of the first stanza in a new arrangement; the envoy repeats all six words in a set pattern. Because of the insistent repetitions of the end-words, the sestina adapts itself to both incantation and polemic. A good example of the incantatory sestina is Auden's "Hearing of harvests rotting in the valley"; of the polemical sestina, Pound's "Sestina: Altaforte."

● Springing   A strong rhythmic disturbance in the metrical line. 'Springing' is only possible in syllable-stress meter; it is a basic conflict between the paradigmatic meter and the disturbing element. It is similar to counterpointing (q.v.); however, in counterpointing the basic metrical structure is still felt. A 'sprung' line loses its sense of firm metrical organization and moves toward greater freedoms. A line may be sprung by an intrusive monosyllabic foot:

> Through sharp | seas | in win | ter nights | doth pass. . .
>
> (Wyatt)
>
> I no long|er strive| to strive| towards| such things. . .
>
> (T. S. Eliot)
>
> No strength | of man, | or fier | cest wild | beast | could with stand. . .
>
> (Milton, Samson Agonistes)

A line also may be sprung by the wholesale use of substitution; the spondee in the third position and trochees in the first, and in the very sensitive fourth position effectively spring this line:

> Look at | the stars! | look, look | up at | the skies!
>
> (Hopkins, The Starlight Night)

● **Sprung Rhythm**　　A verse form invented and described by Gerard Manley Hopkins. In Sprung Rhythm the lines move out of recognizable syllable-stress metric and cannot be scanned by syllable, stress, and foot. Some poems in Sprung Rhythm are actually written in strong-stress meter; other poems are in what amounts to free verse. Hopkins' *The Wreck of the Deutschland* shows a complex stress metric; *The Leaden Echo and the Golden Echo* is a free verse rhapsody.

● **Strong-stress verse**　　Accentual verse as it appears in the basic Old English pattern of the four-stress line. A medial caesura divides the line into two parts:

Across the cloud	pointed with light
Darts the tongue	of the roaring plane
Earth explodes	under its fire
Searing the stone	consuming the air
No hawk, no Harpy	disputes its place
Poised at the sun	death is less sure

● **Substitution**　　In syllable-stress verse the practice of replacing the expected foot with one of a different character. The line below substitutes a trochee for an iamb at the third position:

His sil | ver skin | laced with | his gol | den blood. . .

(Shakespeare, *Macbeth*, II, iii, 118)

Here is a good example of 'counterpoint' rhythm releasing great emotional power.

● **Syllabic verse**　　Strictly speaking, verse measured by count of syllables alone. French prosody is syllable counting; in this stanza by Gautier, we find eight syllables in the line:

> Une femme mystérieuse,
> Dont la beauté trouble mes sens,
> Se tient debout, silencieuse,
> Au bord des flots retentissants.

(Coerulei Oculi)

Many attempts have been made, especially by contemporary poets, to adapt syllabic metric to English. Marianne Moore, W. H. Auden, and Thom Gunn have devised syllabic forms for their poetic contents.

● **Syllable-stress verse**　　The traditional syllable, stress, and foot prosody of English poetry. See Appendix I for fuller explanation and a brief history by examples.

● **Thesis**　　see arsis.